A Guide

MERCURY DIMES,

STANDING LIBERTY QUARTERS,

AND

LIBERTY WALKING HALF DOLLARS

1916–1947

A Complete History and Price Guide

Q. David Bowers

Foreword by Roger W. Burdette

Whitman Publishing, LLC

PUBLISHING SINCE 1934

© 2015 by Whitman Publishing, LLC

3101 Clairmont Road, Suite C, Atlanta, GA 30329

The WCG™ data grid used throughout this publication is patent pending. THE OFFICIAL RED BOOK is a trademark of Whitman Publishing, LLC.

Correspondence concerning this book may be directed to the publisher, at the address above.

ISBN: 079484314X

Printed in the United States of America

Disclaimer: Expert opinion should be sought in any significant numismatic purchase. This book is presented as a guide only. No warranty or representation of any kind is made concerning the completeness of the information presented. The author, a professional numismatist, regularly buys, sells, and sometimes holds certain of the items discussed in this book.

Caveat: The value estimates given are subject to variation and differences of opinion. Before making decisions to buy or sell, consult the latest information. Past performance of the rare coin market or any coin or series within that market is not necessarily an indication of future performance, as the future is unknown. Such factors as changing demand, popularity, grading interpretations, strength of the overall coin market, and economic conditions will continue to be influences.

Other books in the Bowers Series include: *A Guide Book of Franklin and Kennedy Half Dollars; A Guide Book of Double Eagle Gold Coins; A Guide Book of United States Type Coins; A Guide Book of Modern United States Proof Coin Sets; A Guide Book of Shield and Liberty Head Nickels; A Guide Book of Flying Eagle and Indian Head Cents; A Guide Book of Washington and State Quarters; A Guide Book of Buffalo and Jefferson Nickels; A Guide Book of Lincoln Cents; A Guide Book of United States Commemorative Coins; A Guide Book of United States Tokens and Medals; A Guide Book of Gold Dollars; A Guide Book of Peace Dollars; A Guide Book of the Official Red Book of United States Coins; A Guide Book of Civil War Tokens; A Guide Book of Hard Times Tokens;* and *A Guide Book of Half Cents and Large Cents.*

For a complete catalog of numismatic reference books, supplies, and storage products, visit Whitman Publishing online at Whitman.com.

Contents

Foreword

In the 1895 novel *The Time Machine* by H.G. Wells, our first literary time traveler explores the future, only to return to the present; he then vanishes, never to return. Our modern-day time traveler is Doctor Who, a Time Lord who is fully equipped with a living machine called the TARDIS (**T**ime **a**nd **R**elative **D**imension **i**n **S**pace), and the ability to regenerate. While both Wells's time traveler and our modern one have many adventures in time and space, they do so with little more than guesswork as their guide.

Our modern numismatic Time Lord is intrepid author Q. David Bowers. Although he might not have a TARDIS hidden in his New Hampshire office, Bowers has the skill and knowledge to whisk coin collectors into the universe of American numismatic history. As with any expert guide, his journeys are always enjoyable, filled with fresh insights and unexpected tangents.

In this, his latest addition to his series on American coinage, Bowers is our time-travel guide to the newly designed silver coinage of 1916. Each date-and-mint issue is described and accompanied by helpful keys to collecting, aspects of striking, and tips on being a smart buyer. But beyond this, our guide shows us the culture and major events of a century past—a time few today can describe or imagine. This is no small feat. The new coinage designs of 1916 were a product of the training and artistic traditions of their creators. In subtle ways, they embody the aspirations and fears of an America that stepped hesitantly from behind her protective barrier and into the unknown of the larger world. Hermon Atkins MacNeil's quarter dollar demonstrates this uncertainty with clarity, and Bowers gives us the context to understand MacNeil's design and the changes made to it in 1917. German-born Adolph A. Weinman enthralled collectors and the public with a new, beautiful vision of Liberty surrounded by a bowl of shimmering silver and backed with ancient symbols of authority and strength. Weinman's other designs for the half dollar took the hesitancy MacNeil illustrated and turned it into supreme confidence. Miss Liberty strides confidently into the future—a future we understand better because of the insights of Bowers. Weinman's large, powerful eagle stands upon a pier of granite, protecting the pine sapling of freedom and challenging all who might stand in the way.

The symbols—cultural sign posts—are filled with meaning, but to decipher that meaning requires our expert Time Lord and travel guide. As does any astute guide, Bowers provides what is needed to understand these coins and to relate their symbology to the events of their time. Others have written detailed expositions about the origins of these coins, and the multitude of die varieties and unusual pieces that collectors prize, but Bowers stays focused on things we should all know if we are to appreciate what we collect.

This is a book to be read, put aside, then re-read—a refreshment from the commercial and competitive aspects of coin collecting. It will give enjoyment from the first page to the last, and from the first reading to the hundredth.

Roger W. Burdette
Washington, D.C.

Roger W. Burdette is the author of three critically acclaimed numismatic books composing his Renaissance of American Coinage *series. For his groundbreaking work he won the prestigious "Book of the Year" award from the Numismatic Literary Guild in 2006, 2007, and 2008. He has also written numerous articles for numismatic newspapers and magazines, including* Coin World, Coin Values, Coins, *and* The Numismatist. *He is a contributor to the* Guide Book of United States Coins *(the "Red Book"), and to other books in Whitman's Bowers Series, including those on type coins, nickel five-cent pieces, quarter dollars, silver dollars, and double eagle gold coins. He is the author of the* Guide Book of Peace Dollars.

Burdette lives with his daughters near Washington, D.C. Following a successful career with a nationally known non-profit research-and-development corporation, he now devotes his time to numismatic research, writing, publishing, and other projects.

Preface

The first volume of the "Bowers Series" of numismatic references—the *Guide Book of Morgan Silver Dollars*—was published in 2004. As of early 2015 that initial volume plus the 16 that followed it have comprised more than 5,000 pages of information on U.S. copper half cents through gold double eagles, Proof sets, commemorative coins, tokens and medals, and other numismatic collectibles. To that impressive lineup, volume 18 adds three of the most popular U.S. coins ever minted—the Mercury dime, the Standing Liberty quarter, and the Liberty Walking half dollar.

The popularity of these three coin types has long been on our radar at Whitman Publishing. How could it not be? Collectors have bought thousands of Whitman blue folders and albums to save one coin from every date and mint. We get phone calls and letters asking about the coins and their die varieties, how to grade them, and how much they're worth. Until now, we've referred our readers to the *Guide Book of United States Coins* (the hobby's "Red Book," which covers every U.S. coin series), to various books that describe grading or that study one or another of the individual coin types, or, for more detailed exploration of die varieties, to the *Cherrypickers' Guide*. Now collectors have another standard reference, one that brings everything together in a single resource: the *Guide Book of Mercury Dimes, Standing Liberty Quarters, and Liberty Walking Half Dollars*.

The decision of how to present these coins to the hobby community wasn't lightly made. Our intent with the Bowers Series is to study the most popular coin types in books that are affordable, logically organized, and valuable to the reader. These goals brought certain questions to the fore. By 2014, we had no Bowers Series book on dimes, one on quarter dollars (the *Guide Book of Washington and State Quarters*), and one on half dollars (the *Guide Book of Franklin and Kennedy Half Dollars*). Would it make sense to create a *Guide Book of Mercury and Roosevelt Dimes*, covering the last 100 years of that denomination in a single reference? And what to do with the Standing Liberty quarter? Modern quarters, of 1932 to date, were already accounted for, and we knew we would be covering Barber silver coins (dimes, quarters, and halves) all together in a single upcoming volume. That left the Standing Liberty quarter

somewhat orphaned—a relatively short series spread over a span of 15 years, comprising fewer than 40 major date/mintmark varieties, certainly not enough to fill their own 300-page book. A similar question lingered for half dollars, with the Bowers Series already covering that denomination from the present day back to 1948.

I believe our final decision—to present these three coins together in a single volume—is a sound one. Mercury dimes, Standing Liberty quarters, and Liberty Walking half dollars were all part of the elegant "Renaissance of American Coinage" (as Roger W. Burdette termed it in his award-winning book series), the early-1900s rebirth of great U.S. coin design. All three were workhorses of American commerce in their heyday, which spanned from 1916 into the 1940s, from a world war to a gilded age of progress, then through the depths of an unprecedented economic depression and a second global conflagration. The motifs of these working-class coins are widely ranked among America's greatest numismatic designs. They speak to the viewer in a way that the older, grim-faced Barber coins never did, in a way that today's modern presidential-portrait coinage certainly doesn't. Their appeal is not just the sentimental feeling they invoke, and it's not just the vibrancy and action of their designs; it's a combination of everything about them, their ineffable sense of history as well as their old-fashioned but still very robust physicality. We look at them and we think, *This is the United States of America.*

If a Grandpa of a certain age had a cigar box or candy dish that he tossed his pocket change into, chances are good it held a few of these silver pieces. Today they are commonly found in inheritances of old coins—perhaps studiously assembled and proudly displayed, perhaps jumbled haphazardly with vintage bus tokens, World War II ration tokens, and other pocket change. To the community of active hobbyists they are solid "collector" coins, sought by thousands of enthusiasts. Casual collectors fill the holes in their blue folders, eagle-eyed specialists seek out the scarcer die varieties, and deep-pocketed aficionados compete to build the finest registry sets.

For all these reasons—the historical connection of the three coins, their representation of an important generation and era, their unique place in the wider world of American numismatics, and their longstanding popularity among coin collectors and the general public—we decided to combine them into a single standalone book for collectors and historians.

Naturally the perfect author for this subject was Q. David Bowers himself, the "Dean of American Numismatics," after whom the Bowers Series is named. The most widely published numismatic author and researcher of recent generations, Bowers marshals his resources to bring his readers technical, historical, and market-oriented knowledge unavailable in any other single book. The *Guide Book of Mercury Dimes, Standing Liberty Quarters, and Liberty Walking Half Dollars* is the culmination of more than 50 years of research and study, designed to immerse you in the world of these fascinating coins, make you a smarter and more savvy collector, and prepare you to build the greatest coin collection possible.

Dennis Tucker
Atlanta, Georgia

How to Use This Book

Some quoted material has been lightly edited or rearranged, but in all instances the original meaning has been preserved. Common misspellings in quoted material have been corrected. Notes, including in quoted material, are those of the author, Q. David Bowers, unless specifically noted otherwise.

The coin-by-coin catalog section of this book includes the following elements.

The **date** (and, when applicable, the **mintmark**) of the coin is at the top of each listing. Overdates are abbreviated as, for example, *1918/7-S* (for the 1918-S, 8 Over 7, Standing Liberty quarter).

Images of the obverse and reverse of each coin are enlarged to 150% of actual size, to show detail. Actual-size dimes are 17.9 mm; quarters, 24.3 mm; and half dollars, 30.6 mm.

The **circulation mintage** is given for each coin, representing the net quantity of pieces produced *for circulation* by that mint in that year. Similarly, when applicable, a **Proof mintage** is given. Unlike the mintage records of earlier U.S. coins, those of Mercury dimes, Standing Liberty quarters, and Liberty Walking half dollars are well established, with reasonable precision and accuracy supported by solid official documentation. Precise mintages for unusual die varieties typically are unknown, and so these are noted as being included in the regular-issue coin's mintage.

Notes for each coin elaborate on topics of numismatic interest: details about production and distribution, comments from contemporary newspapers or later researchers, and the like. A **Key to Collecting** section gives information intended to make you a smarter and more savvy buyer and seller of each coin—additional historical

notes, current market conditions, details of strike characteristics and planchet quality, analysis of scarcity, and the like.

A **WCG™ pricing grid** (the detailed chart of grades, values, and certified populations) is included for each coin. This includes retail values for circulation strikes and
(when applicable) Proofs, and certified populations as reported by Numismatic Guaranty Corporation of America (NGC). These retail prices are derived from data submitted by a panel of more than 100 professional coin dealers nationwide, and reviewed
by Kenneth Bressett and Jeff Garrett (senior editor and valuations editor, respectively, of the *Guide Book of United States Coins*) and their teams of pricing consultants.
Note that certified-population data from the third-party grading services indicate
what might be called *grading events*, and not necessarily the quantity of individual
coins submitted for grading. This is important because, for example, a collector or
dealer might submit a single 1916-D Mercury dime five or six times, hoping each time
to obtain a higher grade (because a difference of a couple points could mean a market-
value difference of several thousand dollars). Thus the data would suggest that more
individual coins were submitted than is actually the case.

Market Values • Circulation Strikes

G-4	VG-8	F-12	VF-20	EF-40	AU-50	MS-60
$3	$3.25	$3.50	$5	$8	$16	$30
MS-63	MS-64	MS-64FB	MS-65	MS-65FB	MS-66	MS-66FB
$50	$55	$145	$125	$450	$225	$900

Certified Populations

Fair	AG-2	G-4	VG-8	F-12	VF-20	EF-40	AU-50	MS-60
0	0	0	0	1	0	3	24	0
MS-61	MS-62	MS-63	MS-64	MS-65	MS-66	MS-67	MS-68	MS-69
8	32	35	129	115	54	5	0	0

chapter
One

New Coinage of 1916: Beautiful Designs

Traditional Designs

The new coinage of 1916 was the high peak of an evolution that began generations earlier.

From the days of the first federal coinage at the Philadelphia Mint in 1792, the artistry of coin designs was under the supervision of the director of the Mint. The early copper coin dies by Henry Voigt, the Liberty Cap motif by outside-artist Joseph Wright, the silver and gold designs by Chief Engraver Robert Scot, and other motifs were created at and approved within the Mint. Over a period of time assistant engravers and additional outside talent were also used.

Designs tended to be standard, such as common motifs on copper half cents and cents, other motifs replicated across silver series from half dimes to dollars, and still others used on gold coins. Now and again a similar motif would cross the metallic line, such as the Draped Bust obverse used on copper and silver and the Heraldic Eagle used on silver and gold.

Often, designs would be used for long periods of time. Examples include Christian Gobrecht's Liberty Seated motif on silver coins from the late 1830s through 1891 and his Liberty Head on quarter eagles to eagles from 1838 to 1908. Sometimes the starting and ending years would be slightly different, such as the Liberty Head on $2.50 gold coins from 1840 to 1907 and on $5 gold coins from 1839 to 1908.

Minor coins (small-denomination copper, bronze, and copper-nickel pieces) of the second half of the 19th century had designs unique to their denomination—the Flying Eagle and Indian Head cents, Liberty Head nickel three-cent pieces, and Shield and Liberty Head nickels. The obverse of the 1866–1883 Shield nickel was an exception; it copied the two-cent piece of 1864.

Outside artists, employed from time to time to adjust designs or do other work, remained in the background.

Criticisms in the Press

The popular press often commented on new coin designs, usually negatively. The first federal coins were placed into circulation in March 1793. The *Argus*, published in Boston, commented on March 26, 1793:

> The American *cents* (says a letter from Newark) do not answer our expectations. The chain on the reverse is but a bad omen for liberty, and liberty herself appears to be in a fright. May she not justly cry out in the words of the apostle, *"Alexander the coppersmith has done me much harm; the Lord reward him according to his works!"* [1]

The chain of 15 links on the reverse had been intended to represent the 15 states in the Union, not slavery. In response to such criticism the design was soon changed.

The first United States silver dollars were minted in November 1794. Their motif received a mixed review in the *New Hampshire Gazette*.

> Some of the dollars now coining at the Mint of the United States have found their way to this town. A correspondent put one into the editor's hands yesterday. Its weight is equal to that of a Spanish dollar, encircled by *Fifteen Stars*, and has the word "LIBERTY" at the top, and the date, 1794, at the bottom. On the reverse, is the *Bald Eagle*, enclosed in an *Olive Branch*, round which are the words "One Dollar, or Unit, Hundred Cents." The *tout ensemble* has a pleasing effect to a connoisseur; but the touches of the graver are too delicate, and there is a want of that boldness of execution which is necessary to durability and currency.

On balance, reviews of new coins over the years were negative. The *American Journal of Numismatics*, September 1866, included this comment on the new Shield nickel:

> *The New Five-Cent Piece:* After a careful search during the first half of the present year, I have at length succeeded, by the help of a friend, in obtaining a Proof (?) set of the one, two, three, and five cent pieces of 1866; and, inasmuch as the latter piece, particularly, is an "original," both in design and workmanship, perhaps a description of it may prove acceptable.
>
> I say it is an "original," because I have seen nothing like it in my collection, which abounds in all sorts; "bung towns," Chinese cash, German stivers, hellers, and kreatzers; therefore, I think I am correct in the statement.
>
> On the obverse of this remarkable coin, the first *thing* that attracts the attention, is a very elaborate and highly ornamented gridiron, the clumsy handle of which appears to be broken from the body, thus rendering this culinary utensil almost useless. The upper part and sides of this gridiron are hung with leaves of some sort, strongly reminding one of the savory bunches of herbs displayed in a market-

house in autumn, or of a green grocer's sign in huckleberry time. Perhaps the same accident that severed the handle of the gridiron also fractured the lower part, for we notice that it is there skewered by two arrows, pointing in opposite directions. The motto "In God we trust," is very opportune, for the *inventor* of this coin may rest assured that the devil will never forgive him for such an abortion.

The reverse of this thing is less objectionable, for the inventor appears to have almost exhausted his remarkable skill on the obverse. However, he has made a "bold push" and brought forth something. Here we have a circle of stars intersected by thirteen bars of three scratches each (perhaps he never saw a Nova Constellatio) around the top of which are the words "United States of America," in very delicate letters. The make-up of this coin is completed by the insertion in the field, of a big, loud 5, with "cents" in the exergue, which must be pronounced in the peculiar oyster saloon style, thus: "*Five* cents!"

Mr. Editor, did we ever have another such coin?

Yours, truly.

Boston, Aug. 9th, 1866.

Particularly disliked was the reverse of the new 1878 silver dollar designed by George T. Morgan and first minted on March 15 of that year. The Carson City *Morning Appeal*, April 17, 1878, called Morgan's bird a "pelican-bat of the wilderness." Some other papers called it a "buzzard." The Philadelphia *Record* wrote:

Mr. Barber's eagle looks as if it was just recovering from a severe spell of sickness, or that it had been disturbed in its meditations by some unruly schoolboys.[2] Mr. Morgan has a good idea of America's proud bird of freedom, and his original design showed an eagle with wings that nearly enveloped the whole coin. I ts wings were so large that Dr. Linderman, no doubt, feared it might get loose and fly off, so he ordered its wings clipped. In this position it will appear to the public. In its talons is a dart, containing only one feather at the tip of the barb. The director ordered more feathers, so that the barb would present a ship-shape appearance, and not be liable to fly off lop-sided. The head of the Morgan eagle is very poor, and the wings are badly managed. The Barber design shows the eagle with wings as if just unfolding for flight. The motto furnishes the text for many quips, especially from those papers which denounced the 'silver delusion.'"[3]

Charles E. Barber

The tipping point after which more weight was given to public opinion took place during the time that Charles E. Barber was chief engraver at the Mint, from 1880 to 1917. Born in London on November 16, 1840, he came to America with his family in 1852. His father, William, a talented artist and engraver, was hired as chief engraver in January 1869, following the death of Chief Engraver James B. Longacre, who had served in the post since 1844. In the same month, Charles was hired as his father's assistant, although he had very little engraving experience. Charles's talents were viewed as modest at best, although a later generation of numismatists enjoyed his Liberty Head nickel design of 1883 in particular. He was not well liked by his superiors, and after the elder Barber's death on August 31, 1879, some consideration was given to naming George T. Morgan to the post of chief engraver.[4] However, by that time Morgan's mentor, Mint director Henry R. Linderman, who had hired him in 1876, had died, and political situations in the Treasury Department were different.

The Coinage Act of 1890 provided for a change in designs. In 1891 Mint director Edwin O. Leech sent a form letter to artists soliciting ideas for the obverse and reverse of the current silver dollar, as well as new designs for the obverse of the half dollar, quarter dollar, and dime. "The reverse of these last coins will not be changed," it was stated. An award of $500 was to be given for each of the accepted entries.

A wide response was expected, but many artists considered applications to be futile, as only one design would be selected for each denomination. Famous American sculptor Augustus Saint-Gaudens, one of the judges of somewhat more than 200 entries, reported there were but four artists competent to do this class of designing—three Frenchmen and himself. Chief Engraver Charles E. Barber countered that Saint-Gaudens's ideas, including high relief, were impractical for high-speed coinage.

In August 1891, Leech sent this letter:

> It is not likely that another competition will ever be tried for the production of designs for United States coins. The one just ended was too wretched a failure. Doubtless it was the first contest of the sort ever opened by any government to the public at large. The result is not very flattering to the boasted artistic development of this country, inasmuch as only two of the 300 suggestions submitted were good enough to receive honorable mention. So the affair has been handed over to the engraving force of the Philadelphia Mint, which will produce the dies required according to such patterns as its own sense of the beautiful suggests.

The Washington correspondent of the St. Louis *Globe-Democrat* suggested sarcastically:

> There must be a substitute of some kind, representing Liberty, for the Quaker City schoolmarm on the dollar, the reverse of which requires a better type of bird than the present buzzard. Also the unprepossessing female, seated upon a cotton bale is to be removed from the half dollar, quarter, and dime.

Plaster casts of all the patterns evolved will be submitted for approval to the director of the Mint and the secretary of the Treasury, as soon as they have been pronounced satisfactory, dies will be made, and small change of new and lovely mold will soon thereafter jingle in the pockets of the people. No alteration is to be made in the gold coins, because they are really exquisite now and could hardly be improved upon. It is realized that the money of a nation is expressive of its art culture. Therefore, lest posterity imagine the present generation to have been barbarous, it is desirable that our silver pieces should be handsome as may be.

Without fanfare, Director Leech directed Chief Engraver Barber to prepare coinage designs using French coins and medals as a guide for the creation of a Liberty Head motif. This was done, and Barber's new Liberty Head coinage appeared in 1892. The reverse of the dime was unchanged from earlier times, but the reverses of the quarter and half dollar were new, featuring a heraldic eagle.

At this time Augustus Saint-Gaudens was the most honored and admired sculptor in America. Surrounding him were leading sculptors and artists of the day. The work of Charles Barber was dismissed by this community, with Saint-Gaudens calling his work "wretched."

Expected to open in 1892, the World's Columbian Exposition held in Chicago was to observe the 400th anniversary of Christopher Columbus's "discovery" of America. Construction took longer than expected, and the world's fair did not open until 1893. It was envisioned that Augustus Saint-Gaudens would create the official award medal. Offered a fee of $5,000—a remarkable sum for the era—the artist demurred at first, as he was busy with another commission, the Shaw Memorial (today an attraction in Boston Common near the Massachusetts State House). He suggested that the work be placed with an artist in France, where medallic engraving was a high form of art.

Finally, he consented to do the work, if only to keep it out of the hands of Charles Barber. The sculptor prepared suggestions for the design, with the obverse featuring Columbus reaching shore in the New World, a triumphant pose with his cape flared and hand outstretched. The reverse depicted a nude boy holding a torch and several small wreaths against a background of lettered inscriptions.

The depiction of Saint-Gaudens's nude *male* was considered erotic or obscene by some observers, while in the same era nude females in paintings and statues were perfectly acceptable. After much wrangling, an insipid reverse design by Barber was mated with Saint-Gaudens's obverse. The process took a long time, and the medals and accompanying certificates were not issued to awardees until 1896.

Toward Artistic Coin Designs

The Barber designs received no artistic acclaim, and the 1878 silver dollar design by Morgan continued to be criticized. In 1895 the National Sculpture Society, acting with the American Numismatic and Archaeological Society, mounted a campaign to upgrade the art on U.S. coinage. An exhibition was held in May at the Academy of Fine Arts in New York City, and prizes of $300 and $200 were given for the first and second best ideas for a new silver dollar. J.Q.A. Ward, president of the National Sculpture Society, and members Augustus Saint-Gaudens, Richard M. Hunt, and R.W. Gilder all were interested in the project.

"Among the members of the society are Cornelius Vanderbilt, August Belmont, George W. Vanderbilt and almost all the professional sculptors and art lovers in New York City. Powerful efforts will be made to induce the government to adopt the successful designs," a news item related. Nothing came of the idea.

Finally, in 1905 a great leap forward was made. President Theodore Roosevelt, the only chief executive to be deeply interested in coinage designs, commissioned Augustus Saint-Gaudens to redesign the entire coinage spectrum from the cent to the double eagle. This happened after Roosevelt viewed the coins on display at the Smithsonian Institution, admiring the sculpture-like relief of coins of ancient Greece, and he was inspired to have American coinage created of equal merit. He considered the current silver and gold coins to be insipid and unartistic. By early 1907, after Saint-Gaudens had submitted various ideas, sketches, and patterns, designs were ready for the gold eagle and double eagle, the latter possessing the date MCMVII and a very high relief.

Saint-Gaudens died of cancer on August 3, 1907, after which his work was continued by Henry Hering, an assistant at the studio in Cornish, New Hampshire. Chief Engraver Barber protested that the relief was too high on the double eagle to strike up properly. Roosevelt, seemingly as annoyed with Barber as Saint-Gaudens had been, stated that even if only one coin *per day* could be struck, that is the way it would be!

In practice, it took three blows of the press for each coin. After 12,367 of the MCMVII coins had been struck, Barber flattened the relief and changed the date to read 1907. Upon their release through banks in December, the MCMVII coins were praised to the skies by just about everyone. The age of an outside artist doing an entire coin design had arrived!

Artistic Designs Continue

Hoping to continue the new designs and complete the gold series, Roosevelt acted through an intermediary and secured the services of Bela Lyon Pratt, a Boston-area sculptor. Pratt created a design for both the $2.50 and $5 gold coins featuring a realistic Indian-head portrait on the obverse, in contrast to the imaginary head used by James B. Longacre on the Indian Head cent. On the reverse was a standing eagle similar in concept to the one Saint-Gaudens had used on the $10 gold coin of 1907, an adaptation of a motif used on an ancient Greek coin. Both obverse and reverse were intaglio or incuse, sunk below the level of the surrounding field. The collecting community viewed it as inartistic, and letters complaining about it were published in *The Numismatist* and elsewhere.

Next for consideration was the cent. The Indian Head motif in use since 1859 was admired by many, but now, 50 years later, it was time for a change. In 1908 Victor David Brenner, a New York City sculptor who was also a member of the American Numismatic Society, was tapped as the designer. A handsome portrait of Abraham Lincoln was adapted from a plaque Brenner had executed. The new Lincoln cents were released on August 1, 1909, by which time William Howard Taft was in the

White House. The public reception was enthusiastic. The presence of the designer's V.D.B. initials on the reverse caused a minor kerfuffle and they were removed. The portrait lives on to this day, more than a century later—the all-time longevity record for a federal coin design.

In 1912, James Earle Fraser was selected to design a motif to replace the Liberty Head that had been in use on the nickel five-cent piece since 1883. Working with portraits of three Native Americans, he designed a composite "Indian Head" obverse. For the reverse he created a buffalo (American bison), working from the image of Black Diamond in the Central Park Zoo. The first Buffalo nickels were dated 1913 and released that year—to the enthusiasm and acclaim of the numismatic community.

Contemplating the Silver Coinage

Remained to be redesigned were the dime, quarter, and half dollar. Silver dollars had not been minted since 1904; the master hubs for the design had been destroyed, and there was no prospect of ever coining more. Hundreds of millions of Morgan-design dollars dating back to 1878 remained in storage in Treasury vaults, including those of the mints. Accordingly, the old Morgan design was forgotten, and there was no interest in creating new designs for that denomination. The challenge was to replace Charles Barber's disliked Liberty Head design, in use on the dime, quarter, and half dollar since 1892.

At the time, the New York Numismatic Club was one of the most active of such organizations in America. Monthly meetings were held in a private room at Keen's Old English Chop House at 36th Street and Sixth Avenue, New York City, where a fine dinner was followed by discussions, programs, and exchanges of information. On the evening of December 11, 1914, action was taken to encourage the Mint to create new designs. Thomas L. Elder, a member of the executive committee, had severely criticized the existing issues. Members agreed, and William H. Woodin, a longtime collector who controlled the American Car and Foundry Company, was named as chairman. During this era club members also railed against the perceived unattractive surface of Sand Blast Proof gold coins, which attracted a declining number of buyers. (Sand Blast Proof gold coins were discontinued in 1915.)

Elder reinforced his stance in "Some Phases and Needs of American Numismatics," a paper delivered in January to the American Numismatic Society, noting in part:

> I would strongly recommend also that all the numismatic societies interest themselves in a movement to improve the present United States silver coinage of the regular issues. These include the half dollar, quarter, and dime, a type adopted in 1892. The designs may be changed without act of Congress in 1917, when the 25 years of issue

shall have elapsed. These coins are almost unparalleled in modern issues for ugliness, and they are in no way indicative of the power and progress of the United States, in fact they should be considered unacceptable to the smallest islands of the seas. In this movement art alliances and sculptor societies should lend their aid and influence.

Dissatisfaction with the current Barber coins was fully realized by the Mint. Mint director Robert W. Woolley met with the Commission of Fine Arts, the body that reviews coin designs and makes non-binding recommendations, in New York City on December 5 and 6, 1915. By that time artists at the Mint had been working on motifs for about a half year. New designs prepared by Charles Barber were rejected early in the meeting. It was decided that Adolph A. Weinman and Hermon A. MacNeil be invited to submit motifs. A third sculptor was desired, and Albin Polasek was chosen. On December 27 Woolley met with the three sculptors at the New York Assay Office to discuss the project and determine their interest. The answers were affirmative. Models were to be submitted by April 15, 1916.[5]

Success attended these efforts.

New Designs for Silver Coins

A letter from Director Woolley to Weinman on February 28, 1916, gives this information:

> Dear Mr. Weinman:
>
> It gives me pleasure to inform you informally that your models have been accepted for the half dollar and the dime, and that one of the eagles submitted by you is to be used on the reverse of the quarter. In other words, the secretary of the Treasury and I have awarded you tentatively two and one half out of a possible three designs. One of Mr. MacNeil's models has been selected for the obverse of the quarter dollar.
>
> I regret that it will be impossible for me to return your models until Saturday next. I wish to show them to the Fine Arts Commission, and it will be impossible for me to leave Washington before Friday afternoon.
>
> Of course the contents of this letter are to be treated as confidential until such time as the secretary of the Treasury and the director of the Mint decide to make the awards public.
>
> Respectfully.

It developed that the Weinman reverse for the quarter was not used, and the model submitted by MacNeil was chosen as the final design.

In July 1916, *The Numismatist* included this:

> On May 30 Secretary [William G.] McAdoo announced the adoption of the new designs for the subsidiary silver coins. They will probably be issued soon after July 1, the beginning of the new fiscal year. The half dollar and dime were designed by Adolph A. Weinman, and

the quarter dollar by Hermon A. MacNeil. Several sculptors were commissioned to submit sets of sketch models. From more than 50 models Secretary McAdoo and Mr. Woolley, director of the Mint, selected three sets. Not only will there be a change of design, but each of the three denominations will have a different obverse and reverse. This idea was suggested by Mr. Woolley.

The obverse of the half dollar bears a full length figure of Liberty with a background of the American flag flying to the breeze. The goddess is striding toward the dawn of a new day, carrying laurel and oak branches, symbolic of civic and military glory. The reverse shows an eagle perched high up on a mountain crag, wings unfolded. Growing from a rift in the rock is a sapling of mountain pine, symbolic of America.

The design of the 25-cent piece is intended to typify the awakening of the country to its own protection. Liberty, a full figure, is shown stepping toward the country's gateway, bearing upraised a shield from which the covering is being drawn. The right hand bears an olive branch of peace. Above the head is the word "Liberty" and below the feet "1916." The reverse bears a figure of an eagle in full flight, wings extended, and the inscriptions "United States of America" and "E Pluribus Unum." Both the half dollar and quarter bear the phrase "In God We Trust."

The design of the dime is simple. Liberty with a winged cap is shown on the obverse, and on the reverse is a design of a bundle of rods, and a battle-ax, symbolical of unity, "Wherein Lies the Nation's Strength."

Collectors will await with deep interest the appearance of the new coins.

Mercury dimes were released into circulation in October 1916. In December the Treasury Department sent samples of the three coins to the American Numismatic Society, where they were placed on exhibit.

On December 2 this announcement was published:

Washington, D.C. Issuance of the new half dollar coin designed by Adolph A. Weinman, designer of the new dime; and the new quarter designed by Hermon A. MacNeil was deferred today by the Treasury Department until the beginning of 1917. The extraordinary demand for small coins is overtaxing the facilities of the mints, and officials believed calls for the new quarter and half dollar coins would swamp the mints if they are issued at this time.

The new quarters and half dollars were released in January 1917. While the popular press paid much attention to the new dimes, the later-released quarter and half dollar were not as newsworthy as novelties, and fewer articles appeared.

Collectively these three coins spanned the years from to 1916 to 1947, an era that included two world wars, women's suffrage, the recession of the early 1920s (resulting in none of these three denominations being struck in 1922), the "Roaring Twenties" prosperity, the gloom and doom of the Great Depression, the beginning and ending of Prohibition, New Deal changes during the Roosevelt administration, and the advent of the atomic age.

There were vast changes in transportation, communication, science, art, industry, and the American way of life. The world of numismatics changed dramatically as well. In 1916 hardly anyone collected coins by mintmark varieties, there were no standard pricing guides, and albums and folders were far in the future. By 1947, coin collecting was dynamic.

Prelude to 1916

By 1916, the American scene included these situations, elements, and aspects:

President Woodrow Wilson, who defeated his two opponents (William Howard Taft and Theodore Roosevelt) in 1912, was in the White House. Universal women's suffrage was the leading social cause of the era. While women had voting rights in scattered areas, nationally only men were allowed at the polls. Wilson had little sympathy for the movement. He was also a racist. In 1915 D.W. Griffith's epic film *The Birth of a Nation* rekindled nationwide interest in the Ku Klux Klan. At a preview held in Los Angeles, actors dressed in white Ku Klux Klan outfits were showcased, and at the official premiere in Atlanta, real Klansmen were present. One of the film's subtitles was this quotation from *History of the American People*, written by Wilson: "The white men were roused by a mere instinct of self-preservation . . . until at last there had sprung into existence a great Ku Klux Klan, a veritable empire of the South, to protect the Southern country." Child labor was another unresolved issue, as many youngsters of elementary-school age worked in factories, as sorters for coal mines, on farms, and in other pursuits, with little oversight and no compensation for injuries. The work week for many workers of all ages was from Monday through Saturday, often ten hours per day.

By 1915 automobiles were very popular, but horse-drawn vehicles were still familiar sights in towns and cities. Trolley cars for local transportation and trains for long-distance journeys were the favorite ways to travel. Motion pictures were very popular, with subjects ranging from slapstick comedies to the dramatization of Shakespeare and other classic plays and stories. Most theaters had music provided by instruments from photoplayers, which used piano rolls to pipe organs by the Rudolph Wurlitzer Company and others. A piano in the parlor was the sign of a fine home, and models ranged from hand-played to those using perforated paper rolls. Reading, games, amateur theatricals, and other amusements helped while away the evenings.

Most towns and cities were wired for electricity, but many farms and residences in remote areas had no such service. The same was true for telephone service. However, mail delivery was twice daily in many urban places and was very fast. For instant communication, the Western Union and related telegraph companies were used. Shopping, from food to clothing and furniture, was done locally. Many homes had an ice box to preserve food for a period of time, and ice deliveries were made regularly.

On the other hand, the international scene was in turmoil. The Great War, as it was called, was in progress on the European continent, precipitated by the assassination on June 28, 1914, of Archduke Franz Ferdinand of Austria, presumed heir to the Austro-Hungarian throne, and his wife, Sophie, Duchess of Hohenberg. Within a short time much of Continental Europe was involved, as was the United Kingdom. The United States was the main supplier of goods to the United Kingdom and her allies in Europe, giving rise to increased production in U.S. factories and uplift to an already strong economy. There was a call for the United States to join in, which was strongly objected to by prominent pacifists. President Woodrow Wilson called for "preparedness."

On May 7, 1915, the RMS *Lusitania*, with many American passengers aboard, was sunk by German U-boats with a loss of 1,198 lives. Many pacifists changed their position.

Shortly after the sinking of the RMS *Lusitania*, a 57 mm copper medal by Karl Goetz was marketed in Europe. The medal bears the date of May 5, corrected on later versions to May 7, suggesting that Goetz may have prepared the medal before the sinking, which may have been two days later than planned. Death is shown at a ticket window selling tickets to passengers.

Colorful posters encouraged Europeans and, later, Americans to join the war effort.

The Art and Science of Numismatics

By 1916 the collecting of coins, tokens, medals, and paper money was a popular pursuit. Many cities had coin shops with a selection of items for sale. Dealers held auctions on a regular basis, and the presentation of an old-time collection was always a memorable occasion. There were no catalogs listing market values, and there were no grading standards. Because of this, numismatists had to be students of the hobby in order to achieve success. This learning was stimulating and enthusiasm prevailed.

As a result, collecting specialties tended to be diverse and often esoteric. Tokens, medals, obsolete paper money, colonial coins, silver coins prior to 1840, gold coins from 1795 to 1834, and pattern coins were among the favorites. Very few people collected current coins by date and mintmark. The advent of popular albums and folders for the storage of these did not occur until the 1930s. Commemorative coins, from the first Columbian Exposition issues of 1892 to the latest 1915 Panama-Pacific International Exposition issues, were very popular. Proof sets in silver and gold were last made in 1915, as demand for them had been decreasing.

The leading numismatic organization by 1915 was the American Numismatic Association, established in November 1891 at a meeting in Chicago. It published *The Numismatist* monthly, a magazine that had been launched by George F. Heath in Monroe, Michigan, in 1888. Its columns contained the latest news of club meetings, auctions, new coin issues, and feature articles on many subjects.

The American Numismatic Society, founded in New York City in March 1858, was headquartered in a magnificent building in 1908 paid for by Archer Huntington, scion of a railroad family. From time to time the ANS published monographs on specialized subjects, often treating world and ancient issues. Numismatic clubs were also active in many towns and usually met monthly.

The American Scene, 1916–1947

The Year 1916

Current Events. In 1916 America enjoyed prosperity and the relative well-being of its citizens. Popular songs included "Ireland Must Be Heaven for My Mother Came from There," "Roses of Picardy," and "I Ain't Got Nobody." The *Saturday Evening Post* published its first issue featuring a Norman Rockwell painting, *Boy with Baby Carriage*, on the cover. Charlie Chaplin signed with Mutual Studios for a record $10,000. His name on a marquee or banner assured a full house. U.S. Keds, popular rubber-soled "sneakers," were introduced by United States Rubber Co. On August 25 Woodrow Wilson signed legislation creating the National Park Service. What would become Acadia National Park had its beginning when John D. Rockefeller Jr. donated 5,000 acres of Mount Desert Island in Maine to the nation.

The Professional Golfers Association of America (PGA) was formed. The Boy Scouts of America was incorporated. In Browning, Montana, on January 23 and 24 the temperature dropped from 44° degrees Fahrenheit to -56°, a record for a 24-hour change in the United States. Corporations that would evolve to become the Boeing Company and the Lockheed Aircraft Manufacturing Company were formed this year. A pistol-grip electric drill introduced by the Black & Decker Co. was a bestseller and inspired many other types of small power tools. Food prices rose sharply, due to low crop yields plus demand for exports to Great Britain. On November 7 Woodrow Wilson in his bid for reelection to the presidency defeated Charles E. Hughes.

Soldiers in combat in Europe.

In view of the expanding Great War in Europe the National Defense Act was passed by Congress on June 3, 1916, to increase the standing army of 130,000 men to 175,000 over a period of five years and to set up a National Guard with 450,000 troops. On August 29 the Naval Appropriations Act was passed by Congress to provide $313,000,000 to construct dreadnoughts and light cruisers for the Navy, an advance in technology proven effective by the combatants in the Battle of Jutland in Europe. In Santo Domingo in the Caribbean there was great unrest. United States Marines landed there in May to restore order, formally occupied the country on November 24, and would remain until 1924.

On the night of March 8, 1916, extending into the morning of the 9th, Mexican revolutionary Pancho Villa led 1,500 troops in a raid on Columbus, New Mexico, killing 17. The garrison of the United States 13th Cavalry rose to action and drove the invaders off. On March 15, President Wilson ordered 12,000 troops to cross the border to pursue Villa. On March 19, in the first American military action by air, eight planes joined in the hunt. The operation was unsuccessful.

The Numismatic Scene. To *The Numismatist* in this and other years in the era, Commodore W.C. Eaton contributed articles on minute die differences among Flying Eagle cents and mintmark positions on Lincoln cents, this in an era in which few collectors were interested in such varieties. Editor Frank G. Duffield endeavored to compile registries of certain rarities such as 1796 half cents and $3 coins of 1873, 1875, and 1876, and invited readers to contribute. Response was low as most collectors did not want to reveal their holdings. George R. Ross continued his serial study of half cents, noting that from 1793 to 1857 he had identified 122 different varieties. Unrelated to Ross, *The United States Half Cents From the First Year of Issue, 1793, to the Year When Discontinued, 1857. All Dates and Varieties Described and Illustrated*, by Ebenezer Gilbert, was published by Thomas L. Elder. On May 16 Elder held the first of what would be many auction sales. He also issued medals condemning pacifists such as Henry Ford and William Jennings Bryan.

Much space was devoted to the forthcoming new designs for silver coins. The war in Europe had spawned the creation of many commemorative medals, mostly by Germans. From this time continuing for the next several years these were a prime focus of the magazine.

San Francisco was revealed as being the only city in the United States where gold coins were seen more often than paper money in general commerce. "A silver dollar of 1794, the first standard dollar ever coined by the United States, was received at the United States Sub-Treasury Wednesday from a Louisville bank, and it was redeemed with a $1 Silver Certificate," per a notice in the Cincinnati *Times-Star*, April 20, 1916.

In 1916 the San Francisco Mint produced 4,330,000 bronze one-centavo coins for local use in the Philippine Islands, which had been administered by the U.S. Bureau of Insular Affairs since the early 1900s. San Francisco also minted copper-nickel five-centavos and silver twenty-centavos (the latter equivalent in value to a U.S. dime) this year. Such coinage would continue, with the addition of ten-centavo and fifty-centavo coins, until the Manila Mint opened and took over production in 1920.

Beginning on September 23 the annual convention of the American Numismatic Association was held in Baltimore. It was reported that membership totaled 482. Members attending the show numbered 38. H.O. Granberg, the Wisconsin owner of a particularly large coin collection, was elected president for the coming year. In recent times the Philadelphia Mint had been indifferent to the interests of collectors desiring to order Proof coins, and because of this a special resolution was made and passed by the convention:

> Resolved, That this national organization respectfully petitions the Honorable Director of the U.S. Mints to order Proof specimens of all the authorized coins of the United States for the current and subsequent years to be struck according to precedent at the U.S. Mint at Philadelphia and placed on sale with the medal clerk as heretofore, at the usual premium, as has been the rule for upwards of 60 years.

> It is also requested that the coins for this year, 1916, of the design used from 1892 to 1915, and for which dies have been made, be ordered struck and put on sale as aforesaid, and should the dies be ready in 1916 of the contemplated new designs, that they, too, be struck in Proof and also placed on sale; continuing to the end of 1916 to have both sets on sale. . . .

This did not happen, and Matte Proofs of the Lincoln cent and Buffalo were the only special coins made in 1916, after which Proof coinage for collectors was discontinued, not to resume until 1936.

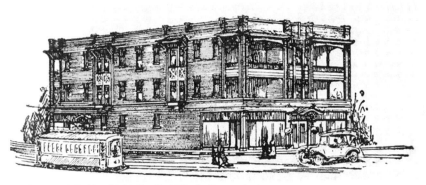

On October 2 B. Max Mehl, the Fort Worth, Texas, dealer, moved into the new Mehl Building completed at a cost of $25,000.

The Year 1917

Current Events. The World War expanded in Europe. Pacifism took a back seat, and precipitated by submarine attacks on shipping, on April 6, 1917, the United States declared war on Germany. The first American combat troops arrived in France. James Montgomery Flagg's "I Want You" Uncle Sam poster was a recruiting sensation. On Mount Wilson in California a 100-inch reflecting telescope was installed and became the world's largest. The United States purchased the Virgin Islands in the Caribbean.

The Numismatic Scene. Chief Engraver Charles E. Barber died on February 18, 1917. He was succeeded in the position by his longtime assistant, George T. Morgan.

No gold coins were minted for circulation in 1917, but the Philadelphia Mint struck about 5,000 McKinley Memorial commemorative gold dollars.

The San Francisco Mint dramatically increased its production of Philippine coinage in 1917, more than doubling the previous year's output and adding two new coins to the lineup: six million ten-centavos and nearly 700,000 fifty-centavos.

In April, editor Frank G. Duffield appealed to readers of *The Numismatist*:

> What does the present war have in store in the United States for collectors of coins, medals, and paper money? The Civil War, the last great war in which this country was engaged, gave collectors

many items of interest in paper money and tokens. *The Numismatist* would like to record in its pages a description of all numismatic issues that have their origin in America's war with Germany. It will illustrate those most worthy if specimens are furnished. Who will report the first?

Attendees at the 1917 American Numismatic Association convention photographed in front of the Memorial Art Gallery in Rochester.

A 1917 silver fifty-centavos coin, designed by Melecio Figueroa and minted in San Francisco for the Philippines. (shown enlarged)

The annual convention was headquartered in the Hotel Rochester, in the Western New York city of the same name, which offered rooms from $1.50 per day upward. Rail connections made it easy to attend. The event opened on Monday, August 27. In attendance were 80 members, a strong showing. The election was held, with most votes being by proxies, the usual method. Carl Wurtzbach won the office of president with 151 votes. Social events included rides through the city in a parade of automobiles and a visit to the amusement park at Manitou Beach.

In October, Henry Chapman advertised that he had purchased a four-story residence at 333 and 335 South Sixteenth Street, at the corner of Pine Street in Philadelphia, and:

After nine months of rebuilding I am moving the 25th of this month into my new home, and in the new building I have three floors devoted exclusively to my numismatic business. When all my stock is ticketed and arranged in the five large burglar-proof safes, as well as some 25 cabinets, I will be able to display what I believe is the finest stock in America of ancient and modern coins of the world.

The Year 1918

Current Events. In March the Spanish influenza epidemic, having raged in Europe for several years, hit America, causing an estimated 500,000 deaths before it ended in June 1920. Worldwide an estimated 20 million to 100 million victims perished; facts were scarce. Theaters, auditoriums, and other places of public entertainment were closed. To conserve electricity, Daylight Savings Time was introduced in many states. With unceasing demand for war goods, many American factories ran three shifts. There were jobs for anyone who wanted them. Unemployment was just 1.4%.

The World War continued with fierce fighting and a terrible toll of lives. The Allied and associated troops of the United States, France, and Great Britain saw action on several fronts including in Russia. The Armistice was signed on November 11, ending the conflict.

The Numismatic Scene. The Pittman Act ordered the melting of many of the Treasury's long-stored silver dollars, and 270,232,722 were converted to bullion in order to provide metal for other denominations and to supply metal for international payments. No record was kept of the dates of the individual coins, thus creating a mystery as to which were melted. During the next two years untold millions of silver dollars were shipped to China. The San Francisco Mint once again increased its production, across all denominations, of coinage for the Philippine Islands, more than tripling its mintage of silver fifty-centavo pieces. In the meantime, the Philippine Legislature passed an appropriations bill that February for construction of a local mint, in Manila; this was seen as more expedient and economical than having coinage shipped from the United States, especially during wartime.

In February the editor of *The Numismatist* observed:

> Commercial numismatics has been held in check internationally since the first months of the war, and with very limited exchanges since unrestricted submarine activities. Necessity has and will continue to force European collections to seek a market, and probably beyond the ability of collectors and dealers to absorb even at investment prices. Numismatic gems, selfishly held for generations, are coming on the market, and rarities at bargain prices—if we may think of them as in the days of tranquility—are to be expected. . . .

In April the well-financed Elmer S. Sears announced his retirement from commercial numismatics, wherein he had been a partner with Wayte Raymond as financial backer of the United States Coin Company. Sears announced that his stock would be sold by B. Max Mehl, who in Fort Worth, Texas, probably had the largest volume of any dealer in America. Raymond announced that he would henceforth conduct business in his own name, moving at the time to the new building of the Anderson Studios at Park Avenue and 59th Street in New York City.

It was stated that the production of commemorative war medals had expanded, and that one collector in Holland had more than 600 varieties, purchased at a cost of about $10,000.

Throughout the summer ANA members had been planning for the annual convention to be held in Philadelphia from October 5 to 9. A great show was in the offing. That was not to happen. *The Numismatist* reported the action of the head of the Committee on Arrangements:

> At 2:00 p.m. on the afternoon of October 3 the Board of Health of Philadelphia had placed on the bulletin boards an order prohibiting all public assemblages, including those at churches, schools, theatres, moving-picture theaters, conventions, banquets at hotels, etc. "I saw this notice as soon as it was posted, and immediately endeavored to get into communication with the other members of the committee. . . . In consultation with other members of the committee . . . we concluded that the convention must be postponed, and the president ordered it postponed indefinitely.
>
> At midnight we sent several telegrams and letters to members who had announced their intention to attend, and sent additional messages during the forenoon of Friday, until all those who had informed the committee that they expected to be present were sent telegrams. Two Chicago members, Messrs. W.F. Dunham and Theo. E. Leon, and Mr. Hillyer Ryder of Carmel, New York were already on their way before the telegrams were received. Mr. Geo. H. Blake of Jersey City, who did not notify us he was coming, also arrived. Messrs. Fred Joy of Boston, M. Marcuson of Cleveland, and H.H. Yawger of Rochester, though informed, came on to enjoy meeting any members that might have arrived.
>
> We had small social gatherings at the Hotel Stenton and at the homes of two of the members of the committee, and all enjoyed the opportunities for conversation on the study in which we are all mutually interested."

On December 11 an ANA business meeting was later held at the Chamber of Commerce in Springfield, Massachusetts. Proxies were counted, and Carl Wurtzbach was reelected as president.

Following a similar action by his brother Henry, S. Hudson Chapman announced that had moved his office to a more central location, in his residence at 1128 Spruce Street, Philadelphia. Further:

> My residence of four stories, which I have owned for 20 years, is in the very center of the city, within three squares of the principal

hotels and railroad stations, where many of the principal banks and trust companies, new Stock Exchange, Union League, Art and Manufacturer's Clubs are also located, and towards which other banks are gravitating, and I see it will now be more convenient for both city and out-of-town patrons.

In November the war was over, and the prospects for numismatics appeared to be bright.

Just over 100,000 commemorative silver half dollars (with a beardless portrait of young Abe Lincoln) were struck in 1918 to mark the centennial of Illinois statehood.

The Year 1919

Current Events. In France the Versailles Treaty was signed, incorporating President Wilson's draft of the Covenant of the League of Nations, to promote international harmony. The Allies and Germany signed it, but it was rejected by the United States Senate. Placed under heavy restrictions, Germany soon sought to rebuild its former glory.

Race riots, inspired in part by *The Birth of a Nation*, broke out in 26 U.S. cities. The 26th amendment to the Constitution was ratified on January 16, inaugurating Prohibition (the ban of the manufacture, transportation, and sale of intoxicating liquors), which would last until 1933. This spawned a counterculture of smugglers and secret distillers challenged by federal agents. Jazz was the new wave of music, replacing ragtime and ballads. Movie-going became increasingly popular. In order to move profits from studios to themselves, leading players Mary Pickford, Douglas Fairbanks Jr., and Charlie Chaplin, together with director D.W. Griffith, formed the United Artists studio. Hollywood was the center of the industry, as it had been in recent years. On May 16 a Navy NC-4 Curtiss aircraft made the first trans-Atlantic flight, departing from Newfoundland, landing at the Azores, and then continuing on to Lisbon.

The Numismatic Scene. The Treasury Department declared that any and all Confederate paper money was the property of the government, the heir to the assets of the Confederate States of America. Scattered seizures took place, causing a great outcry from collectors. The idea was quickly dropped.[1]

Longtime stamp and coin dealer John Walter Scott died on January 4, 1919, at the age of 74. His name lives on today with the attribution of postage stamps to Scott numbers.

The March 1919 issue of *The Numismatist* reported that 125 bushels (an unusual measurement) of silver dollars had been shipped from Treasury vaults to the Philadelphia Mint to be melted. Further:

> With such a wholesale melting process going on, the mint reports of dollar coinage will cease to be of any value in estimating the rarity of any date between 1878 and 1904, and time alone will tell the story. The dollars coined since 1878 have not been popular with collectors, compared with other United States issues, and the number in the hands of dealers or collectors is probably small. None, or very few, are in circulation, and probably few of those that will finally be left in the Treasury will ever be in circulation again. It would seem as if these considerations might tend to popularize this coin with collectors, with a possibility that in the future some very great rarities may be determined.

In May, Henry Chapman advertised: "1919 regular coinage, 1c, 5c, 10c, 25c, 50c Unc. set $1.10."

The July issue of *The Numismatist* began with an article, "A Trial List of the Countermarked Modern Coins of the World," by Frank G. Duffield, the first in a continuing installment which was to become the standard reference on the subject.

American Numismatic Association convention attendees gathered in Philadelphia on Sunday, October 5, and were treated to an automobile trip in open cars to Valley Forge and other points of interest, concluding at six in the evening, by which time those participating had no other discomforts than the usual one of such a trip—a very heavy coat of dust. The event officially opened in the Bellevue-Stratford Hotel on Monday. On that afternoon a trip was made to the Mint. That evening Henry Chapman conducted an auction in the billiard room of his home while Mrs. Chapman entertained the ladies. On Tuesday evening Mr. and Mrs. S. Hudson Chapman invited visitors to their home, where a program was conducted in their lecture hall, and saw films of Hudson's travels in Europe. The Philadelphia dealers lived in grand style! ANA membership stood at 489, with not much of a change in recent years. Waldo C. Moore, an Ohio banker and an enthusiastic researcher in the field of tokens and obsolete paper money, was elected president. Sixty members were in attendance.

Toward the end of the year large quantities of silver dollars were shipped from the San Francisco Mint to China and valued at $1.35 per ounce, rather than face value. No account was kept of the dates involved. San Francisco's production of coinage for the Philippines, under U.S. sovereignty, dramatically decreased this year. On May 20, 1919, Philippine Insular Treasurer Albert P. Fitzsimmons, formerly a mayor of Tecumseh, Nebraska, was named director ad interim of the Mint of the Philippine Islands, then being organized in Manila.

The Year 1920

Current Events. Although radio had been used in earlier times, including in maritime and military communications, it was not until 1920 that KDKA, a Pittsburgh station, transmitted the first radio broadcast. This and related events launched a passion for radios, including crystal sets and tube models, in the home—a great growth industry in the coming decade. The nation's thirst for alcohol was unabated, and private clubs known as speakeasies (from entrants softly giving a code word at the door) were opened all across the country.

On August 26 women's suffrage became a reality when Tennessee ratified the 19th amendment to the U.S. Constitution.

A great controversy erupted after the arrest on May 5 of two Italian immigrants and acknowledged anarchists, factory worker Nicola Sacco and fish peddler Bartolomeo Vanzetti, who were accused of a murder in the armed robbery of a factory Braintree, Massachusetts, on April 15. They were convicted in 1921, after which appeals were filed and continued as testimonies were changed and new facts uncovered, creating by 1925 major demonstrations claiming their innocence in cities around America and in some foreign countries. By that time the evidence was viewed as very flimsy. The two died in an electric chair on August 23, 1927, but the *cause célèbre* of the era echoed for many years afterward.

The November 2, 1920, presidential election pitted Republican Warren G. Harding and his running mate Calvin Coolidge against Democrat James M. Cox and Franklin D. Roosevelt. For the first time nationwide, women were allowed to vote. Harding won in a landslide.

The Numismatic Scene. During the war the demand for silver and gold had reached an unprecedented high. No new gold coins had been made for circulation from 1917 to 1919. Beginning in 1918, banks stopped paying out gold coins. The situation settled in 1920, coinage resumed, and new coins were minted. The only city in America in which gold coins were widely seen in commerce was San Francisco. Beginning this year quarter eagles were virtually absent from circulation.

In 1920 the San Francisco Mint produced no coinage for the Philippine Islands. Instead, the new Mint of the Philippine Islands opened in Manila and started local production of bronze, copper-nickel, and silver coins. (Since shortly after the end of the Spanish-American War in 1898, much of the Philippines' civilian government had been overseen by the U.S. Bureau of Insular Affairs, part of the War Department.) The new mint's machinery had been designed and built in Philadelphia under the supervision of U.S. Mint chief mechanical engineer Clifford Hewitt, who also coordinated its installation. The Manila Mint was opened, with celebrations and machine exhibits, on July 15, 1920.

A commemorative silver medal was struck in Manila to celebrate the new Philippine mint there. Collectors call it the "Wilson dollar" because of its bold portrait of the president.

On January 6, 1920, the Treasury Department issued a ruling prohibiting the photography of paper money or other financial obligations of the United States. This had a chilling effect on the dissemination of numismatic information, and it was not until the 1950s that the ban was rescinded. In the intervening decades no illustrations of federal paper money appeared in print.

In February an article by Theodore J. Venn in *The Numismatist*, "Creating a Permanent Interest in Numismatics," noted in part:

> My observation has been that the majority of collectors either have been so from early manhood or else have taken it up as a diversion after the more active portion of their life had been spent. In other words, few numismatists are made between the ages of 25 and 50.

In March, editor Frank G. Duffield commented:

> Coins Were Never Cheaper: In the report of the United States Coin Committee of the American Numismatic Society, at the annual meeting in January, the statement is made that while the price of coins did advance slightly during the war, the advance was not at all in keeping with the increase in the cost of clothing and food. . . . The wise collector will not need to be urged to buy now to the best of his ability.

The annual American Numismatic Association convention was centered in the Hotel Sherman, Randolph and Clark streets, Chicago, which offered accommodations beginning at $2.50 per day for a room without a bath, to $9 upward for two connecting rooms with a bath. The event opened on Monday afternoon, August 23, with a welcoming address by President Waldo C. Moore, who was reelected at the show. In due course Moritz Wormser, chairman of the board of governors, berated dealers who came to such gatherings with the intention of selling coins.[2] S. Hudson Chapman countered with the comment that if there were not coins for sale, many members would not attend. Membership had increased to 603, a heartwarming situation inasmuch as membership had been a prime order of concern during the past year.

A discussion was held as to whether the ANA should combine with the American Numismatic Society, "a society of art members and not a national organization at all," and whether the ANS with its own building and vast collection would be interested. The matter was dropped. Samuel S. Brown, formerly employed at the Philadelphia Mint, was on hand for a short time on Monday and showed five 1913 Liberty Head nickels, a variety not earlier known to exist. On the social side, on Monday afternoon Mrs. Alden S. Boyer, wife of the president of the Chicago Coin Club, held a reception for the ladies at her home. That evening the women went to the theater and about 25 men called upon Virgil M. Brand at his home/business on Elston Street and were warmly received.

1920 drew to a close, the hobby riding a crest of enthusiasm the equal of which had not been seen for a long time. The American economy was good, the coin market was strong, and all seemed to be well.

The Year 1921

Current Events. Economic recession swept America, and hardships were experienced throughout the country. By August 5,735,000 were unemployed. By September there were nearly 20 million business failures. Prices of agricultural products fell across the board.

Warren G. Harding and his Cabinet.

President Warren G. Harding was inaugurated on March 4, beginning what some historians would call the least effective presidential administration in history. Speakeasies continued to proliferate. Druggists had a rush of business filling prescriptions for alcohol as a medicine, prompting a songwriter to compose "The Drugstore Cabaret." General William ("Billy") Mitchell flying over the Atlantic Ocean off the Virginia coast dropped a bomb and sunk the German battleship *Ostfriesland*, which eventually changed the strategy of naval warfare. Work began on the USS *Jupiter*, an 11,000-ton collier ship, to convert it to an aircraft carrier. Upon completion in 1922 it was named the USS *Langley*.

The Bank of Telluride, Colorado, announced that it would no longer pay out paper money of any kind, and that change for large transactions would be given only in silver dollars and $5, $10, and $20 gold coins.

The Numismatic Scene. Recessionary times reduced demand for nearly all products, including coins. Mintages were very low. Morgan silver dollars were coined for the first time since 1904. In December the new Peace dollars were released. Quarter eagles were longer paid out by banks or the government.

Although the economy was in the doldrums in 1921, the rare-coin market remained strong. The annual ANA convention was held at the Copley Plaza Hotel in Boston, which offered rooms for $5 per day and up. For those wanting cheaper accommodations, from $4 up, several alternative suggestions were given. The event opened on Saturday afternoon, August 20. The election of Moritz Wormser as president was announced. Membership had climbed to an all-time high of 704. Eighty members and twenty guests were in attendance. Only one new publication had been received in the past year, a pamphlet by Theodore J. Venn on the subject of coin investment. Lively discussions were held as to whether sales of coins should be permitted at conventions, a debate that ended without resolution.

Cabinets such as this were the main way to display coins in the 1920s.

The new Peace dollar design placed into circulation in December attracted attention and was admired. During this era commemorative half dollars were issued on multiple occasions, and many accounts were given of them in *The Numismatist*. There were no price guides, no grading standards, and no albums or pages to store and display coins. Most coins were kept in drawers in cabinets or in 2x2-inch paper envelopes.

The Year 1922

Current Events. The Lincoln Memorial was dedicated on May 30, in Washington, D.C. Although business improved in some areas of the United States, with a sharp upturn in automobile sales, an economic recession continued in other areas, notably agriculture. In protest to wage cuts, coal miners went on strike for many months. This action by United Mine Workers had far-reaching effects on U.S. industry. A 13% wage cut was announced on May 28, 1922, affecting 400,000 workers, who went on strike from July 1 through the rest of the summer.

The first issue of *Reader's Digest* was published in February. On November 26 the tomb of Egypt's King Tut (Tutankhamen) was discovered.

War debts were a cause of dispute among various countries, with Germany struggling to pay huge amounts to its victors. Chaos erupted in Germany, and in August the value of the mark, already an inflated 162 to the American dollar, depreciated to more than 2,000 for the dollar; even this would be high by the later standards of 1923.

The Numismatic Scene. Demand for American coinage hit a low point, and the only denominations minted for circulation were the cent, silver dollar, and double eagle.

The annual convention of the American Numismatic Association was headquartered at the Great Northern Hotel at 118 West 57th Street, at which location rooms were available for $3 and up. The event was held from August 26 through 31. On Saturday the 26th the conventioneers took a boat cruise around Manhattan on the *General Meigs*. In the evening a smoker was held for the men, while many of the ladies went to the Capitol Theatre to see the film *Rich Men's Wives* (whether it related to their husbands was a point of discussion). F.C.C. Boyd conducted an auction of about 800 lots, including these rarities: 1875 Proof gold dollar, $100; 1849 Oregon $5, Fine, $117; 1852 Wass, Molitor $5, $100; 1851 Augustus Humbert $50, Good, $140; and 1879 $4 Stella, Very Fine, $100.

Medal struck in honor of American Numismatic Association president Moritz Wormser.

Starting on Monday, president Moritz Wormser, who was reelected and would be again in the next four elections, moderated the meetings, the first of which was held in the American Fine Arts Society Building. That afternoon tours to the American Museum of Natural History and the Metropolitan Museum of Art were conducted. On Tuesday evening three buses were hired to take the attendees to Coney Island for a dinner followed by fun in Luna Park. The Honeymoon Express was the most popular ride, and one couple spent most of the evening on it. Despite the travails of the national economy, the coin hobby was in a growth stage. ANA membership hit a new high of 811. Among the presentations, S. Hudson Chapman talked about varieties of 1794 cents, illustrating them on a screen. More than two dozen members set up exhibits.

Despite continuing travails in the national economy, 1922 was a very good year for numismatics.

The Year 1923

Current Events. President Warren G. Harding died on August 3 in San Francisco from congestive heart failure and complications while on a speaking tour. Vice President Calvin Coolidge was sworn in as president at his family home in Plymouth, Vermont. Coolidge gained a reputation for reticence and became known as "Silent Cal." On October 25, Congress began investing the Teapot Dome scandal, which began in 1921 when Secretary of the Interior Albert Fall secretly leased the Teapot Dome government oil reserve in California to private operators Harry Sinclair and Edward Doheny. The DuPont Corporation marketed cellophane. In August the U.S. Steel Corporation reduced its work day from 12 to 8 hours and raised wages, but profits increased. Business across the nation regained strength, and the recession was over, or nearly so. An era of prosperity was in the offing.

The first issue of *Time* magazine was on newsstands on March 3. Economic chaos prevailed in Germany. By December it took 4.2 trillion marks to buy a United States dollar. Many municipalities issued their own provisional currency known as *notgeld*. At age 34, Adolf Hitler staged the "Beer Hall Putsch" in Munich. Hitler's National Socialist German Workers' (Nazi) party achieved increased power, which would become absolute within a decade.

The Numismatic Scene. In 1923 the numismatic scene was one of varied activity. Most numismatists collected a variety of coins, and while some specialized in U.S. pieces by date and mintmark, most seemed to have eclectic and far-ranging interests, from Hard Times tokens to current medals, to European crowns, to ancient coins. Relatively little attention was paid to current coins, and even scarce issues such as the 1916-D dime, the 1916 Standing Liberty quarter, and the low-mintage half dollars of 1921 were nearly completely overlooked in print. In the largest-ever American numismatic transaction, M. Knoedler & Co., New York City art dealers, brokered the $100,000 sale of the James Ellsworth Collection to Wayte Raymond and Ambassador John Work Garrett (who selected the pieces he wanted, after which Raymond sold the others).

In the spring the Mint Collection in Philadelphia was transferred to the Smithsonian Institution in Washington, on a loan of unspecified length. This collection was *merged* with that already on hand, but does not seem to have been specified as a gift.[3] The annual ANA convention was held in Montreal, Canada, from August 25 to 30, where the Windsor Hotel offered a single room without a bath for $3 or with a bath from $3.50 to $5. Membership stood at 830, a new high.

The Year 1924

Current Events. In the presidential election in November, using the theme "Coolidge Prosperity," Republican incumbent Calvin Coolidge handily defeated his opponent, Democrat John W. Davis. In Florida, real estate was booming, as salesmen, including William Jennings Bryan, extolled the virtues of living in the sunny South. International Business Machines Corporation was formed in New York. In due course IBM data-processing cards would become popular; they were made the size of American currency, to facilitate the public's becoming used to handling them. The first Chrysler automobile was made. More than half of the world's cars were Model T Fords, priced then as low as $290. President of the American Tobacco Company James B. Duke offered Trinity College in Durham, North Carolina, $40 million to change its name to Duke University; this was eventually done amid much criticism that the educational institution was prostituting itself.

Radio was a national fascination, with more than three million Americans owning them, mostly of the crystal-set variety. In Chicago, Al Capone and other gangsters raked in untold profits from bootleg liquor and other activities made possible by Prohibition and by lax law enforcement. The first product of New York's newly established publishing firm Simon & Schuster was a crossword-puzzle book. Soon these puzzles became all the rage. Clarence Birdseye, after seeing how the Inuit fishermen laid freshly caught fish on the ice to freeze them quickly, went home and established Birdseye Seafoods, later expanding his business to include meat, fruits, and vegetables.

More and more dirigibles were seen in the skies around the world. The *ZR-3*, made in Germany, flew from Friedrichshafen to Lakehurst, New Jersey. The United States Navy acquired the craft and renamed it the *Los Angeles*. Vladimir Ilich Lenin died on

January 1, 1924, and Petrograd was renamed Leningrad in his honor. The new German reichsmark was issued, 30% backed by gold, ending runaway inflation.

The Numismatic Scene. The annual convention of the American Numismatic Association was held at the Hollenden Hotel in Cleveland from August 23 to 28.

Slightly more than 80 enthusiasts attended. Membership had again increased and now stood at 938. Henry Chapman conducted a 321-lot auction.

George Hetrich was in attendance and announced that his book on Civil War store cards, prepared with the assistance of Julius Guttag, was scheduled to be published by the Guttag Brothers, New York City securities brokers who had entered the coin trade in 1920. The firm was prominent for most of the decade but failed after the Wall Street crash in 1928. National Coin Week was launched and would continue for years afterward, sometimes under variant names.

The Year 1925

Current Events. In July, John T. Scopes, a teacher arrested for teaching the theory of evolution, was defended by Clarence Darrow during the famous "Monkey Trial" in Dayton, Tennessee. Scopes was found guilty and was fined $100. Prosecutor William Jennings Bryan died of apoplexy on July 26, 1925, several days after the end of the trial, possibly from the strain caused by the case.

On March 18 the worst tornado in America's history leveled sections of eastern Missouri, southern Illinois, and southern Indiana, killing 689 people. On August 8, 1925, 40,000 hooded Ku Klux Klan members staged a march in Washington, D.C. The Florida land bubble continued to inflate for a time, only to break later in the year, ruining many investors. Old Gold, Lucky Strike, and Chesterfield, among many others, were popular cigarette brands. Two firms merged to form the Caterpillar Tractor Company, which would later build a huge factory in Peoria, Illinois. Radio program "WSM Barndance" in Nashville, later to become "The Grand Ole Opry," aired in November 1925. Popular songs of the year were "Collegiate," "Don't Bring Lulu," "I'm Sitting on Top of the World," "Moonlight and Roses," "Jalousie," "Show Me the Way to Go Home," and "Five Feet Two, Eyes of Blue." The season's best-known musical was *No, No, Nannette*.

Books published included Theodore Dreiser's *An American Tragedy*, Sinclair Lewis's *Arrowsmith*, Anita Loos's *Gentlemen Prefer Blondes*, and *The Great Gatsby* by F. Scott Fitzgerald. The last typified the excesses of the increasingly prosperous era.

Adolf Hitler's *Mein Kampf* was published in Germany while the author was serving a prison sentence.

The Numismatic Scene. U.S. Mint chief engraver George T. Morgan died suddenly on January 4 at his home at the age of 79. He was succeeded in the post by John R. Sinnock.

What may have been the first radio programs on rare coins were broadcast on February 20. One of them, by American Numismatic Association president Moritz Wormser, was carried on WGY, New York City, and the other, on Mint history, was given by Frank H. Stewart on WLIT, Philadelphia.

It was a banner year for commemorative half dollars with the release of Stone Mountain, Fort Vancouver, and Lexington-Concord issues.

In the July issue of *The Numismatist* E.S. Thresher reported that on June 1, 1919, he had started to search for every variety of regular coin in general circulation. He lacked only these:

> *Cents:* 1924-S, 1925-D , 1925-S.
>
> *Nickels:* 1913 Liberty Head; 1924-S, 1925-D, 1925-S.
>
> *Dimes:* 1893-O, 1894-S, 1896-S, 1901-S, 1915-S, 1924-S, 1925, 1925-D, 1925-S.
>
> *Quarter dollars:* 1893-S, 1896-S, 1899-S, 1901-S, 1909-O, 1909-S, 1911-D, 1913-S, 1914-S, 1915-S, 1923-S, 1925, 1925-D, 1925-S.
>
> *Half dollars:* 1893-S, 1895-S, 1897-O, 1904-S, 1905, 1908-S, 1919-S, 1921, 1925, 1925-D, 1925-S.
>
> *Silver dollars:* 1878-S 8 tail feathers, 1884-CC, 1885-CC, 1889-S, 1892; 1893-S, 1894, 1897, 1899, 1923-D, 1925-D, 1925-S.

> I have also kept a record of other oddities found in circulation. I have received no Liberty Seated dollars, but have found 16 half dollars, 12 quarters and 21 dimes of the Liberty Seated type, many with the dates illegible; 67 nickels of the old 5 type, of which I could read the date on only eight.

The annual convention of the ANA was held at the Hotel Statler in Detroit starting on Monday, August 24. That evening was Dealers' Night, "when everybody was invited to buy and sell coins to his heart's content." Membership had reached 970, and it was stated that incoming applications would easily take it across the 1,000 line. An auction cataloged by Henry Chapman included the sale of a 1795 $10, Fine, for $40; an 1881 $3, EF, $19; a Boyd Park Lesher dollar, $25; and a "semi-Proof" 1796 quarter, $20.

To *The Numismatist* in December Thomas L. Elder contributed an article, "Pre-War and Present-Date Coin Prices and Value," that included this:

> In this present day of $9 grand opera orchestra seats, of $3.50 sirloin

steaks, and of $16-a-day wages for stone masons, one cannot help pausing to inquire whether coin values and coin prices have kept step with these things. The answer must be definitely no.

This was true, indeed. Although the American economy was expanding at an exponential rate, including from investment by amateurs in real estate and securities, it still took quite a bit of study to be a successful numismatist, a challenge that relatively few people were prepared to undertake.

The Philadelphia Mint struck more than 1.3 million silver half dollars in 1925 to commemorate the Stone Mountain Memorial outside Atlanta, Georgia.

The Year 1926

Current Events. In 1926 no half dollars were coined for circulation, nor had any been since 1923, although there had been commemorative issues. The denomination was only lightly used, and silver dollars were hardly ever seen. It was reported that in common change the nickel was seen more often than the dime.

Prosperity continued, new construction reached a record, businesses reported record profits, and the stock market surged. The "Roaring Twenties" era was in full swing.

The Army Air Corps was established on July 2, 1926. Later, it would become known as the United States Air Force. Rear Admiral Richard Byrd and Floyd Bennett made the first successful flight over the North Pole on May 9.

For children, A.A. Milne's *Winnie-the-Pooh* and Watty Piper's *The Little Engine That Could* were published.

Josef Stalin named himself dictator of the Soviet Union in 1926, beginning a 27-year reign of terror over Russian citizens and their neighbors.

The Numismatic Scene. The annual convention of the ANA was held at the Washington Hotel in Washington, D.C., and opened on Monday, August 23. Not only had the 1926 membership of 970 failed to increase to cross the 1,000 mark, but, alas, there had been a decrease to 966. Harry H. Yawger was elected president. It rained all week, dampening excursions. The Treasury Department, located opposite the hotel, was paying out long-stored 1882-CC silver dollars at face value, to the delight of the conventioneers.

H.A. Sternberg showed a very clever coin puzzle. "The trick is to take seven coins— half dollar, quarter dollar, nickel and four pennies, totaling 84 cents—and arrange them in two rows, five coins in each row, each row totaling 82 cents. Sounds impossible, but it can be done. Try it."

The coin market was strong throughout the year. Prices remained stable. In contrast, stamp collecting was booming, and thousands attended a philatelic convention held in New York City in October.

The Year 1927

Current Events. On August 2, 1927, when asked if he would seek the presidential nomination in 1928, Calvin Coolidge said "I do not choose to run." Charles Lindbergh left Long Island's Roosevelt field alone in his Ryan monoplane, *The Spirit of St. Louis*, at 7:55 a.m. on May 20 and arrived in Paris 33 hours and 29 minutes later, making headlines all over the world and winning a $25,000 prize. Pan-American Airways was founded by Juan Trippe and grew to become America's preeminent flag carrier through the 1930s and 1940s, after which competition and diffidence toward its passengers led to its decline and eventual bankruptcy.

After 15 million Model T Fords had exited the assembly lines, the Model A Ford was introduced at a cost of $200 million for retooling, which took six months. In 1927 more than 20 million automobiles were registered in the United States. Television was first demonstrated on April 7, 1927, by the Bell Telephone Company. John Willard Marriott opened his Hot Shoppe in Washington, D.C., laying the foundation for his vast hotel and restaurant empire. *The Jazz Singer*, starring Al Jolson, captured the imagination of Americans, with its limited singing and dialogue sections. Catalyzed by this, most studios would add soundtracks to films in the early 1930s. The Academy of Motion Picture Arts and Sciences was founded on May 11. The first award statuette, later named "The Oscar," was given for the film *Wings*.

The Numismatic Scene. The yearly American Numismatic Association convention was headquartered at the Hotel Bond in Hartford, rates for which ranged from $2.50 for a single room without a bath to $8 for a deluxe double room with a bath. The Connecticut State Library, which displayed the extensive Joseph C. Mitchelson Collection, was the main attraction. The first session opened on Monday, August 22, in the State Library. Finally the association's membership at 1,002 had crossed the magic 1,000 line. Charles Markus was elected president. Among the proposals raised was the establishment of a grading system:

> The old description of "Fine for coin" is one of the most meaningless sentences ever introduced in a catalogue. As it is today, every dealer and cataloguer has a standard of his own, and it is a sliding scale at that. A coin is either Fine or Good or Poor; if Poor, but rare, let us say so.

It was also felt that if more reference books were published this would boost the hobby. At the time such books were few and far between and mostly out-of-date.

Vermont's statehood sesquicentennial was celebrated in 1927 with a commemorative silver half dollar. 28,142 of them were distributed.

The Year 1928

The Ford Motor Co. assembly line.

Current Events. Republican presidential candidate Herbert Hoover, a statesman and businessman who had a reputation for accomplishments, ran against Democratic candidate Governor Alfred E. Smith of New York, a Catholic who was in favor of repealing Prohibition. Smith's religion was attacked in a negative campaign. Hoover's statement that progress was changing from a full dinner pail to the full garage was misquoted by his opponent as saying "A chicken in every pot and two cars in every garage." Hoover won by a landslide.

The economy continued to boom, and soaring stock prices led the way. Pledging their assets and buying on margin, many citizens contemplated their paper profits. The Bank of America, based in California, was the country's largest banking institution.

The antibacterial property of penicillin was discovered, and soon caused a revolution in the medical treatment of infection.

On May 11 the first scheduled television program was broadcast by WGY in Schenectady, New York. On radio, the 15-minute *Amos 'n Andy Show* made its debut on March 19, 1928, in Chicago. The next year the show would be broadcast nationally and it soon captured about two-thirds of the available radio audience, 40 million listeners. Theaters, seeking to maintain their trade, interrupted their programs to broadcast Amos and Andy each evening. Walt Disney introduced Mickey Mouse in *Plane Crazy*, a black-and-white cartoon, Disney Productions' first release.

Most families in 1928 had automobiles. The Ford Motor Company assembly lines were busy turning out the new Model A. During this time there was a tremendous outflow of American gold coins to foreign banks and other entities. In 1928 the Bureau of Engraving and Printing developed new small-size paper money, to be circulated beginning in July 1929, ending the large-size format in use since the Civil War.

The Numismatic Scene. In March the Beistle Company of Shippensburg, Pennsylvania, announced the availability of Unique Coin Holders, albums with insertable pages. This was a watershed moment in American numismatics. Beginning this year a number of collectors and dealers started putting away inventories of bank-wrapped current coins.

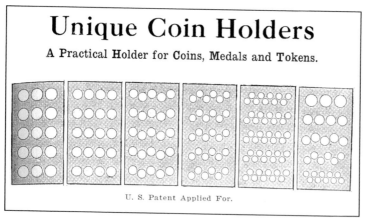

The time was not far distant when coin collecting in America would be transformed by these and related holders, and a new generation of numismatists would direct their efforts to filling in holes, much as the crossword puzzle fan enjoys filling in the last word. Commemoratives were active, and prices had been rising in recent times.

The ANA convention was held at the Hotel Seneca in Rochester, New York, from August 18 to 23, with the first business session on Monday the 20th. The membership was at a new high of 1,105. Charles Markus was reelected president. At the banquet attended by 97 members and guests a new song, "Coin Bugs," sung to the tune of "It Ain't Gonna Rain No More," was introduced and with new verses lampooning people and events it would become a staple at such gatherings.

The Year 1929

Current Events. The St. Valentine's Day gangland massacre in Chicago on February 14 received nationwide headlines and showcased the widespread corruption in Chicago, mostly financed from the illicit liquor trade. Prohibition continued to be a profitable opportunity for the underworld. It was an era of unprecedented wealth for those in the upper reaches of society. Automobiles were the height of transportation luxury as were Pullman coaches on railroads. Wooden-hulled sports boats and larger yachts were in great demand. Mansions were built in record numbers. Entrepreneurs, envisioning even more expansion, planned more skyscrapers, and construction begun. The stock market reached record highs, driven to a large extent by the public buying on margin. $1,000 in capital would allow the purchase of $10,000 in stock—seemingly risk free, as stocks had been going up ever since the early 1920s.

Storm clouds were gathering on the economic horizon, however, and some businesses and projects began to experience a diminishing of demand. On March 25 the Federal Reserve warned of excessive speculation in stocks, causing a temporary drop in the market, soon forgotten when prices continued upward. Agricultural interests had not shared in much of the growth of the decade, and their plight was recognized. Consumer credit was at a record high, with buyers betting on future prosperity. Automobile sales slackened. These situations surely would pass and were not widely publicized. In August 1929 the Guttag Brothers, securities brokers who were also important in professional numismatics during the decade, disregarded such warnings and proudly announced that they had purchased a large parcel of land at 42 Stone Street in New York City and were to erect a three-story financial center.

After financier Roger Babson warned that "a crash was coming," the market took a hit on September 18. However, optimism prevailed and prices resumed their upward trend.

The death knell, or almost, of the market took place on "Black Thursday," October 24, 1929, when at the opening bell the stock market lost 11% of its value, part of which was recovered by the end of the day. On "Black Monday," October 28, the Dow Jones Industrial Average lost 13% of its value, as investors were forced to sell in face of margin calls they could not meet. On "Black Tuesday," the next day, the DJIA lost another 12%. The volume record for that day would not be broken until nearly 40 years later.

Wealthy traders, financiers, and industrialists announced they were confident and amid enthusiastic announcements made scattered purchases in the market. It was to no avail. The Great Depression had started.

The Numismatic Scene. M.L. Beistle announced the publication of his book on early half dollars, joining A.W. Browning's volume on early quarter dollars as two important references on federal coinage issued in the 1920s.

The ANA convention was held in the Congress Hotel in Chicago from August 24 to 29. In attendance were B. Max Mehl and his family, recently returned from a grand tour of Europe. Membership increased slightly to 1,125. The attendance comprised 103 members and about 30 guests. Alden Scott Boyer of Chicago was elected president. A new song, "Coin Days," was introduced, but the previous year's "Coin Bugs" continued to be the favorite. A splendid view of the *Graf Zeppelin* was had by members as it flew over Chicago on the last lap of its around-the-world trip.

By December, when the stock-market crash dominated the news, no setback was seen for the prices of rare coins.

The Year 1930

Current Events. Unemployment rose to 8.9%, and President Hoover appointed a committee for relief. The Hawley-Smoot Tariff Act was passed by Congress in an effort to strengthen domestic industry. Foreign countries reciprocated, and international trade went into a sharp decline, an unintended consequence. Historians would later ascribe this as a major factor causing the Depression.

Clyde Tombaugh discovered Pluto, the ninth planet (the status of which was modified generations later). Vannevar Bush constructed the "differential analyzer," the first analog computer.

First-day-of-issue envelope with the three *Graf Zeppelin* stamps and the signatures of the postmaster general and other Post Office officials.

The large and impressive *Graf Zeppelin* continued to make the news. In 1930 its Europe–Pan America round-trip flight formed the occasion for the Post Office to issue a set of three stamps of $0.65, $1.30, and $2.60 denominations, which were eagerly snapped up by collectors and which remain as classics today.

The Numismatic Scene. As a result of alloy debasement of coins in many countries the price of an ounce of silver dropped to 44 cents early in the year, giving a U.S. silver dollar a melt-down value of just 35 cents. The Treasury Department officially discontinued the quarter eagle on April 11. Although they had been coined as recently as 1925 to 1929, they sold at a premium when found at banks. Liberty Standing quarters were minted for the last time.

NOW COMPLETE

The National

Coin Album

Pages for all dates of U. S. Silver and Copper Coins, each opening stamped with date.

At all times your coins are in plain view but are insured complete protection.

This remarkable Album makes your coin collection as easy to handle as a collection of stamps.

Window sections of transparent celluloid cover each row of coins, and are easily moved by friction of the fingers. Both sides of the coins may be seen.

It may be purchased in sections.

Descriptive Circular on request.

Scott Stamp & Coin Co.

1 West 47th St., New York

The Scott Stamp & Coin Company, operated by Wayte Raymond, began to market its "National" albums made by Beistle—presaging a new world of collecting. Raymond commented that the company had discontinued selling coins some years earlier because:

> At that time the collection of coins required bulky cabinets; such things as were available were not only expensive but were ugly in appearance. They had no place in the home, excepting perhaps some out of the way corner in the cellar.

Devising a grading system for coins had been an active topic since the 19th century, but especially since the American Numismatic Association convention in Hartford in 1928. In a January article Robert H. Lloyd laid the problem on dealers, who often used meaningless descriptions. In 1930 more proposals were advanced, including one using numbers, but it was generally conceded that opinions varied and no consensus would please all.

The Guttag Brothers had guessed wrong in 1929 when they set about building a financial center for their securities business. They were forced to liquidate their stock in 1930 and failed soon afterward.[4]

The annual ANA convention was held at the Statler Hotel in Buffalo from August 23 to 28. Membership was 1,196, representing an increase of 71 during the year. George J. Bauer was elected president. A vigorous debate took place when Frank G. Duffield, editor of *The Numismatist*, suggested that no one under age 21 should apply to join the ANA. Others suggested that youngsters were the brightest and best in the hobby. The matter was not resolved. A paper by George A. Pipes, "How Not to Do It," held that most collectors enjoyed the variety and history of the pieces they owned, but for some that was changing:

> This can best be demonstrated by describing a species of collectors who, alas! are becoming too common. Such a one is he who has permitted avarice to absorb his entire interest in numismatics. He knows little about his coins, and desires to know no more. He is only interested in their value. . . .

In contrast to the situation on Wall Street, the rare-coin market showed strength in all areas, with prices considerably advanced over what they had been a year or two earlier. A complete set of 1915 Panama-Pacific coins fetched $600, an Uncirculated 1796 quarter eagle without stars brought $225, an Uncirculated 1826 $5 brought $385, a Very Fine 1792 half disme fetched $63, a 1793 Chain AMERICA cent, "Extremely Fine for coin," went to a buyer for $44.50, a 1796 half cent with pole in Fine grade commanded $155, an 1861 Confederate restrike half dollar brought $26, and an Extremely Fine 1652 Massachusetts Pine Tree shilling sold for $47.25.

The year 1930 closed on a favorable note. In complete contravention to the national economy, the hobby of coin collecting was strong and growing stronger. The Scott albums had a lot to do with this.

The Year 1931

Current Events. Al Capone was sentenced to 11 years in prison for tax evasion. Congress adopted "The Star Spangled Banner" as the national anthem over protests that "America the Beautiful" was easier to sing and had nicer lyrics.

Construction of the Empire State Building, the world's highest structure, was completed, but tenants were hard to find. The electric Frigidaire made by General Motors accelerated the demise of the traditional ice box. Automobile sales continued to decline. Construction of the Hoover Dam began on the Colorado River; it would be completed in 1936.

The Numismatic Scene. The annual convention of the ANA was held in Cincinnati from August 29 to September 3 at the Netherland Plaza Hotel, where rooms were $3 per day and up. Membership had grown by 48 names during the year and stood at a record 1,244. George J. Bauer was reelected as president. He remarked how fortunate coin collectors were to be part of a dynamic and growing hobby when national economic conditions were growing increasingly gloomy.

The Great Depression took its toll on some numismatists. Baltimore bank president Waldo C. Newcomer was having difficulties and turned over his magnificent collection to B. Max Mehl to sell. This would be accomplished in 1932 and 1933. Prices of some commemorative coins fell slightly.

The Year 1932

Current Events. Despite President Herbert C. Hoover's comment that "prosperity is just around the corner," the Great Depression deepened. Congress established the Reconstruction Finance Corporation in an effort to stimulate the economy. Tens of thousands of Bonus marchers, as they were called, marched in Washington, claiming monetary bonuses earlier promised for their service in the World War. Most left after Congress rejected their plea, and Army troops led by Douglas MacArthur forcibly removed the others. Unemployment was at a record 24.1%. Radio City Music Hall opened in New York City and featured the Rockettes chorus line and the largest Wurlitzer theater pipe organ ever made.

Franklin D. Roosevelt.

The new Washington quarter, introduced in 1932.

The November 8 election drew more interest than any other such contest in American history. Incumbent Republican Herbert Hoover sought reelection on his record (which he thought was excellent) and the promise that good economic times were in the offing. Democrat Franklin D. Roosevelt saw no such possibility and offered a "New Deal" for Americans, with specific plans for new programs. On September 9, 1932, with the election looming, the Dow-Jones Industrial Average closed at 41.63, down 91% from its level on the same day in 1929. More than 5,000 banks had failed. Roosevelt won in a landslide.

The Numismatic Scene. Through the efforts of Nelson Thorson, a governor of the American Numismatic Association, the Treasury Department in Washington was persuaded to offer for the first time a selection of older as well as current coins at face value. This was in response to the difficulty some collectors had experienced in filling the spaces in their collections, as stocks held by banks were erratic. By autumn these were available:

> *Philadelphia Mint coinage:* 1¢: 1929, 1930, 1931, 1932. 5¢: 1929, 1930. 10¢: 1929, 1930, 1931. 25¢: 1929, 1930. $1: 1921 Morgan and Peace, 1924, 1925, 1926, 1927, 1928. $5: 1929. $10: 1932. $20: 1931, 1932.

> *Denver Mint coinage:* 1¢: 1930, 1931, 1932. 5¢: 1929. 10¢: 1931. 25¢: 1928. 1929. 50¢: 1929. $1: 1921, 1922, 1926. $5: 1907, 1909. $10: $20: 1925, 1926, 1927, 1931.

> *San Francisco Mint coinage:* 1¢: 1929, 1930, 1931. 5¢: 1929, 1930, 1931. 10¢: 1929, 1930, 1931. 25¢: 1928, 1929, 1930. 50¢: 1929. $1: 1921, 1922, 1923, 1924, 1925, 1926, 1927, 1928. $5: $10: 1930. $20: 1925, 1926, 1927, 1930.

The new Washington quarter released on August 1 was the focus of much attention. Wooden nickels were introduced in Tenino, Washington, for use in local commerce after the town's only bank closed. This launched a nationwide passion for such pieces. Collecting coins from circulation, especially one-cent pieces, became very popular, leading the way to widespread interest in mintmarked coins. The Raymond "National" albums continued to be popular.

A Little News From
ALDEN SCOTT BOYER
PRESIDENT
of the A.N.A.

The annual convention of the American Numismatic Association was in Los Angeles at the Biltmore Hotel from August 20 to 26. The summer Olympic Games had been held in the summer and had closed on August 14. Alden Scott Boyer was elected ANA president. For the first time in many years the Association's membership dropped, with a loss of 93 names. Fewer than 50 people registered at the event, a situation ascribed to its location in the West, remote to most of the Association's membership.

The Year 1933

Current Events. Franklin D. Roosevelt was inaugurated on March 4. "The only thing we have to fear is fear itself," he stated. In view of the failure of President Hoover to do much about the Great Depression, Roosevelt offered hope.

William H. Woodin, one of America's most prominent numismatic scholars, was appointed secretary of the Treasury. On March 6, President Roosevelt announced a "complete bank holiday in the United States for the period Monday March 6th to Thursday, March 9, 1933, both inclusive. . . ." The Bank Holiday, which was extended for some institutions, permitted solidly based banks to reopen if they passed the scrutiny of auditors. Many others were forced by the Treasury Department to close or to be consolidated with other banks, with bank officers having little say in the matter.

On March 12 the president gave his first radio address, inaugurating a series of popular "fireside chats." A few days later on March 15 the Dow Jones Industrial Average went up from 53.84 to 62.10, or a gain of 15.34%—the highest one-day percentage gain before or since.

On April 3 Roosevelt ordered that all gold coins held by the public (above an allowance for up to $100 per person, and with numismatic collectibles excepted), must be surrendered to the government, through banks and Federal Reserve offices. Despite this, the minting of double eagles continued. Of the 445,500 pieces struck of the 1933 $20, 100,000 were minted in March 1933, 200,000 in April, and 145,500 in May. Was it intended to resume the use of these in circulation? No logical reason has ever been found for their production. Nearly all would later be melted by the government.

Unemployment stood at 25.5%. History would show that 1933 was the low point in the business slump. Prohibition was repealed, and liquor became an open business. Frequency Modulation (FM) radio was announced, bringing new clarity to the airwaves. The Century of Progress Exposition in Chicago drew many visitors.

The Numismatic Scene. The February 1933 issue of *The Numismatist* included an article, "Enthusiasm," by Waldo C. Moore. Enthusiasm and collecting went hand in hand, the author noted, and a spirit such as this was "a fine thing to keep this old world going."

The annual ANA convention was held from August 26 to 31 in Chicago at the Congress Hotel, directly across the street from the entrance to the Century of Progress. The membership declined by 54 names during the year, with the roster standing at 1,094. Nelson T. Thorson was elected president.

The coin market continued to be strong. B. Max Mehl said the "New Deal" of Roosevelt was responsible for record prices in one of his auctions. On the other hand, with the nation in distress, discretionary money became scarce, and behind the scenes many rarities were available for prices lower than two years earlier. Across the country coin collecting continued to surge in popularity with people looking through pocket change for scarce cents and nickels in particular, but some higher denominations as well.

The Year 1934

Current Events. By 1934 business conditions in the United States had improved, but not greatly, and social conditions were unsettled. In January the Treasury set the price of gold at $35 per ounce, up from the traditional $20.67 per ounce value in effect when gold coins were recalled in 1933. Citizens who turned in their coins were the losers.

Henry Ford's business had taken an uptick, and he restored the $5 per day minimum wage to 47,000 of his 70,000 workers. The Chrysler Airflow car featuring overdrive was introduced, bringing streamlining to the car business, but the model sold in only limited numbers. American Airlines and Continental Airlines were formed.

Vast dust storms swept through Oklahoma, Kansas, Texas, and other Midwestern states, stripping tens of millions of acres of valuable topsoil, eventually leading to several hundred thousand farmers leaving the Dust Bowl. Many moved west, primarily to California.

On January 1, 1934, Dr. Frances E. Townsend proposed a pension scheme, popularly called the Townsend Plan, that would furnish a stipend to everyone over 60 years of age. Louisiana senator Huey Pierce ("Kingfish") Long controlled the government of his state and suggested a wealth-distribution plan that would make "every man a king." Many get-rich-quick schemes were propounded across the country.

Father Charles Coughlin attracted wide radio audiences by preaching his view of social conditions and condemning President Roosevelt. The Nazi party was in firm control in Germany, and the Japanese were building strength in the Far East.

On May 23 a barrage of bullets ended Clyde Barrow's and Bonnie Parker's two-year rampage of murder and robbery. On July 22, Public Enemy No. 1, John Dillinger, who had spent 11 years robbing banks ("because that is where the money is") in Midwestern states, was shot dead by FBI agents as he left the Biograph Theater in Chicago.

The Federal Communications Commission (FCC) was created. Shirley Temple made her first full-length film, a first step in her becoming the child sweetheart of millions.

The Numismatic Scene. The years 1931, 1932, and 1933—the depth of the Great Depression—had seen a sharply reduced production of regular coinage at the three United States mints (Philadelphia, Denver, and San Francisco). In 1934 signs of an economic recovery began appearing, and with this came a demand for new coins, starting an upward trend.

Across the nation hobbies were booming. A lot of people had spare time on their hands. Jigsaw puzzles, crossword puzzles, stamps, and other pursuits drew millions. At a hobby show in Rockefeller Center from April 25 through 30 the American Numismatic Association set up a display, including coins from members' collections. It was always crowded with spectators standing three or four deep, according to a report.

The first large edition of Wayte Raymond's *Standard Catalogue of United States Coins* was issued for $2.50, to be followed by other editions, 18 in all, through 1957. Now, for the first time in a single book, valuations and mintage figures were available. The prices it reported were what the Scott Stamp & Coin Co. would sell the coins for if they were in stock (but inventory was modest at the time). Raymond revived the *Coin Collector's Journal* title and commenced to issue monographs on specialized subjects. With his National albums selling well, he was leading the hobby.

The annual ANA convention was held in Cleveland from August 18 to 25 at the Carter Hotel. Membership increased by 91 during the year and now stood at 1,160. Nelson T. Thorson was reelected president. For the first time a dealers' bourse was set up. More than 100 members attended the show.

Commemorative coins were creating a lot of interest and rising in price, which in turn stimulated even more activity. In 1934 several issues appeared including the Maryland Tercentenary and the Texas Centennial (although the Texas centennial of independence would not be celebrated until 1936).

All told, 1934 was the most active year that the hobby of coin collecting had ever seen up to that point.

1934 was the first year of the Daniel Boone Bicentennial half dollar; the commemorative would also be issued annually from 1935 through 1938.

The Year 1935

Current Events. The Rural Electrification Administration (REA) was established. At that time only about 10% of America's 30 million people living on farms had electrical service, but thanks to the REA and other efforts the figure would climb to 90% within 15 years. Congress passed the Social Security Act on August 14, 1935, to provide income for retirees (also see 1940).

On September 8, Governor Huey Long of Louisiana was assassinated by Carl Austin Weiss, M.D., who sought to save America from an aspiring dictator.

Canned beer was introduced by Krueger of Newton, New Jersey. Alcoholics Anonymous was founded in New York on June 10, 1935.

Beginning an era of trans-Atlantic "palace" liners, the SS *Normandie* went into service for the French line.

William Randolph Hearst reportedly earned the highest salary in the United States in 1935, with sex-symbol movie actress Mae West ("Why don't you come up some time, and see me") earning the second highest. The first football bowl game was held in Miami on January 1, 1935, when Bucknell defeated Miami 26–0. The first major-league night baseball game was played on May 14 at Crossley Field in Cincinnati. The real-estate–trading game Monopoly was introduced by Parker Brothers, bringing a fortune to Charles B. Darrow of Pennsylvania, who laid out the game board by using street names from Atlantic City, New Jersey.

The B-17 bomber was demonstrated by the Boeing Aircraft Company. Experiments continued with radar, which would play an important role in World War II several years later.

Adolf Hitler denounced the Treaty of Versailles, which provided for the disarmament of Germany, and organized the Luftwaffe to give Germany a military air force.

Nazi leader Heinrich Himmler proposed a breeding program to create a pure Aryan "super race" of blonde, blue-eyed children, and encouraged young women "of pure blood" to mate with SS officers. The Nuremberg Laws enacted by the Nazi party on September 15 deprived Jews of German citizenship and set up other restrictions, beginning widespread officially sanctioned persecution that would accelerate to become the Holocaust.

The Numismatic Scene. Numismatically the year 1935 was one to be remembered. Coin collecting went into the fast lane. Newly issued commemorative half dollars were in short supply, and the Hudson (New York) Sesquicentennial issue, of which 10,000 were made for distribution at $1 each, zoomed in value to $5, then $7 per coin. Old Spanish Trail halves did likewise, and a special issue of 1935 Boone half dollars with a small "1934" on the reverse multiplied from $3.70 for a pair of Denver and San Francisco coins to $50, in a fraudulent promotion by issuer C. Frank Dunn. Many collectors complained that distribution practices were unfair. By year's end, as more new commemoratives were planned for the year ahead, there was great controversy surrounding them.

Lee F. Hewitt launched the *Numismatic Scrapbook Magazine*, soon to be the most popular coin periodical ever. Gold coins, including large denominations, attracted many buyers who felt they were a good store of value in an economy viewed by many as having an uncertain future. In an article, Thomas L. Elder reminded readers that gold coins are indeed "tangible assets."

Henry Chapman died in Philadelphia on January 4 at the age of 75, having been in professional numismatics since he was a teenager. His company continued to be conducted by his secretary, who used his name in print, not mentioning that he was deceased. This continued into the 1940s.

In 1935 B. Max Mehl (in his own building, since 1916, in Fort Worth, Texas) was the leading dealer in the country. He boasted a capital of $250,000 and made most of his money by selling *The Star Rare Coin Encyclopedia*, a premium guide advertised in print and on the radio, suggesting that 1913 Liberty Head nickels and other rarities could be found in pocket change. In New York City the Stack brothers, Joseph and Morton, conducted their first auction.

Whitman Publishing Company gained a foothold in numismatic supplies by acquiring the business of J.K. Post of Neenah, Wisconsin, and expanding it, with 1935 seeing the popularity of the "penny board," in which Lincoln cents could be placed from circulation including, hopefully, the highly prized 1909-S V.D.B. and 1914-D.

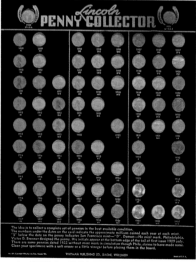

In 1935 the Whitman "Lincoln Penny Collector" board created a sensation.

The annual convention of the American Numismatic Association was held in Pittsburgh at the Webster Hall Hotel from August 24 to 29. Many of the activities were conducted nearby at the Carnegie Institute. During the year membership had jumped by 223 to a record 1,398. T. James Clarke was elected president.

The Year 1936

Current Events. On November 3 the nation's presidential election pitted incumbent Franklin D. Roosevelt against Republican challenger Alf Landon. Roosevelt triumphed with 523 Electoral College votes against Landon's pitiful 8. Unemployment improved and was at 16.9%.

Electric guitars were introduced. Already, the Hammond electronic organ was a great success.

The Numismatic Scene. Fort Knox was established in Kentucky as a repository for United States gold bullion. The commemorative boom continued with a record number of new issues. However, by the summer, continuing into the autumn, the momentum had been lost, sales were slower, and some prices suffered a setback. The euphoria was over, and large numbers of commemorative coins remained unsold—to be shipped to the Mint to be melted or to be wholesaled at a few cents over face value.

Proof sets were issued for the first time since 1916. The cost was $1.81 for a full set, but coins could be ordered individually from the Mint as well. W.R. Anderson, a Chicago dealer, announced his Daily Coin Auction. Items were put on display each day, and 10 days later they were awarded to the highest bidders.

The annual American Numismatic Association convention was held in Minneapolis from August 22 to 37 at the Nicollet Hotel. The membership in the past year had jumped by 460 to stand at 1,863. T. James Clarke was reelected president.

In 1935 the U.S. Congress had granted the Philippines commonwealth status. This gave the islands a great deal of self-governance under their own constitution—an important step toward full independence. To celebrate the transition, in 1936 the Manila Mint struck a set of three silver commemorative coins, with an issue price of $3.13.

1936 silver commemoratives celebrating the transition of the Philippines to commonwealth status.

The Year 1937

Current Events. On February 5 President Roosevelt, taking issue with the U.S. Supreme Court resisting his innovations, proposed adding more judges, whom he would appoint. This proposed "packing" of the Court caused public outrage, and the Senate rejected the plan.

On May 6 the hydrogen-filled German dirigible *Hindenburg* exploded while landing at Lakehurst, New Jersey, killing 36 people and ending that method of passenger transportation. Amelia Earhart and her co-pilot Fred Noonan set out on a round-the-world flight, but disappeared near some remote islands in the South Pacific Ocean.

The U.S. gunboat *Panay* was sunk on December 12 by the Japanese on the Yangtze River in China. Japan was pursuing a policy of dominating its section of the world, while in Germany the Nazis were building military strength and persecuting minorities.

U.S. unemployment improved and was at 14.3%.

In New York City the Glenn Miller Band made its debut. It was the beginning of the age of "swing."

The Numismatic Scene. The San Francisco Mint moved to a new facility in the city. It was dedicated on May 15. In May in *The Numismatist* editor Frank G. Duffield commented on the increasing number of coin collectors, including this:

> Anyone, without the expenditure of a dollar, may start a collection of small cents. This makes that series of coins attractive to both sexes of all ages. Its attractiveness has been stimulated by the cardboard holders for the series placed on the market by novelty dealers. . . .

The Whitman Publishing Company offered "Whitman Coin Collector Boards" consisting of pieces of rectangular cardboard with cutouts for Lincoln cents, titled "Lincoln Head Penny." These boards retailed for 25 cents each. Also available were boards for Indian Head cents, Liberty Head nickels, Buffalo nickels, Morgan [sic] dimes (a misnomer for Barber dimes), Mercury dimes, Standing Liberty quarters from 1916, Morgan [sic] quarters, and commemorative half dollars. "Whitman Coin Collector Boards for United States coins of current and recent issues now in circulation or available are developing thousands of new coin collectors—the numismatists of tomorrow," an advertisement noted. How true these words were! Any slack in the coin market caused by the slump in commemorative half dollar prices was more than made up by valuations for Indian Head and Lincoln cents, Liberty Head nickels, and other issues, all of which were achieving new highs.

The *Annual Report of the Director of the Mint* for fiscal year 1936, which ended on June 30, 1937, revealed that $600,000,000 face value in gold coins had been melted, including 1,271 $3 pieces and 4,423 gold dollars. Thomas L. Elder was keeping busy by sending letters to bank tellers advising of the premiums he would pay for rare issues. Employees of the Philadelphia Mint earned extra money privately by switching common gold coins for rare ones—a quid pro quo situation as the coins were to be melted anyway. Dealers in New York City took advantage of buying rare-date double eagles such as those of 1932 in particular, but also of 1933, and many other coins.

The annual American Numismatic Association convention was held at the Hotel Washington in Washington, D.C., from August 21 to 26. Membership stood at a high of 2,577. Nearly 200 members attended the show, another record. J. Henri Ripstra was elected president. It rained most of the week, causing discomfort for those who stayed in the hotel in an era before air conditioning. Field trips included the Smithsonian Institution, the Bureau of Engraving and Printing (specially opened after hours), Arlington Cemetery, and Mount Vernon.

The Year 1938

Current Events. In September the worst hurricane on record wreaked havoc on Long Island and much of coastal New England, causing an unprecedented loss of life and property.

On October 30 Orson Welles broadcast "War of the Worlds" on the radio. Although it was pure fiction, it sounded like a real newscast and created a nationwide panic as listeners believed that aliens had landed in New Jersey.

The national unemployment rate rose to 19.0%. The New York Yankees, the winningest team in baseball, once again took the World Series. Chester F. Carlson produced the first xerographic copy, heralding what in later years would become the Xerox Corporation. Non-stick Teflon was introduced.

The Numismatic Scene. By year's end the Treasury had melted all gold coins on hand, except for those recently turned in. The Buffalo nickel was replaced by the Jefferson design. Concerning the one gloomy spot in the otherwise dynamic market, B. Max Mehl advertised:

Commemoratives have taken an awful spanking in recent months. And those who have large stocks (and I am one of 'em) have taken more than a mere spanking! Now, I don't intend to publicly undermine the market—but, if you are really and truly in the market for commemoratives, and will send me your want list, I will make you a price that will surprise you and one you couldn't resist.

The convention of the American Numismatic Association this year was held at the Neil House in Columbus, Ohio, from August 13 to 18. Membership stood at 2,673, a gain of 144 for the year. J. Henri Ripstra was reelected president, despite allegations he had misappropriated or misspent $5,000 in association funds including for excessive travel. It was an era of rumors and name-calling. Entertainment at the ANA convention included a concert by the Columbus Chamber Orchestra, organized by the Federal Music Project, a unit of the Works Progress Administration.

A silver commemorative half dollar in 1938 marked the 250th anniversary of the founding of New Rochelle, New York.

The Year 1939

Current Events. The World's Fair opened on Flushing Meadow near New York City and was a great success. The pavilion for Czechoslovakia stood vacant, as that country had been overwhelmed by a Nazi invasion in March.

Benito Mussolini, dictator of Italy, took over Albania, and Germany invaded Poland. This signaled the beginning of World War II. President Roosevelt submitted a $1,319,000 defense budget and declared a limited emergency, but stated that America would become neutral. The arms embargo was lifted, and American munitions began to be shipped in record numbers to Great Britain.

In Washington the Daughters of the American Revolution refused to allow African-American singer Marian Anderson to perform at Constitution Hall.

The first federal food-stamp program was launched. Unemployment dropped slightly to 17.2%.

Taking nearly four hours to view, *Gone with the Wind* was the film sensation of the year. For months people had been speculating as to whether Rhett Butler (Clark Gable) would dare to speak the word "damn." He did. The "Batman" cartoon series was introduced.

Albert Einstein, a German refugee, wrote to President Roosevelt to suggest the possibility of using uranium to initiate a nuclear chain reaction. Neoprene was developed by a Harvard chemist, to become the first effective substitute for rubber. Nylon hosiery was first marketed on May 15. The first helicopter capable of sustained flight was unveiled by Igor Sikorsky.

The Numismatic Scene. Finally, the Mint's commemorative coin program ended completely with the distribution of Oregon Trail and Arkansas Centennial coins. No more would be made until 1946.

The "brilliant is best" philosophy pervaded the hobby, and most silver coins in collections were cleaned or dipped to brighten them.

In April, American Numismatic Association president J. Henry Ripstra gave this bad advice—guaranteed to *ruin* coins:

> There is no use of coin collectors having tarnished silver coins in their collection any longer, as they can safely remove the tarnish discoloration from an Uncirculated Proof coin by using the following instructions without any possible danger of injuring the coin whatsoever:
>
> Lay the coin on a small piece of cotton flannel in a saucer. Squeeze lemon juice on the coin, then apply common baking soda on a wad of cotton batting and gently rub the coin. Add lemon juice and soda until the tarnish is removed. Then dip the coin in boiling water and wipe off with a cotton flannel cloth, and you again have a brilliant coin.

Albert Einstein had left Germany in the early 1930s to escape Nazi oppression. In 1939 he was prominent in scientific development in the United States.

> To properly clean medals of bronze or gold I use common laundry soap and the ordinary household ammonia and scrub well with a bristle brush. Where coins and medals have been lacquered, I remove the lacquer with alcohol. This will not injure the article the least bit.
>
> I have demonstrated the above in various parts of the country with absolute success.

The ANA convention was held in New York City at the Hotel Pennsylvania from September 30 to October 5. Membership had jumped by 431 to a new high of 3,104 names. L.W. Hoffecker, a coin dealer and also an untruthful distributor of commemoratives (the 1935 Old Spanish Trail issue), was elected president.

Grading remained a controversial topic. Although the *Standard Catalogue* gave guidelines for Proof, Uncirculated, Very Fine, Fine, Very Good, Good, and Fair, nothing was official, and usage and terminology varied widely. A high-grade coin is either Very Fine or it is Uncirculated, with no in-betweens, commented a reader. "Was Proof, now Uncirculated" was a phrase in common use. (This makes no sense, as *Proof* is a method of manufacture, and not a grade as such. Once a Proof, always a Proof, whether perfect or impaired.)

By the end of 1939, scarce dates and mintmarks were bringing more than common ones, and in the Liberty Head nickel series, for example, such low-mintage varieties as 1885 and 1886 were becoming recognized. A decade earlier, just about all Proof Liberty Head nickels had sold for about the same price, regardless of date. Whitman and Raymond panels and albums had changed the market.

The Year 1940

Current Events. In preparation for war the Selective Service Act became law, allowing the draft for military service. The first Social Security checks reached their recipients. The unemployment rate dropped to 14.6%.

The Pulitzer Prize for literature was awarded to John Steinbeck for *The Grapes of Wrath*, his story of the Dust Bowl. The Columbia Broadcasting System (CBS) demonstrated color television. WNBT, the first regularly-operating TV station, went on the air in New York City and drew an estimated 10,000 viewers. The *Superman* radio show made its debut.

Plasma was found to be an effective substitute for blood in transfusions.

In rapid succession Nazi Germany conquered Denmark, Norway, Holland, Belgium, and France, encountering little resistance. Holland and Belgium were to suffer greatly. In London the German Blitz destroyed extensive property.

On November 5, incumbent Franklin D. Roosevelt in his bid for an unprecedented third presidential term overwhelmed Republican challenger Wendell Willkie, 449 to 82 electoral votes.

The Numismatic Scene. In *The Numismatist* in July 1940 editor Frank G. Duffield, in "Is This Numismatics" column, took exception to collectors who studied variations in mintmark positions, the number of rays on a coin, and other details. He could not, however, stem the tide of interest in such details. In the meantime it became increasingly evident that many coins prior to the 1930s, including high-mintage issues, were rare in Mint State, as few people had had any interest in preserving them at that time.

The war raging in Europe had slowed communications to and from numismatists there. Foreign mail had to pass examination by postal inspectors.

The annual ANA convention was held at the Detroit Leland Hotel, a 21-story edifice with rooms priced at $2.50 and up, from August 24 to 29. Membership had increased by 636 during the year and was now 3,176, even though European memberships dropped precipitately. L.W. Hoffecker was reelected president.

The convention auction sale, conducted by Stack's, included the following prices:

> 1856 Flying Eagle cent, Proof, $53; 1796 quarter dollar, VF $24.50; 1836 reeded edge half dollar, Uncirculated $15; 1836 Gobrecht dollar, Proof $33; 1739 Higley threepence, Broad Axe variety, Fine or better $160; 1879 $4, Proof $175; and 1887 Proof $20, $155.

The Year 1941

Current Events. On December 7 the surprise Japanese attack on the U.S. naval fleet in Pearl Harbor, Hawaii, brought the United States into World War II. War was declared against Japan, Germany, and Italy. Unemployment dropped to 9.9%. Factories everywhere began to gear up to do defense work.

Orson Welles's film *Citizen Kane* fictionalized the life of William Randolph Hearst and would come to be a cinematic landmark.

The Numismatic Scene. Whitman Publishing Co. issued the *Handbook of United States Coins*, a guide to wholesale prices dealers were paying, on average, for collectible coins. Nicknamed the *Blue Book*, it would go on to be produced annually. Wayte Raymond's *Standard Catalogue of U.S. Coins*, now containing an extensive section on tokens, was the source for retail market values, although in a rising market many listings were soon out of date.

In January in *The Numismatist* editor Frank G. Duffield observed:

> During the course of the past five years there has been a curious trend in numismatics. Perhaps this is best explained by observing that in former years numismatics was not the popular pastime it is today in thousands of homes.
>
> The numismatist was for the most part an older person seriously delving into the subject in accordance with limitations of time and purse. In the later years there has come a marked change; numismatists, today (if we may call them that), are a younger lot, filled with enthusiasm.
>
> Far more written material on the subject is available, and it has been popularized. To the penny board and its cousins, the nickel, dime, and quarter boards, we have to express thanks for having wrought this change. It has placed numismatics on a simplified basis

U.S. Navy sailors rescuing a survivor of the sinking USS *West Virginia*, Pearl Harbor, December 7, 1941.

never before thought possible. It has made it a subject which anyone can master in its elementary phases. We ask, then, what does the numismatist of old then have before him?

We can answer that it is our mission. It is up to the numismatic generation of today to train these erstwhile penny-board collectors into numismatists. They must be shown the greater values in the hobby than the mere collecting of dates and mintmarks from circulation. If the hobby had nothing but dates and insignificant letters to offer it would not be the fascinating science the real numismatist considers it to be.

This plea was to no avail. Most new collectors were primarily interested in rarity and value, not in the art and science of numismatics.

Gimbel Brothers, the New York City department store, opened a coin department managed by Robert Friedberg, whose name was not mentioned in publicity. Among items for sale was a 1787 Brasher doubloon on consignment from the Virgil M. Brand estate. In June, B. Max Mehl's sale of the William F. Dunham Collection caused a lot of attention.

The 1941 American Numismatic Association convention was held in Philadelphia at the Benjamin Franklin Hotel, which offered a special rate of $3 including a private tub and bath and circulating ice water. Most hotels of the era had shared baths. The event ran from August 16 to 21. J. Douglas Ferguson, a Canadian, was elected president. The membership stood at 3,282, a slight increase from the year before. Unlike recent gatherings, there were few controversies about grading or other matters.

Among the convention's advertisers, William Rabin, of Philadelphia, advertised a 1793 Strawberry Leaf copper, calling it "the rarest of all cents" and pricing it $2,500. I. Snyderman (the Art Trading Company), The Numismatic Gallery (Abe Kosoff with Hans M.F. Schulman also on hand), Stack's, and the New Netherlands Coin Company invited collectors to stop by and visit on the way to or from the ANA convention in Philadelphia. "Remember, only one hour and forty minutes to New York, for a grand sale," enticed Kosoff in an advertisement. From Holland, Jacques Schulman advised readers: "Please remember my address, and as soon as this war is over I will gladly take up again the agreeable relations with all my old clients and with many new ones. Meanwhile, correspondence by air mail invited."[5]

1941 would be the final year the Manila Mint struck coins for the Philippines as a U.S. commonwealth. The Japanese invasion that year interrupted all coinage.

The end of the year 1941 saw the numismatic hobby in a state of mixed emotions. The uncertainties of World War II were just beginning, and soon profound effects would be felt upon numismatics and every other aspect of human endeavor.

The Year 1942

Current Events. The war continued apace and overwhelmed everything else on the American scene. Factories that once made automobiles were converted to produce Jeeps, tanks, and airplanes. Others made ammunition, uniforms, navigation devices, and other military supplies. On the home front citizens were united in their backing of the government's action and the restrictions placed on domestic categories. Unemployment was down to 4.7%.

Many Germans and German-Americans were viewed with suspicion. Even worse, more than 120,000 Japanese and people of Japanese ancestry on the West Coast were sent to "relocation centers," some until 1945.

In Boston a fire in the Coconut Grove nightclub killed 491.

In November *Casablanca* premiered on the movie screen. Set in wartime Africa, it would go on to be one of the most acclaimed American films of all time.

The Numismatic Scene. The nation's first full year of World War II had a profound effect on U.S. numismatics. Proof coins were made in 1942, and then discontinued, not to be struck again until 1950. The composition of the nickel-five cent piece was changed to an alloy of silver, as nickel was a strategic material.

The overprint HAWAII was added to paper money circulated in those islands, so they could be repudiated if they fell into Japanese hands.

While national focus was on the war, collectors were reminded that numismatics offered an escape from everyday reality, a chance to relax and enjoy, if only for brief periods. The hobby of numismatics grew by leaps and bounds, not necessarily as a method of relaxing, but as a place to put money when consumer goods were scarce. The investment record of coins had been phenomenal since the mid-1930s, and this created even more attention and demand. For example, B. Max Mehl pointed out that a complete collection of Uncirculated Mercury dimes from 1916 onward, plus Proofs of later dates, cataloged $37 in 1937 but by 1942 had climbed to $118.

Joseph B. and Morton Stack bought the John H. Clapp collection of United States coins for $100,000, tying the Ellsworth Collection transaction price of 1923, and sold it to Louis E. Eliasberg of Baltimore, who then determined to obtain one of each federal-coin date and mintmark variety from the 1793 half cent to the 1933 double eagle (in November 1950 he accomplished this goal).

"Casablanca," the winner of the "Best Picture" Academy Award for 1944, had a wartime setting.

Amid some controversy the ANA convention was held in Cincinnati from August 22 to 27 at the Netherland Plaza Hotel. It was agreed by most that it was a welcome break from the stress of the war. The event was attended by 149 members and 70 guests. J. Douglas Ferguson was reelected president. Membership had increased by 127 to 3,541. There was an air of satirical humor in the air. The dealers' bourse was called Robbers' Row. The Pirates' Den name was given to the hospitality suite sponsored by Thomas G. Melish, who hired a local artist to depict certain collectors and dealers as buccaneers. Each lady was given a "dime and ring." An auction of 1,190 lots was conducted by Abe Kosoff.

The Year 1943

Current Events. Prices were frozen on goods and salaries. The Office of Price Administration (OPA) issued ration coupons. Scrap-metal and other drives took place. The Pentagon was completed as the largest office building in the world. Unemployment dropped to just 1.9%. Factories continued to work around the clock to make military vehicles, planes, ammunition, and other war supplies.

In July Mussolini resigned as head of Italy. American and British forces invaded Sicily.

The Numismatic Scene. Some gold double eagles were used in the North Africa campaign, but the Mint either would not or could not say where they came from.[6] Zinc-coated steel replaced the bronze alloy for Lincoln cents in 1943, but in 1944 bronze was resumed.

On September 10 and 11 in New York City the Numismatic Gallery offered at auction the Michael F. Higgy Collection with about 1,850 lots, including scarce and rare issues. Action was intense, and Abe Kosoff stated that prices were double and triple his expectations. This was the jumping-off point for very large increases in coin values during the next several years.

Many new buyers knew little or nothing about grading, with the result that the market was flooded with overgraded coins, including some polished circulation strikes offered as Proofs.

The American Numismatic Association held a business meeting in Chicago from September 11 to 13, and members were invited to attend. There were to be no programs or exhibits, but the Chicago Coin Club set up a display. About 200 people attended, to the surprise of everyone. ANA membership stood at stood at 3,638, an increase of 173 from the previous year. Martin F. Kortjohn was elected president.

The zinc-coated steel cent introduced in 1943 to save copper for the war effort. (shown enlarged)

The Year 1944

Current Events. In November, Franklin D. Roosevelt, seeking a fourth presidential term, handily defeated Republican challenger Thomas Dewey. The GI Bill of Rights was passed, providing educational and other benefits for veterans of the armed services. Unemployment was 1.2%.

Fighting was intense in many theaters of war, including in the far reaches of the Pacific Ocean. On June 6, "D Day," Allied forces left England and landed on the beaches of Normandy in France, with 176,000 men, 400 war ships, 4,000 landing and other craft, and 11,000 planes providing cover. For some time B-17 and B-24 planes of the 8th Air Force based in England, and planes of the Royal Air Force (RAF), had been bombing German cities. The liberation of Continental Europe had begun. Paris was set free on August 24. In September, Germans launched V-2 rockets or "buzz bombs" in attacks on London. Many were shot down by the RAF.

At Dunbarton Oaks, a mansion in Washington, plans were laid for the formation of the United Nations. In the Mount Washington Hotel in Bretton Woods, New Hampshire, an international monetary convention was held in July, to hash out a post-war global monetary strategy.

Boeing B-17E Flying Fortress bomber.

The Numismatic Scene. The coin market continued upward, and even commemorative coins, the prices for which had crashed in late 1936 and in 1937, were in demand. Gold double eagles in any grade found ready buyers. Cash was plentiful and many consumer products continued to be unavailable. The Flanagan and Bell auctions conducted by Stack's set records.

Plastic holders became very popular in 1944 and 1945, inaugurating an age in which individual coins as well as sets could be placed in three Lucite plastic sheets, the center one with holes for individual pieces. The sheets were held together by plastic or metal screws on the edges. These holders protected the coins from handling and from most atmospheric effects, and also made a nice display.

From August 26 to 28 the American Numismatic Association held a convention at the Hotel LaSalle in Chicago. ANA membership was reported as "close to 4,200," as compared to 3,638 the previous year. Martin F. Kortjohn was reelected president. The event was attended by 139 members and 51 visitors. William Rayson conducted an auction with 203 lots.

It was estimated that in 1944 more than $1 million had been realized in auctions, and that private sales totaled an even greater amount.[7] Although *The Numismatist* contained many offerings of coins for sale, the publication was eclipsed in size by Lee F. Hewitt's *Numismatic Scrapbook Magazine*, which in 1944 carried more pages of advertisements than any other magazine in coin-collecting history.

The Philadelphia, Denver, and San Francisco mints all contributed to the Pacific War effort in 1944 by producing bronze, copper-nickel-zinc, and silver coins for the Philippines. The coins were shipped to the islands to enter circulation as U.S. and Philippine military forces fought the Japanese troops who had invaded in 1941.

One of the 58 million one-centavo coins struck by the San Francisco Mint for the Philippines in 1944. (shown enlarged)

The Year 1945

Current Events. On April 12, Franklin D. Roosevelt died in Warm Springs, Georgia. Harry S Truman, his vice president, was sworn in as president. On March 18, Allied B-17, B-24, and other bombers—1,250 of them—rained destruction on Berlin. In desperation, the next day Adolf Hitler ordered that all industries, military installations, machine shops, transportation systems, and communication facilities in Germany be destroyed. His underlings disobeyed the order. On May 8, Germany surrendered. After VE (Victory in Europe) Day, Allied forces went through Germany and Poland and discovered horrific conditions in concentration camps.

On July 16 as part of the Manhattan Project the first atomic bomb was successfully tested in Alamogordo, New Mexico. On August 6 and 9, atomic bombs were dropped on the Japanese cities of Hiroshima and Nagasaki. The war officially ended with the surrender of the Japanese on September 2, known as VJ Day.

By the end of the war, 1.6 million Americans had served, and in the military 405,399 had died and 672,846 had been wounded. In Europe the toll far exceeded 10 million deaths, including civilians. Germany was divided into two parts: East under the control of the Soviet Union and West under joint supervision by the United States, Great Britain, and France. Reconstruction began and massive aid was sent to distressed victims of the conflict.

The high and low figures for the Dow Jones Industrial Average for the year were 195 and 155. Unemployment was at 1.9%. The Federal Communications Commission set up 13 channels for commercial television broadcasting and received 130 applications for licenses. Channels were regional, and the same channel number could be used in several places. The first all-electronic computer, ENIAC (Electronic Numerical Integrator and Calculator), was completed, and in 1946 it would be dedicated at the University of Pennsylvania.

The Numismatic Scene. As the year 1945 opened the coin market was strong and throughout the hobby an air of enthusiasm prevailed. Military successes of the American forces and their allies resulted in victory, and everyone was looking forward to worldwide peace and prosperity. The Denver and San Francisco mints continued a herculean effort of producing hundreds of millions of coins for the Philippines (where legal-tender coins had disappeared from circulation, many shipped to Japan to be melted and remade into imperial coinage). As an example, the Denver Mint made more Philippine twenty-centavo pieces in 1945 than the Philadelphia Mint's production of Washington quarters for domestic use that year. The coins were shipped overseas to accompany the U.S. military as Americans and Filipinos fought to liberate the islands.

"Cabinet friction" was a term in popular use to describe an "Uncirculated" coin that had rubbing on the higher areas. Most collectors continued to demand brilliant silver coins, necessitating repeated dipping each time they regained natural toning.

President Harry Truman.

The Numismatic Gallery offered the F.C.C. Boyd Collection of silver coins as "The World's Greatest Collection." Never mind that it lacked many rarities as well as mint-marked issues.

An executive board meeting of the American Numismatic Association was held in New York City from August 25 to 27. Membership jumped to 5,004 as growth continued unabated. Only a small percentage of collectors were ANA members. Probably well over 100,000 enthusiasts kept busy filling Whitman folders and National albums. V. Leon Belt was elected ANA president. Outgoing president Martin F. Kortjohn gave this message:

My second and last term of office as your president has drawn to a close. The two years during which I served you were for most people filled with hard work, great sorrow, and gradual hope and in the very recent past with the happiness that military victory brings. We shall endeavor to hide the past except as a lesson of what the world must not tolerate again in the future. We must look forward to the day when peace and contentment reign supreme. And with that peace and contentment we shall find the time to sit down and enjoy our numismatic pursuits or to get together at informal gatherings, club meetings and conventions to discuss numismatic subjects as our special form of entertainment or educational research.

The Year 1946

Current Events. President Harry S Truman in his first year in office had to endure extensive criticism, particularly from Republicans, that he was unqualified for the position. He would be elected in 1948 and serve until 1953. Many modern historians consider him to have handled the presidency very well.

On March 5 at Westminster College in Fulton, Missouri, Winston Churchill coined a new term in his speech, which included, "From Stettin in the Baltic to Trieste in the Adriatic, an iron curtain has descended across the Continent." This brought to the forefront the Iron Curtain imposed by dictator Josef Stalin over countries in Eastern Europe that were once under Nazi domination, but were now satellites of the Union of Soviet Socialist Republics (USSR). For years afterward the Soviets would be viewed as ready to precipitate an atomic war, causing domestic and military operations in America as a counter to this. Both sides engaged in testing improved atomic weapons. At the time there was little knowledge of the danger of radioactive fallout. On a lighter note the bikini bathing suit was introduced, named for Bikini Atoll in the South Pacific, a site for atomic testing.

On July 4, the Philippine Islands were granted independence from the United States, part of a transition of power scheduled in 1935. This ended a colorful chapter in American numismatics, as Philippine coins had been struck by U.S. mints off and on since the early 1900s.

On August 21 the Atomic Energy Commission was formed to regulate the use of such power.

In the autumn, trials in Nuremburg, Germany, sentenced 12 Nazi leader (one in absentia) to hang and 7 to prison; 3 were acquitted.

It was a time of labor unrest, and throughout the year there were many strikes and work stoppages, including in the steel, coal, and electrical industries. The future was certain; employment was anything but guaranteed. On the consumer front appliances, automobiles, and other manufactured goods were scarce, as production of civilian products could not take place until factories were converted back to their former status. Black markets arose in used cars and other items. Cash was common, and prices of many things, including rare coins, rose sharply. *The Best Years of Our Lives* was popular in theaters and dealt with the readjustment families faced when members returned from the war.

Winston Churchill (seen during the war, and in a 2015 British Royal Mint commemorative).

The Numismatic Scene. The composition of nickel five-cent pieces was restored from its wartime silver alloy to 75% copper and 25% nickel. The Mercury dime was replaced by the Roosevelt design by Chief Engraver John R. Sinnock. Commemorative coins were issued for the first time since 1939—the Iowa Centennial and Booker T. Washington half dollars.

Whitman Publishing Company issued the first of what would become many annual editions of *A Guide Book of United States Coins* (the hobby's popular "Red Book"). Richard S. Yeoman was editor and Stuart Mosher was hired to compile facts and figures. Released in November 1946, its cover bore the date 1947, so as to give it longer shelf life in hobby centers and bookstores.

Bank-wrapped rolls of coins became very popular in the marketplace—an ideal way for casual investors to purchase quantities of brilliant Uncirculated coins. Charles H. Fisher reported record-breaking prices for his recent sale, asking, "Where is it going to stop?" A Proof 1856 Flying Eagle cent fetched $180, while a Proof 1877 Indian Head cent brought $52.50, an 1873 two-cent piece sold for $40, a Proof 1877 nickel three-cent piece went for $52.50, and an 1877 Proof Shield nickel found a new home at $80.

The Year 1947

Current Events. The fear of the USSR continued, and rumors ran rampant of various Americans having Communist tendencies or, worse, being spies. The House Un-American Committee, supervised by Senator Joseph McCarthy, created a Hollywood "black list" and dragged actors and actresses to declare if they had ever attended a Communist party meeting or had read related publications such as the *Daily Worker*. The proceedings were broadcast on television. In view of dropping attendance during viewing hours, many department and other stores installed TV sets on their premises.

Unemployment inched up to 3.9%.

Consumer goods remained scarce in many sectors. Many prices rose, causing inflation and reduced buying power of the dollar. *Meet the Press* was launched on television and in time became the longest-running series ever. Inventions included carbon-14 dating of historical objects, the transistor, and the microwave oven. Flying a Bell X-1 rocket plane USAF captain Chuck Yeager broke the speed of sound.

The first edition of the *Guide Book of United States Coins* brought a revolution to American coin collecting.

The Numismatic Scene. Chief Engraver John R. Sinnock died on May 14.

The coin market paused to rest, and instead of numerous "buy" advertisements, such terms as "wholesale," "closeout prices," and "better buys" appeared in headlines. Cash that might have gone into rare coins now had many more uses. Consumer goods such as automobiles and appliances were becoming increasingly available, and new homes (including entire communities) were being built at a record rate. B. Max Mehl offered selected Proof coins at discounts of 25% to 50% off catalog prices. Bank-wrapped rolls continued to be popular with investors. Scott Stamp & Coin Company endeavored to liquidate a hoard of hundreds of low-mintage 1879 and 1880 gold dollars, in Mint State, for $15 and $20 each respectively.

The American Numismatic Association convention was held in Buffalo, New York, at the Hotel Statler from August 23 to 27. The association apologized that due to inflation the rates earlier quoted were now obsolete, and that new tariffs were in effect. For example, a room that used to be $3.85 per day was $4, an $8.80 double-bedded room was now $10, and a $9.35 twin-bedded room was raised to $9.50. The tourist business was good, and the hotel took a take-it-or-leave-it attitude. ANA membership stood at 7,326. At the event M. Vernon Sheldon was elected president.

The convention auction conducted by the Numismatic Gallery included these prices:

> A New England shilling $270, a rare NE sixpence at $630, and a seldom-seen Willow Tree sixpence at $210. Two George Clinton cents sold for $250 and $225 respectively. A Washington Roman Head cent brought $150. The finest known 1799 cent from the Sheraton Collection $1,500. Among gold coins: 1808 $2.50 EF $210, 1821 $5 EF $600, 1831 $5 Uncirculated $340, 1834 $5 With Motto Uncirculated $300, 1883 $20 Proof $1,050, 1884 $20 Proof $1,625, 1887 $20 Proof $500. A five-piece Panama-Pacific Exposition set realized $1,025.

By year's end the strength of the coin market had recovered slightly. Challenging times lay head. Prices would fall in 1949 and 1950, but in 1951 a long upward trend would begin. By that time the heyday of the Mercury dime, Standing Liberty quarter, and Liberty Walking half dollar would be numismatic history.

By the late 1940s, all three of the silver coins that had debuted in 1916 would see their designs replaced by modern portraiture.

Mercury Dimes, 1916–1945

The 1916 dime as adopted for circulation, the style used from 1916 to 1945.

The Design of the New Dime

On the afternoon of May 30, 1916, Secretary of the Treasury William G. McAdoo announced that new designs had been adopted for the dime, quarter, and half dollar. Three sculptors were commissioned to prepare sketches, and 50 were submitted. Mint Director Robert W. Woolley selected the designs. Adolph A. Weinman was named as the designer of the dime and half dollar, and Hermon A. MacNeil would create the quarter.

> The design of the dime, owing to the smallness of the coin, has been held quite simple. The obverse shows a head of Liberty with winged cap. The head is firm and simple in form, the profile forceful.
>
> The reverse shows a design of the bundle of rods, with battle ax, known as "fasces," and symbolical of unity, wherein lies the nation's strength. Surrounding the fasces is a full foliaged branch of olive, symbolical of peace.[1]

For a long time afterward, the motif was formally known as the Winged Liberty Head within the halls of the Treasury Department, including in correspondence well into the 1940s, but not in many other places, although "Head of Liberty with Winged Cap" would have been more correct, per the original announcement. The designer, sculptor Adolph A. Weinman, was not mentioned—standard policy at the time for press releases on new designs. His identity was not kept secret, however.

The alignment of the fasces on the reverse fools the eye—an optical illusion. When the bundle of sticks is upright it appears to lean slightly to the right.

Frank G. Duffield, editor of *The Numismatist*, contacted Weinman to learn more about his creation of the design. His reply:

> Dear Sir—
>
> In response to your letter of November 14, requesting a word of explanation as to my reasons for selecting a winged female head for the design of the obverse, and the fasces for the reverse of the new dime, permit me to say that the law on the coinage of the United

States stipulates that on all subsidiary coins there shall appear upon the obverse a figure or representation of Liberty. Hence the head of Liberty, the coin being obviously too small in size to make the representation of a full-length figure of Liberty advisable.

The wings crowning her cap are intended to symbolize liberty of thought.

As to the reverse of the dime, the law does not stipulate what is to appear upon this side of the coin, while it does specifically state that upon the reverse of the quarter dollar and the half dollar shall appear the figure of an eagle.

I have selected the motive of the fasces and olive branch to symbolize the strength which lies in unity, while the battle-ax stands for preparedness to defend the Union. The branch of olive is symbolical of our love of peace.

Very truly yours,
A.A. Weinman

Numismatic historian Roger W. Burdette described the portrait on the coin:

The image on the 1916 dime was derived from two sources:

The first was a 1912-1913 portrait bust of Elsie Katchel Stevens, wife of lawyer Wallace Stevens. The couple rented an apartment above Weinman's studio, and Stevens and Weinman convinced Elsie to pose for the bust. Elsie had been a sales clerk in a store, and Wallace wanted to boost her status among the other wives at the insurance company where he worked. A portrait by a nationally-known artist was just the thing. By 1916 the Stevenses had moved to Connecticut, so Weinman used the model of Elsie as one source.[2]

The second and probably stronger source was Weinman's *Union Soldiers and Sailors Memorial* dedicated on November 6, 1909, in Baltimore. It sits on a high pedestal base making the lowest portions of the figures difficult to see from ground level. When photographs of the dime are compared with the head of *Victory* from the Memorial

Elsie Stevens with newborn daughter Holly in 1924.

Weinman's *Union Soldiers and Sailors Monument* in Baltimore and a view of Victory.

A depiction of Mercury with wings on his head from a $10 note of the Bank of Ann Arbor in Michigan. The vignette engraved by George W. Hatch shows Mercury bringing a cornucopia filled with coins to the seated Moneta, who is holding the key to a strongbox protected by a griffin, the mythological guardian of treasure.

the resemblance is unmistakable. On the dime *Liberty* wears the same breastplate and cap as *Victory*. Both have hair curls flowing in a similar manner and matching profiles.[3] As the Baltimore monument predates Weinman's meeting the Stevens, the model is obviously is not Elsie.

At present I do not know who the model was, although it was common for most artists to use composite figures in their allegorical works. It is only with the Washington quarter that our circulating coinage begins to have recognizable individuals' portrait on the obverse.[4]

Release and Distribution

Minting of the new design began in October 1916, and the first coins were distributed later that month. The release of the dime was described in the December issue of *The Numismatist*:

> The new silver dime was given to the public during the last days of October, and by the time this issue reaches its readers it will be in general circulation. For five months collectors have been anxiously waiting to get a glimpse of what we were told was to be a beautiful coin, and we have not been disappointed.
>
> The opinion of a single man, whether he be artist, sculptor, numismatist, or layman, as to its merits or the beauty of the design, should not weigh heavily. But when a number of men familiar with the coinages of the world from the earliest times all pronounce it a very creditable piece of work and perhaps the most attractive coin this government has ever put in circulation, its popularity with collectors cannot be a matter of doubt.
>
> During the past month *The Numismatist* has received a number of letters from prominent numismatists of the United States, expressing their opinions of the new coin, which we print below. It will be noted that there is not an unfavorable opinion expressed, though there are varying degrees of approval.

Miss Liberty was fitted with a winged cap, as noted. Collectors quickly nicknamed it the "Mercury" dime, never mind that the messenger-god Mercury of fame was a *male*. Today it continues to be referred to as such, although some sources, *Coin World* being an example, use "Winged Liberty Head" and the *Guide Book of United States Coins* notes both monikers.

The first delivery from the Philadelphia Mint of the new dimes was on October 17, 1916. From a large mintage of 22,180,080, coins quickly reached circulation, including to the numismatic community, and inspired many comments such as those quoted above.

The first delivery of coins from the San Francisco Mint was on October 24. In time the generous mintage of 10,450,000 was widely scattered, including many in Rocky Mountain states.

The first delivery of Denver Mint coins did not take place until December 29. By the time these reached circulation in early 1917 the design was no longer a novelty, and the public saved very few. This and the low mintage of 264,000 combined to make the 1916-D dime rare in all grades.[5]

Comments and Reviews

The new dime furnished the opportunity for well-known numismatists to make comments, published in *The Numismatist* in December. Edgar H. Adams, the most honored numismatic writer and researcher of the time, wrote from New York City:

> The new dime, in my opinion, is one of the handsomest coins of the denomination that has been issued for regular circulation in this country. There are a few minor features which may be criticized, but the general effect is very commendable. I hope the designs for the new half and quarter dollars will be as satisfactory.

John W. Scott, who had been in the coin trade for many decades and was now retired, said,

> The new dime is the best piece of work that the United States Mint has turned out in a century.

Farran Zerbe, former president of the American Numismatic Association and in 1915 the distributor of the Panama-Pacific International commemorative coins, stated succinctly,

> I am delighted with the new dime.

From Philadelphia, Henry Chapman, a coin dealer since 1875, when at the age of 16 he went to work in the shop of J.W. Haseltine, wrote

> I think the new dime a very creditable production, and am glad to see such an artistic coin come out from this country.

Wayte Raymond, whose career star was in the ascendancy in New York City, weighed in:

> I think very favorably of the new dimes. The head of Liberty has considerable resemblance to some coins of the Roman Republic and is very artistic. The only criticism I have to make is the fact that the words "In God We Trust" and the date seem to be placed on the die as an afterthought, as there is really no place for them on the obverse.

B. Max Mehl, of Fort Worth, Texas, shared this:

> To my mind it did not require very artistic efforts to excel the old issue. The new issue is indeed a welcome addition to our coinage, and one which I think will meet with the approval of thinking numismatists. From a business standpoint I think any new issue is a good thing for the numismatic profession, as it seems to stimulate interest not only among collectors, but among non-collectors, and is the means of bringing out a considerable number of new collectors.

T.L. Comparette, curator of the Mint Collection, shared this:

> I am for the most part very favorably impressed with its general appearance. The head is very good, one of the best on our coins. Personally, I should have been glad to see the coin appear with a simpler reverse design.
>
> I should much prefer to see the fasces a simple type, similar to the one on the piece just supplanted, that is, with merely the denomination of the coin within the wreath. Persons inclined toward criticism will find several features justly open to attack, but they are rather in the details of the subject of the types than in the execution of them.

Howland Wood of the American Numismatic Society in New York City:

> The new dime by Adolph A. Weinman is without doubt the finest example of our new coinage which was begun in 1907 with the advent of the $20 and $10 gold pieces. . . .

Thomas L. Elder, the most important coin dealer in New York City, gave this view:

> We have in the new United States dime, designed by Adolph Alexander Weinman, the handsomest American coin. The winged head of Liberty is a real portrait of great beauty and finish. Our American girl in this instance is youthful, refined, and of gentle expression. The addition of wings to the head is taken from ancient art of emblems. The head is not unlike those of Roty and Chaplain shown on so many modern French coins and medals. The obverse lettering is beautifully simple. The spacing of the letters is not a new idea, and was used on a number of dies rejected by the United States. Like the tiny monograms which covered nearly all the ancient Greek coins, Mr. Weinman has added his minute "A.W." joined. The motto "In God We Trust" on the obverse will stop any criticism of religionists.
>
> The reverse is beautiful, but not original. The chief types, a fasces and olive branch joined, are both ancient symbols. The fasces is quoted as "a bundle of rods containing an axe, carried by the lictors before the magistrates of ancient Rome as a symbol of authority." In this case the olive branch partially obstructs our view of the fasces, so that the first glance is puzzling, leaving the reverse not as satisfactory as the obverse. Numismatists will all remember that Anthony Paquet designed some pattern half dollars in 1859 with the figure of Liberty sitting by a shield, holding a fasces in her hand, so this is not a new idea in United States coins. The fasces was a favorite emblem on the later coins of Louis XVI of France, and not a few are seen on other French coins, including those of the Mayence siege. The Roman Republic used it also. The "E Pluribus Unum" on the reverse seems small and hard to read, and the balance of the lettering is badly

crowded, but we must admit the artist had no other alternative than to insert it the best way he could. So, after years of waiting and not a little agitation, in which I claim a share, we have here a coin which is second to none we have issued, and it will compare favorably with any in Europe, which is saying much. Let us hope the new quarter and half dollar, soon to appear, will be as creditable.

The same coin prompted an editorial by Frank G. Duffield:

Perhaps one reason why the new dime has made such a hit with numismatists is because the designer has given us innovations on both the obverse and reverse. The female head has been used to typify Liberty on most of our coins, and the conceptions of the designers have varied greatly. The head with the flowing hair on our earliest coins was perhaps the least attractive of all. That on the 1793 Chain cent was a nightmare. Throughout the cent series there was a gradual improvement with the aid of the turban and the coronet. But throughout the entire series of U.S. coins there has been about the head of Liberty an appearance of maturity. It was not youthful. The designer of the new dime has given us a youthful, even girlish head. But the innovation on the obverse consists in adding wings to the head. This, of course, is not a new type for a coin; it is only new for the United States. The winged head was used almost exclusively on one side of the family or consular coins of the Roman Republic before the Christian era. . . .

The girlish Miss Liberty with wings on her cap has already won a place in the numismatist's heart. Of course, dimes are only bits of change in this busy old world, and no one expects to keep them in his pocket for any length of time. They come to us quickly, and go from us even more quickly, without the aid of wings; but this is not an objection to the new coin; those of the old type were equally active in their flights in both directions. The dime has always been a good friend to man, woman and child; it opens many doors to pleasure and amusement. The new one will be fully as good a friend, and a bit of art to admire as well.

The Mercury dime was widely admired by collectors and the public alike and would be minted continuously through 1945 with the exceptions of 1922, 1932, and 1933.

Hub Changes

The Mercury dimes of 1916 were made in higher relief than were later issues. This caused some problems in coin-operated machines. The relief was lowered slightly—most noticeable in the hair curl over Miss Liberty's ear. The front or leading edge of the wing was lowered as well.

In 1918 the obverse hub was modified slightly. Numismatic historian David W. Lange describes the difference:

> The new obverse hub of 1918 varies only in the details of Liberty's hair and in the contour and detailing of the wing. Liberty's wing follows the contour of her head on both the type of 1916 and the type of 1917, curving away from the viewer and toward the coin's field. On the type of 1918 the wing projects straight backward and remains within a single plane. The tip of each long feather is clearly highlighted by a raised outline not seen on the earlier hubs. The gaps between each of the smaller feathers have been increased to make the feathers more easily distinguished.[6]

These hub differences have not been widely noticed by collectors, but are interesting to contemplate upon close viewing of the coins.

Mercury Dimes in Circulation

Except for the initial interest on the part of the public and collectors alike concerning the new Mercury dime design when it appeared in circulation in late 1916 and early 1917, attention faded. In the absence of albums and folders to display coins and without any pricing or grading guides, numismatic interest in dimes was apathetic at best. Even when low mintage figures were published, as for 1921 and 1921-D, there was no excitement. Because of this the survival of Mint State coins after 1916 was a matter of chance.

When coin albums became available in the early 1930s that changed, and dramatically. All of a sudden there was a great demand. By that time the dates from 1916 to the early 1920s in circulation were usually well worn, with Very Fine being a typical grade. Few were Extremely Fine or About Uncirculated, accounting for the rarity of 1916-D, 1921, and 1921-D at those levels. The hunt for Mercury dimes continued nonstop through the mid-1960s, after which silver coins of all denominations became worth more for their precious metal than their face value and disappeared from circulation. By that time the early issues, if found in pocket change, were apt to be About Good or Good.

Countless millions of worn Mercury dimes of the 1930s and 1940s were melted from 1965 through the late 1970s during the great silver speculation that resulted in the metal reaching an all-time high of $50.35 per ounce on Comex on January 18, 1980, giving a silver dime the melt-down value of $3.64.

A 1916 dime with the lower obverse rim flatly struck, although the other details are sharp.

The last digit of the date is weak on this 1920 dime.

Aspects of Striking

Detail of the reverse center of a 1945 dime showing the bands fused together.

Full Bands (FB) on the reverse of a 1942/1-D dime. The FB feature barely makes the cut. The definition of the bands can vary, and some have a deeper horizontal line and have the bands rounded, unlike here.

Full Bands on the reverse of a 1921-D dime are more boldly separated than on many certified FB coins. FB coins that have the bands rounded are more desirable than ones in which the bands are barely split. To determine this, you need to inspect coins carefully.

Full Bands on the reverse of a Proof dime. Proofs typically have a deep line separating the bands.

The striking sharpness or lack thereof in this series has not been carefully studied, although David W. Lange in *The Complete Guide to Mercury Dimes* has published more information than can be found anywhere else.

The sharpness of details is determined by the spacing of the dies in a coining press. If the dies are positioned closely apart, all details will be struck sharply, but the dies will wear more quickly. If they are spaced father apart, the features deepest in the dies (creating the highest parts on the coin) will not be struck up and will be flat or weak.

On Mercury dimes flatness can occur mainly on the obverse on the hair covering Liberty's ear, on the last digit of the date, and on the rim. Scarcely any numismatic attention has been paid to this.

On the reverse, flatness occurs mostly on the bands across the fasces, especially the middle bands, and on the sticks in the fasces. The bands are composed of two parallel lines with a separation or "split" between. Sometimes the bands are barely split, and other times they have a deep line separating them and the bands are rounded. Coins with the latter feature are far more preferable.

If you are a connoisseur you will want to examine both sides carefully and pick a coin that has full details. *Simplicity* is the byword for descriptions in the marketplace, and to do the foregoing takes time and care. A quick fix is the designation Full Bands (FB), which satisfies the vast majority of coin buyers. This designates a coin in which the two center bands in the fasces show a division or recess separating them—but as noted above, further inspection is necessary if you are a connoisseur. Such coins can bring great premiums, never mind that other areas of the coin might be weak!

A dramatic example is provided by the listing of a 1945 Philadelphia Mint dime in the first issue of the *Guide Book of United States Coins, Deluxe Edition*. A regular MS-65 is priced at $28 while one with FB is priced at $10,000!

For a really deluxe specimen of any Mercury dime, find one with FB *plus* sharp striking in other areas as well. This is best done by checking the reverse for FB and then inspecting the obverse. An obverse with full details will cost no more than one with lightness in some areas.

Proof Mercury Dimes

Proofs are available of the years from 1936 to 1942, after which production was stopped due to the national need to spend more time on the war effort. The mintages increased gradually over this span of years. Today Proofs exist in proportion to their original mintages.

Proofs were struck from completely polished dies, including the portrait. Certain early issues of 1936 are exceptions and are not from fully polished dies.

Grading Mercury Dimes

1919-S. Graded MS-65.

MS-60 to 70 (Mint State)

Obverse: At MS-60, some abrasion and contact marks are evident on the highest part of the portrait, including the hair immediately to the right of the face and the upper left part of the wing. At MS-63, abrasion is slight at best, less so for 64. Album slide marks on the cheek, if present, should not be at any grade above MS-64. An MS-65 coin should display no abrasion or contact marks except under magnification, and MS-66 and higher coins should have none at all. Luster should be full and rich. **Reverse:** Comments apply as for the obverse, except that the highest parts of the fasces, these being the horizontal bands, are the places to check. The field is mainly protected by design elements and does not show contact marks readily.

1942, 2 Over 1. Graded AU-55.

AU-50, 53, 55, 58 (About Uncirculated)

Obverse: Light wear is seen on the cheek, the hair immediately to the right of the face, the left edge of the wing, and the upper right of the wing. At AU-58, the luster is extensive, but incomplete, especially on the higher parts and in the field. At AU-50 and 53, luster is less.

Reverse: Light wear is seen on the higher parts of the fasces. An AU-58 coin has nearly full luster, more so than on the obverse, as the design elements protect the field areas. At AU-50 and 53, there still is significant luster. Generally, the reverse appears to be in a slightly higher grade than the obverse.

1921. Graded EF-40.

EF-40, 45 (Extremely Fine)

Obverse: Further wear is seen on the head. Many of the hair details are blended together, as are some feather details at the left side of the wing.

Reverse: The horizontal bands on the fasces may be fused together. The diagonal bands remain in slight relief against the vertical lines (sticks).

1942, 2 Over 1. Graded VF-20.

VF-20, 30 (Very Fine)

Obverse: The head shows more wear, now with the forehead and cheek mostly blending into the hair. More feather details are gone.

Reverse: Wear is more extensive, but the diagonal and horizontal bands on the fasces still are separated from the thin vertical sticks.

1916-D. Graded F-12.

F-12, 15 (Fine)

Obverse: The head shows more wear, the hair has only slight detail, and most of the feathers are gone. In the marketplace a coin in F-12 grade usually has slightly less detail than stated by the ANA grading standards or *Photograde*, from modern interpretations.

Reverse: Many of the tiny vertical sticks in the fasces are blended together. The bands can be barely discerned and may be worn away at the highest-relief parts.

1916-D. Graded VG-8.

VG-8, 10 (Very Good)

Obverse: Wear is more extensive on the portrait, and only a few feathers are seen on the wing. The outlines between the hair and cap and of the wing are distinct. Lettering is clear, but light in areas.

Reverse: The rim is complete, or it may be slightly worn away in areas. Only a few traces of the vertical sticks remain in the fasces. Current interpretations in the marketplace are given here and are less strict than those listed by the ANA grading standards and *Photograde*. Often, earlier issues are graded more liberally than are later dates.

1916-D. Graded G-4.

G-4, 6 (Good)

Obverse: Wear is more extensive, with not all of the outline between the hair and the wing visible. The rim is worn into the edges of the letters and often into the bottom of the last numeral in the date.

Reverse: The rim is worn away, as are the outer parts of the letters. The fasces is flat or may show a hint of a vertical stick or two. The leaves are thick from wear. The mintmark, if any, is easily seen.

1916-D. Graded AG-3.

AG-3 (About Good)

Obverse: The rim is worn further into the letters. The head is mostly outline all over, except for a few indicates of edges. Folds remain at the top of the cap. The date is clearly visible.

Reverse: The rim is worn further into the letters. The mintmark, if any, is clear but may be worn away slightly at the bottom. The apparent wear is slightly greater on the reverse than on the obverse.

1939. Graded PF-67.

PF-60 to 70 (Proof)

Obverse and Reverse: Proofs that are extensively cleaned and have many hairlines, or that are dull and grainy, are lower level, such as PF-60 to 62. These are not widely desired, and represent coins that have been mistreated. With medium hairlines and good reflectivity, assigned grades of PF-63 or 64 are appropriate. Tiny horizontal lines on Miss Liberty's cheek, known as *slide marks*, from National and other album slides scuffing the relief of the cheek, are common; coins with such marks should not be graded higher than PF-64, but sometimes are. With relatively few hairlines and no noticeable slide marks, a rating of PF-65 can be given. PF-66 should have hairlines so delicate that magnification is needed to see them. Above that, a Proof should be free of any hairlines or other problems.

Being a Smart Buyer

There are enough Mercury dimes in the marketplace that with very little effort the typical or casual collector can easily acquire a full set of dates and mintmarks in MS-64 or MS-65 in a short time. Probably all but a handful can be purchased on the Internet in a single afternoon. Quality, however, will be a mixed bag under such a buying plan.

My advice is to be a connoisseur. Buy only certified coins, such as from PCGS or NGC, the two leading professional third-party grading services. Coins are marked with grades. The only distinction made for striking sharpness is FB for coins with Full Bands on the reverse. Sometimes + signs, stars, or other notations are added, but these do not signify sharp striking overall and can be confusing. As mentioned above, the FB notation can be one thing, and on certified coins the quality of the division between the bands can range from minimal to well separated and rounded. Moreover, coins can be certified as FB, but be weak in other areas.

If you feel that having an FB coin is desirable in view of the great premium often required, then be certain that the coin has the bands nicely split and has full details everywhere else. Otherwise you are wasting your money, in my opinion.

You will get the most value for your money if you ignore FB designations for varieties in which this feature costs a tremendous premium, and do your best to buy Mercury dimes that lack this feature, but are sharp in all other details.

Eye appeal is another consideration. A certified MS-65 dime can be dark, spotted, or as ugly as a toad, in which case I suggest you avoid it. Among Mint State coins look for pieces that have rich frosty mint luster and are brilliant or with light iridescent toning. Most "rainbow" toning is artificial. Bear in mind that better coins can be deceptively made through chemistry, as they say, and adding toning to a brilliant Mercury dime is easy enough for a "coin doctor" to do.

Furthermore, over the years there has been "gradeflation" with certified coins. Many that were certified as MS-64 20 years ago are graded MS-65 or even higher today. In the late 1980s MS-66 and MS-67 grades were few and far between in the population reports published by PCGS and NGC. Today, such grades are very common. "Cracking" coins out of holders and resubmitting them in the hopes of a higher grade has become an industry in itself. Often "low end" (more common) coins are left in holders and "high end" (rarer, and thus more valuable) coins are resubmitted in hopes of getting a higher grade. The cost of doing this repeated times can be small in comparison to the extra value received when, for example, an MS-65 graduates to become MS-66. Some years ago a leading dealer told me that he had a 1916-D dime that was certified as MS-64. He submitted it repeated times, and on the 24th try it graduated to MS-65 and gained thousands of dollars in value.

Not everyone can afford a Mint State 1916-D, 1921, 1921-D, 1942/1, or 1942/1-D dime. If this includes you, cherrypick nice VF, EF, or AU coins with care, selecting only coins with nice eye appeal.

Take your time. All the coins that meet your particular requirements are in the marketplace, but to find them may take a few weeks or months. Study each coin carefully before making a purchase decision. The thrill of the chase is part of the fun of numismatics.

A complete set of Mercury dimes is beautiful to behold.

Mercury Dimes
Standing Liberty Quarters
Liberty Walking Half Dollars

1916 Mercury Dime

Circulation-strike mintage:
22,180,080

Notes. The first Winged Liberty Head or "Mercury" dimes were released on October 28, 1916. By December they were widespread, resulting in many comments sent to newspapers and magazines, nearly all lauding the new design. In contrast the new-design quarters and half dollars were not released until January 1917.

Key to Collecting. 1916 dimes are available in all grades from well-worn to Mint State. Enough were saved in the first year of issue that Mint State coins are easy to find. Most are well struck, resulting in Full Bands coins selling for a modest premium in comparison to most FB dimes in the series. The worn coins are those taken out of circulation after the early 1930s, when collecting by dates and mints became popular.

Market Values • Circulation Strikes

G-4	VG-8	F-12	VF-20	EF-40	AU-50	MS-60
$4	$5	$7	$8	$15	$25	$35
MS-63	MS-64	MS-64FB	MS-65	MS-65FB	MS-66	MS-66FB
$48	$60	$70	$120	$175	$190	$450

Certified Populations

Fair	AG-2	G-4	VG-8	F-12	VF-20	EF-40	AU-50	MS-60
26	29	4	3	1	2	6	88	0
MS-61	MS-62	MS-63	MS-64	MS-65	MS-66	MS-67	MS-68	MS-69
26	144	278	771	728	433	110	15	0

1916-D Mercury Dime

Circulation-strike mintage:
264,000

Notes. Four reverse dies were used for the 1916-D coinage. As the first delivery of these coins did not take place until December 29, they did not circulate until early 1917, by which time public interest and newspaper articles about the new design had diminished. Some of these were distributed in Montana.[7] Very few numismatists of that time collected by mintmark varieties. As a result the survival of Mint State coins is a matter of rare chance. When mintmark collecting did become popular in the 1930s, the 1916-D dime became an object of desire. By that time most in circulation were well worn.

Mathematics based on the mintage figures of 264,000 Denver coins versus 22,180,080 made in Philadelphia suggests that 1 Mint State 1916-D should exist for every 84 Philadelphia coins. However, as Philadelphia dimes were saved for their novelty value and 1916-D dimes were released after the fact, likely the 1916-D is 300 to 500 times rarer.

On November 24, 1915, newly installed Mint director F.J.H. von Engelken called a halt to Mercury dime coinage in Denver so that the Mint could fill a huge order for 1916-D Barber quarters, of which 6,540,800 were eventually struck. Regional demand for Mercury dimes was subsequently mostly filled by San Francisco coins.

Fakes of the 1916-D made by affixing a spurious D mintmark to Philadelphia Mint coins were once so common in the marketplace that in the 1970s John J. Ford Jr. said that more than half he saw at a large convention were alterations. Today the leading third-party certification services guarantee authenticity, providing valuable protection. Fakes still abound on the Internet and elsewhere. Advice: do not buy a 1916-D for any price unless it is certified by PCGS, NGC, or another leading grading service.

Key to Collecting. The 1916-D dime is the key date and mintmark in the Mercury dime series. Most circulated examples range from About Good to Good, as found in circulation in the 1940s to the mid-1960s. Very Good to Very Fine coins are those mostly found and set aside in the 1930s and 1940s.

Most 1916-D dimes are well struck, and among high-grade issues many have Full Bands, but these sell for a significant premium.

Market Values • Circulation Strikes

G-4	VG-8	F-12	VF-20	EF-40	AU-50	MS-60
$1,000	$1,500	$2,600	$4,200	$6,000	$9,000	$13,500
MS-63	MS-64	MS-64FB	MS-65	MS-65FB	MS-66	MS-66FB
$17,000	$19,000	$22,500	$28,000	$45,000	$34,000	$55,000

Certified Populations

Fair	AG-2	G-4	VG-8	F-12	VF-20	EF-40	AU-50	MS-60
472	1,671	663	341	126	142	77	136	1
MS-61	MS-62	MS-63	MS-64	MS-65	MS-66	MS-67	MS-68	MS-69
28	47	33	70	32	7	2	0	0

1916-S Mercury Dime

Circulation-strike mintage:
10,450,000

Notes. 1916-S dimes were widely distributed from the West Coast to the Midwest, in the latter location taking the place of Denver Mint coins that normally would have been used (see preceding entry). Many were saved by the public. The small S mint-mark is very high on most dies.

Key to Collecting. Most 1916-S dimes are well worn, in grades from Good to Very Fine—pieces taken from circulation starting in the 1930s. These are very common. Mint State coins are easily enough found from pieces saved by the public at the time of issue. Many show light striking at the centers, most evident on the hair covering Liberty's ear and on the fasces on the reverse, on which the vertical sticks can be light, especially in the lower areas. Some have Full Bands, even though there is weakness in the hair and on some sticks. As this is not widely known, if you are seeking a Full Bands coin take your time and find one that has full details overall. It will cost no more.

Market Values • Circulation Strikes

G-4	VG-8	F-12	VF-20	EF-40	AU-50	MS-60
$4	$6	$9	$12	$20	$25	$42
MS-63	MS-64	MS-64FB	MS-65	MS-65FB	MS-66	MS-66FB
$65	$90	$170	$215	$700	$400	$1,300

Certified Populations

Fair	AG-2	G-4	VG-8	F-12	VF-20	EF-40	AU-50	MS-60
48	16	1	2	0	1	8	43	0
MS-61	MS-62	MS-63	MS-64	MS-65	MS-66	MS-67	MS-68	MS-69
19	63	144	337	170	77	10	0	0

1917 Mercury Dime

Circulation-strike mintage:
55,230,000

Notes. America was at war in 1917, and large mintages were the rule across all copper, nickel, and silver denominations. 1917 dimes were struck with both the old 1916 hub style in higher relief (David W. Lange estimates about 12% of the mintage) and in the modified 1917 style. No attention is paid to such differences in the marketplace.

Key to Collecting. 1917 dimes are as common as can be in well-worn grades— coins taken from circulation starting in the 1930s. Mint State coins are plentiful by virtue of the large production quantity. Full Bands coins are not rare on an absolute basis, but in higher grades they command a sharp premium.

Market Values • Circulation Strikes

G-4	VG-8	F-12	VF-20	EF-40	AU-50	MS-60
$3	$3.25	$3.50	$6	$8	$12	$30
MS-63	MS-64	MS-64FB	MS-65	MS-65FB	MS-66	MS-66FB
$60	$80	$100	$170	$400	$360	$850

Certified Populations

Fair	AG-2	G-4	VG-8	F-12	VF-20	EF-40	AU-50	MS-60
1	0	0	2	5	6	6	69	1
MS-61	MS-62	MS-63	MS-64	MS-65	MS-66	MS-67	MS-68	MS-69
21	86	125	277	138	52	10	0	0

1917-D Mercury Dime

Circulation-strike mintage:
9,402,000

Notes. Most 1917-D dimes (David W. Lange suggests about 88%) are from the 1916 hub. All 1917-D dimes were widely distributed at the time.

Key to Collecting. Made in large quantities, 1917-D dimes are common today. Most range from Good to Very Fine. Mint State coins are encountered with frequency. FB coins are in the distinct minority and when seen are usually of the 1917 or new hub. Many with FB are weak in other areas—another opportunity for cherrypicking.

Market Values • Circulation Strikes

G-4	VG-8	F-12	VF-20	EF-40	AU-50	MS-60
$4.50	$6	$11	$22	$45	$95	$145

MS-63	MS-64	MS-64FB	MS-65	MS-65FB	MS-66	MS-66FB
$350	$400	$1,250	$1,050	$5,000	$2,100	$10,000

Certified Populations

Fair	AG-2	G-4	VG-8	F-12	VF-20	EF-40	AU-50	MS-60
0	1	2	3	1	3	5	86	0

MS-61	MS-62	MS-63	MS-64	MS-65	MS-66	MS-67	MS-68	MS-69
24	102	123	159	32	8	2	0	0

1917-S Mercury Dime

Circulation-strike mintage:
27,330,000

Notes. The high mintage is accounted for by the great demand for coins of all denominations during the first year the United States was directly involved in the World War. These were widely distributed at the time of issue.

Key to Collecting. As is true of other high-mintage Mercury dimes of the era, most survivors are very worn and were taken from circulation after a new boom in coin collecting started in the 1930s. Mint State coins survived as a matter of chance as there was not a strong numismatic interest in Mercury dimes after the novelty of the 1916 issues passed.

Many are well struck. Full Bands coins sell at a premium, but at not high multiples of the regular price.

See next page for chart.

Market Values • Circulation Strikes

G-4	VG-8	F-12	VF-20	EF-40	AU-50	MS-60
$3	$3.25	$4	$7	$12	$30	$60

MS-63	MS-64	MS-64FB	MS-65	MS-65FB	MS-66	MS-66FB
$180	$265	$425	$500	$1,000	$750	$1,800

Certified Populations

Fair	AG-2	G-4	VG-8	F-12	VF-20	EF-40	AU-50	MS-60
0	1	2	4	2	5	5	69	2

MS-61	MS-62	MS-63	MS-64	MS-65	MS-66	MS-67	MS-68	MS-69
14	67	109	167	82	27	6	1	0

1918 Mercury Dime

Circulation-strike mintage:
26,680,000

Notes. This wartime issue was made in large numbers and widely circulated at the time. For the next several years, until 1921, mintages were generous.

Key to Collecting. As is true of all other early Mercury dimes with very high mintages, examples are very common today in worn grades, and many Mint State examples exist as well, the latter mainly from pieces saved by chance as opposed to being deliberately set aside by collectors. Full Bands coins sell at a sharp premium, but are not rarities.

Market Values • Circulation Strikes

G-4	VG-8	F-12	VF-20	EF-40	AU-50	MS-60
$3	$4	$6	$12	$25	$40	$70

MS-63	MS-64	MS-64FB	MS-65	MS-65FB	MS-66	MS-66FB
$125	$160	$350	$425	$1,200	$1,150	$2,000

Certified Populations

Fair	AG-2	G-4	VG-8	F-12	VF-20	EF-40	AU-50	MS-60
0	1	0	3	0	1	3	41	1

MS-61	MS-62	MS-63	MS-64	MS-65	MS-66	MS-67	MS-68	MS-69
19	50	66	137	80	20	3	0	0

1918-D Mercury Dime

Circulation-strike mintage:
22,674,800

Key to Collecting. As is true of the others with production quantities over 5,000,000, well-worn coins attract little notice, this being true of all other varieties after 1916-D and before 1921. 1918-D dimes are mostly lightly struck. Full Bands coins are quite rare and command a dramatic premium.

Market Values • Circulation Strikes

G-4	VG-8	F-12	VF-20	EF-40	AU-50	MS-60
$3	$4	$6	$12	$24	$50	$125

MS-63	MS-64	MS-64FB	MS-65	MS-65FB	MS-66	MS-66FB
$250	$310	$3,200	$600	$25,000	$1,400	$80,000

Certified Populations

Fair	AG-2	G-4	VG-8	F-12	VF-20	EF-40	AU-50	MS-60
3	0	2	1	3	5	7	55	1

MS-61	MS-62	MS-63	MS-64	MS-65	MS-66	MS-67	MS-68	MS-69
16	70	82	209	54	12	3	0	0

1918-S Mercury Dime

Circulation-strike mintage:
19,300,000

Key to Collecting. 1918-S dimes are mostly lightly struck. Full Bands coins are seldom seen and command a high premium. Among FB examples 1918-S is a true rarity.

See next page for chart.

Market Values • Circulation Strikes

G-4	VG-8	F-12	VF-20	EF-40	AU-50	MS-60
$3	$3.25	$5	$10	$18	$40	$120

MS-63	MS-64	MS-64FB	MS-65	MS-65FB	MS-66	MS-66FB
$275	$450	$2,500	$725	$6,750	$1,950	$11,500

Certified Populations

Fair	AG-2	G-4	VG-8	F-12	VF-20	EF-40	AU-50	MS-60
1	1	1	0	1	4	1	41	3

MS-61	MS-62	MS-63	MS-64	MS-65	MS-66	MS-67	MS-68	MS-69
17	48	69	133	45	17	3	1	0

1919 Mercury Dime

Circulation-strike mintage:
35,740,000

Key to Collecting. Examples are plentiful in all grades. Most Mint State coins were saved by chance, as collecting Mercury dimes by date and mint was not popular at the time. Most are well struck. Full Bands coins are easy enough to find but make up only a small percentage of the population.

In early 2015, a previously undiscovered doubled-die 1919 dime was reported, quickly making headlines in *Coin World* and other hobby media. "An exciting new doubled die error has been found on a 1919 Winged Liberty or Mercury Head dime," wrote Tom DeLorey in *Numismatic News*, March 17, 2015. "In terms of the degree of rotation between the two impressions it is almost as great as that seen on the famous 1955 doubled die obverse (DDO) cent, but because of a quirk of fate, the doubling is confined to only one small area of the die." The doubling is evident on the upper right portion of the motto IN GOD WE TRUST.

Market Values • Circulation Strikes

G-4	VG-8	F-12	VF-20	EF-40	AU-50	MS-60
$3	$3.25	$4	$6	$10	$30	$45

MS-63	MS-64	MS-64FB	MS-65	MS-65FB	MS-66	MS-66FB
$150	$180	$275	$375	$725	$1,200	$1,700

Certified Populations

Fair	AG-2	G-4	VG-8	F-12	VF-20	EF-40	AU-50	MS-60
0	2	0	1	0	4	4	50	0

MS-61	MS-62	MS-63	MS-64	MS-65	MS-66	MS-67	MS-68	MS-69
18	75	79	143	73	21	3	0	0

1919-D Mercury Dime

Circulation-strike mintage:
9,939,000

Key to Collecting. Most 1919-D dimes are lightly struck. Mint State coins are elusive in comparison to the demand for them. Full Bands coins are quite rare and command a dramatic premium. Most are not deeply split with rounded bands, so be careful when selecting for your collection. Also be sure that *other* areas of the coin are sharply struck.

Market Values • Circulation Strikes

G-4	VG-8	F-12	VF-20	EF-40	AU-50	MS-60
$4	$7	$12	$24	$35	$75	$200

MS-63	MS-64	MS-64FB	MS-65	MS-65FB	MS-66	MS-66FB
$450	$725	$5,750	$1,800	$32,500	$4,500	$125,000

Certified Populations

Fair	AG-2	G-4	VG-8	F-12	VF-20	EF-40	AU-50	MS-60
0	1	1	2	2	6	7	40	1

MS-61	MS-62	MS-63	MS-64	MS-65	MS-66	MS-67	MS-68	MS-69
21	55	84	119	35	4	1	0	0

1919-S Mercury Dime

Circulation-strike mintage:
8,850,000

Key to Collecting. Most 1919-S dimes are lightly struck. Similar to the situation for 1919-D, Mint State coins are scarce in proportion to the demand for them. There is no evidence that any were saved in quantity beyond whatever supplies Henry Chapman and John Zug, and to a lesser extent William Pukall, had on hand to accommodate clients wanting current issues. Full Bands 1919-S coins are quite rare, although not quite as rare as those of 1918-S, and they command a dramatic premium.

See next page for chart.

Market Values • Circulation Strikes

G-4	VG-8	F-12	VF-20	EF-40	AU-50	MS-60
$3.50	$4	$8	$16	$35	$75	$200

MS-63	MS-64	MS-64FB	MS-65	MS-65FB	MS-66	MS-66FB
$450	$700	$6,200	$1,200	$14,000	$1,500	$67,500

Certified Populations

Fair	AG-2	G-4	VG-8	F-12	VF-20	EF-40	AU-50	MS-60
0	1	1	1	1	5	11	67	1

MS-61	MS-62	MS-63	MS-64	MS-65	MS-66	MS-67	MS-68	MS-69
16	29	27	54	30	16	0	0	0

1920 Mercury Dime

Circulation-strike mintage:
59,030,000

Key to Collecting. The last digit of the date often is weak, as are the rims. Cherry-picking is advised. Dimes with Full Bands are easy enough to find, although they do command a premium.

Market Values • Circulation Strikes

G-4	VG-8	F-12	VF-20	EF-40	AU-50	MS-60
$3	$3.25	$3.50	$5	$8	$15	$35

MS-63	MS-64	MS-64FB	MS-65	MS-65FB	MS-66	MS-66FB
$75	$100	$150	$260	$500	$540	$900

Certified Populations

Fair	AG-2	G-4	VG-8	F-12	VF-20	EF-40	AU-50	MS-60
0	2	1	1	1	3	3	25	0

MS-61	MS-62	MS-63	MS-64	MS-65	MS-66	MS-67	MS-68	MS-69
17	55	107	299	148	40	17	3	0

1920-D Mercury Dime

Circulation-strike mintage:
19,171,000

Key to Collecting. The 0 of the date is often weak due to its closeness to the rim. Cherrypicking is advised. Full Bands coins are rare and command a dramatic premium.

Market Values • Circulation Strikes

G-4	VG-8	F-12	VF-20	EF-40	AU-50	MS-60
$3	$3.50	$4.50	$8	$20	$45	$145

MS-63	MS-64	MS-64FB	MS-65	MS-65FB	MS-66	MS-66FB
$350	$400	$1,150	$775	$4,500	$2,000	$6,750

Certified Populations

Fair	AG-2	G-4	VG-8	F-12	VF-20	EF-40	AU-50	MS-60
0	2	1	1	3	1	3	53	1

MS-61	MS-62	MS-63	MS-64	MS-65	MS-66	MS-67	MS-68	MS-69
17	74	74	109	44	23	6	0	0

1920-S Mercury Dime

Circulation-strike mintage:
13,820,000

Key to Collecting. The last digit of the date is often weak, a characteristic on dimes of this year from all three mints. Full Bands coins are rare and command a dramatic premium. If you seek a FB coin, be sure all other parts are sharply struck.

See next page for chart.

Market Values • Circulation Strikes

G-4	VG-8	F-12	VF-20	EF-40	AU-50	MS-60
$3.25	$4	$5	$8	$18	$45	$145

MS-63	MS-64	MS-64FB	MS-65	MS-65FB	MS-66	MS-66FB
$325	$465	$2,300	$1,450	$6,500	$2,850	$15,000

Certified Populations

Fair	AG-2	G-4	VG-8	F-12	VF-20	EF-40	AU-50	MS-60
0	0	0	1	1	1	2	44	1

MS-61	MS-62	MS-63	MS-64	MS-65	MS-66	MS-67	MS-68	MS-69
13	44	42	75	42	13	0	0	0

1921 Mercury Dime

Circulation-strike mintage:
1,230,000

Notes. The Philadelphia Mint coins of 1921 were made in the smallest quantities since the mintage of 1916-D. A nationwide financial recession reduced the demand. No dimes at all were struck in 1922. The date on the 1921 and 1921-D is high and is usually bold on the coins.

Key to Collecting. The 1921 dime commands a good premium in all grades from About Good upward. This was a favorite date for collectors to look for in circulation in the 1930s, and duplicate coins when found were kept. By the 1950s nearly all had disappeared from circulation. The 1916-D, 1921, and 1921-D were the key dates although the 1931-D and 1931-S were scarce as well.

Most 1921 dimes are well struck, and many have Full Bands. Because of this the premium of the FB price is low in relation to the price for regular coins.

Market Values • Circulation Strikes

G-4	VG-8	F-12	VF-20	EF-40	AU-50	MS-60
$65	$80	$130	$320	$600	$925	$1,200

MS-63	MS-64	MS-64FB	MS-65	MS-65FB	MS-66	MS-66FB
$2,200	$2,300	$2,850	$3,500	$4,200	$4,500	$7,500

Certified Populations

Fair	AG-2	G-4	VG-8	F-12	VF-20	EF-40	AU-50	MS-60
7	208	190	92	93	150	78	85	0

MS-61	MS-62	MS-63	MS-64	MS-65	MS-66	MS-67	MS-68	MS-69
14	20	28	79	65	25	5	0	0

1921-D Mercury Dime

Circulation-strike mintage:
1,080,000

Notes. For this coinage 11 obverse dies and 8 reverse dies were made, although it is not certain that all were used. Reverses could be held over for use later. If all obverses were used this indicates a production of about 100,000 coins per die. This is a low figure. For most dates and mints, Mercury dime dies struck 200,000 pieces or more.

Key to Collecting. Similar to the Philadelphia dimes of this date the 1921-D coins command a good premium in all grades from About Good upward. This was a favorite date for collectors to look for in circulation in the 1930s, and if multiples were found they would be set aside. By the 1950s nearly all had disappeared from pocket change. Finding one was worthy of an announcement at a coin-club meeting.

The 1921-D dimes are well struck, similar to the Philadelphia coins, and many have Full Bands. Because of this the premium of the FB price is low in relation to the price for regular coins.

Market Values • Circulation Strikes

G-4	VG-8	F-12	VF-20	EF-40	AU-50	MS-60
$80	$130	$210	$420	$775	$1,250	$1,500

MS-63	MS-64	MS-64FB	MS-65	MS-65FB	MS-66	MS-66FB
$2,600	$2,700	$3,200	$3,500	$5,000	$5,000	$8,500

Certified Populations

Fair	AG-2	G-4	VG-8	F-12	VF-20	EF-40	AU-50	MS-60
4	135	189	162	145	135	82	67	0

MS-61	MS-62	MS-63	MS-64	MS-65	MS-66	MS-67	MS-68	MS-69
7	33	33	97	52	24	2	0	0

1923 Mercury Dime

Circulation-strike mintage:
50,130,000

See next page for chart.

Notes. Dimes of this date are common, the start of a string of high-mintage dimes of more than two million per year that extended to 1931, with the exception of 1926-S. Philadelphia Mint coins were made by the tens of millions, as that mint served most of the American population. Denver and San Francisco coins were made in lesser quantities, but still by the millions. Counterfeit "1923-D" dimes were made in the 1920s and circulated widely.

Key to Collecting. 1923 dimes are common in all grades. Full Bands coins are common on an absolute basis but represent only a small fraction of the total population.

Market Values • Circulation Strikes

G-4	VG-8	F-12	VF-20	EF-40	AU-50	MS-60
$3	$3.25	$3.50	$5	$7	$16	$30
MS-63	MS-64	MS-64FB	MS-65	MS-65FB	MS-66	MS-66FB
$45	$55	$65	$130	$350	$450	$625

Certified Populations

Fair	AG-2	G-4	VG-8	F-12	VF-20	EF-40	AU-50	MS-60
0	0	2	3	2	9	5	42	1
MS-61	MS-62	MS-63	MS-64	MS-65	MS-66	MS-67	MS-68	MS-69
13	60	96	285	218	116	35	1	0

1923-S Mercury Dime

Circulation-strike mintage:
6,440,000

Key to Collecting. 1923-S dimes are common in worn grades in proportion to their mintage. Most were saved beginning in the 1930s. Mint State coins are elusive. Full Band dimes are rare, and most of these do not have rounded bands and can be weak in other areas. Great care is urged when buying FB pieces.

Market Values • Circulation Strikes

G-4	VG-8	F-12	VF-20	EF-40	AU-50	MS-60
$3	$4	$8	$18	$65	$105	$160

MS-63	MS-64	MS-64FB	MS-65	MS-65FB	MS-66	MS-66FB
$400	$575	$2,150	$1,250	$5,800	$2,400	$18,500

Certified Populations

Fair	AG-2	G-4	VG-8	F-12	VF-20	EF-40	AU-50	MS-60
0	1	2	0	2	6	13	51	1

MS-61	MS-62	MS-63	MS-64	MS-65	MS-66	MS-67	MS-68	MS-69
22	53	52	92	26	5	1	0	0

1924 Mercury Dime

Circulation-strike mintage:
24,010,000

Key to Collecting. Due to the generous mintage 1924 dimes are common in well-worn grades and are easy enough to find in Mint State as well, although these represent only a tiny proportion of survivors. Full Bands coins are readily available but command a premium, as in all cases.

Market Values • Circulation Strikes

G-4	VG-8	F-12	VF-20	EF-40	AU-50	MS-60
$3	$3.25	$4	$6	$15	$30	$45

MS-63	MS-64	MS-64FB	MS-65	MS-65FB	MS-66	MS-66FB
$100	$125	$160	$210	$500	$450	$975

Certified Populations

Fair	AG-2	G-4	VG-8	F-12	VF-20	EF-40	AU-50	MS-60
0	0	0	3	1	0	0	17	1

MS-61	MS-62	MS-63	MS-64	MS-65	MS-66	MS-67	MS-68	MS-69
8	20	56	150	147	102	20	2	0

1924-D Mercury Dime

Circulation-strike mintage:
6,810,000

Key to Collecting. Most 1924-D dimes are fairly well struck. Full Bands coins are plentiful in comparison to those of other branch-mint Mercury dimes of the era.

Market Values • Circulation Strikes

G-4	VG-8	F-12	VF-20	EF-40	AU-50	MS-60
$3.50	$4.50	$8	$24	$70	$110	$175
MS-63	MS-64	MS-64FB	MS-65	MS-65FB	MS-66	MS-66FB
$500	$600	$775	$950	$1,200	$1,700	$2,100

Certified Populations

Fair	AG-2	G-4	VG-8	F-12	VF-20	EF-40	AU-50	MS-60
0	0	3	2	2	6	9	41	0
MS-61	MS-62	MS-63	MS-64	MS-65	MS-66	MS-67	MS-68	MS-69
15	39	57	150	57	32	7	0	0

1924-S Mercury Dime

Circulation-strike mintage:
7,120,000

Key to Collecting. Although 1924-S is common in lower grades from About Good through VG and is readily available in higher circulated grades as well, in Mint State it is one of the rarer issues in the Mercury dime series. Most at that level are in lower ranges such as MS-60 to 63. With Full Bands this date/mintmark is very rare.

Market Values • Circulation Strikes

G-4	VG-8	F-12	VF-20	EF-40	AU-50	MS-60
$3.50	$4	$6	$10	$60	$110	$200

MS-63	MS-64	MS-64FB	MS-65	MS-65FB	MS-66	MS-66FB
$500	$600	$2,900	$1,250	$15,000	$3,000	$45,000

Certified Populations

Fair	AG-2	G-4	VG-8	F-12	VF-20	EF-40	AU-50	MS-60
0	0	1	0	3	4	12	50	2

MS-61	MS-62	MS-63	MS-64	MS-65	MS-66	MS-67	MS-68	MS-69
23	59	42	103	26	5	0	0	0

1925 Mercury Dime

Circulation-strike mintage:
25,610,000

Key to Collecting. Following the trend of Philadelphia Mercury dimes of the decade the 1925 is very common in worn grades, less so in Mint State, but at any level there is no scarcity. Many if not most are lightly struck in one area or another. Full Bands coins are scarce and can be less than optimal. Again, cherrypicking is advised.

Market Values • Circulation Strikes

G-4	VG-8	F-12	VF-20	EF-40	AU-50	MS-60
$3	$3.25	$4	$5	$10	$20	$30

MS-63	MS-64	MS-64FB	MS-65	MS-65FB	MS-66	MS-66FB
$85	$130	$225	$225	$875	$550	$1,600

Certified Populations

Fair	AG-2	G-4	VG-8	F-12	VF-20	EF-40	AU-50	MS-60
0	0	0	0	0	4	7	25	0

MS-61	MS-62	MS-63	MS-64	MS-65	MS-66	MS-67	MS-68	MS-69
8	23	39	118	76	25	4	0	0

1925-D Mercury Dime

Circulation-strike mintage:
5,117,000

Key to Collecting. 1925-D dimes are common in lower grades. In Mint State they are somewhat scarce. Many if not most are weakly struck in one area or another, suggesting that care is needed to find quality coins. The same is true for FB coins, which are elusive and often have problems, revealed when they are studied carefully.

Market Values • Circulation Strikes

G-4	VG-8	F-12	VF-20	EF-40	AU-50	MS-60	
$4	$5	$12	$45	$120	$200	$375	
MS-63	MS-64	MS-64FB	MS-65	MS-65FB	MS-66	MS-66FB	
$800	$950	$1,250	$1,700	$3,550	$3,000	$8,000	

Certified Populations

Fair	AG-2	G-4	VG-8	F-12	VF-20	EF-40	AU-50	MS-60
0	0	1	1	0	9	16	60	1
MS-61	MS-62	MS-63	MS-64	MS-65	MS-66	MS-67	MS-68	MS-69
7	32	46	76	19	16	4	0	0

1925-S Mercury Dime

Circulation-strike mintage:
5,850,000

Key to Collecting. In his *Complete Guide to Mercury Dimes* David W. Lange states: "In the opinion of the author and many others 1925-S holds the record for the most poorly made issue in the series. Both obverse and reverse are plagued by heavy die polishing and erosion and a generally weak strike throughout."

This is an ideal example illustrating that a grade assigned to a professionally certified coin can be one thing, but *quality* can be something else entirely. As is true in nearly all federal series, 90% or more of today's buyers simply read the labels on holders. The secret for you is that cherrypicking for quality costs no more—but it does take time. Full Bands coins are quite rare and must be checked for quality. The Lange guide is highly recommended for additional information on the series.

Market Values • Circulation Strikes

G-4	VG-8	F-12	VF-20	EF-40	AU-50	MS-60
$3.25	$4	$8	$18	$70	$110	$180

MS-63	MS-64	MS-64FB	MS-65	MS-65FB	MS-66	MS-66FB
$500	$700	$1,375	$1,400	$3,100	$2,600	$7,000

Certified Populations

Fair	AG-2	G-4	VG-8	F-12	VF-20	EF-40	AU-50	MS-60
0	0	1	1	1	4	5	35	1

MS-61	MS-62	MS-63	MS-64	MS-65	MS-66	MS-67	MS-68	MS-69
9	18	39	76	32	14	5	0	0

1926 Mercury Dime

Circulation-strike mintage:
32,160,000

Key to Collecting. By virtue of its large mintage the 1926 is very common in worn grades and is easily found in Mint State. Most are decent strikes. Full Bands coins are plentiful.

Market Values • Circulation Strikes

G-4	VG-8	F-12	VF-20	EF-40	AU-50	MS-60
$3	$3.25	$3.50	$5	$7	$16	$25

MS-63	MS-64	MS-64FB	MS-65	MS-65FB	MS-66	MS-66FB
$65	$100	$145	$250	$400	$475	$900

Certified Populations

Fair	AG-2	G-4	VG-8	F-12	VF-20	EF-40	AU-50	MS-60
0	0	0	0	0	2	5	36	1

MS-61	MS-62	MS-63	MS-64	MS-65	MS-66	MS-67	MS-68	MS-69
11	69	103	266	138	47	11	0	0

1926-D Mercury Dime

Circulation-strike mintage:
6,828,000

Key to Collecting. The 1926-D is easily found in circulated grades. Mint State coins are common as well. The Denver Mint spaced the dies too far apart, with the result that most have weakness in some areas. There is a caveat concerning Full Bands coins: they may be weak in other areas. Be careful.

Market Values • Circulation Strikes

G-4	VG-8	F-12	VF-20	EF-40	AU-50	MS-60
$3.25	$4.50	$6	$10	$28	$50	$125
MS-63	MS-64	MS-64FB	MS-65	MS-65FB	MS-66	MS-66FB
$275	$380	$700	$600	$1,850	$1,450	$3,500

Certified Populations

Fair	AG-2	G-4	VG-8	F-12	VF-20	EF-40	AU-50	MS-60
0	0	2	2	2	2	9	43	2
MS-61	MS-62	MS-63	MS-64	MS-65	MS-66	MS-67	MS-68	MS-69
18	61	60	151	72	19	3	0	0

1926-S Mercury Dime

Circulation-strike mintage:
1,520,000

Notes. The mintage of the 1926-S is one of just a few Mercury dimes that dipped below two million coins.

Key to Collecting. In worn grades the 1926-S is not scarce, but fewer examples are around than are of other issues of the era. Mint State 1926-S coins are elusive in comparison to most other date/mintmarks and are very rare if MS-65 or better with Full Bands, sharp in all other areas and with good eye appeal.

Market Values • Circulation Strikes

G-4	VG-8	F-12	VF-20	EF-40	AU-50	MS-60
$13	$15	$26	$60	$250	$450	$825

MS-63	MS-64	MS-64FB	MS-65	MS-65FB	MS-66	MS-66FB
$1,500	$1,875	$3,600	$2,850	$6,000	$4,600	$15,000

Certified Populations

Fair	AG-2	G-4	VG-8	F-12	VF-20	EF-40	AU-50	MS-60
0	0	10	6	18	63	57	77	2

MS-61	MS-62	MS-63	MS-64	MS-65	MS-66	MS-67	MS-68	MS-69
6	21	16	49	23	7	2	0	0

1927 Mercury Dime

Circulation-strike mintage:
28,080,000

Key to Collecting. 1927 Philadelphia Mint dimes are easily available in any grade desired. In the 1950s scattered rolls of this date were sometimes seen.

Market Values • Circulation Strikes

G-4	VG-8	F-12	VF-20	EF-40	AU-50	MS-60
$3	$3.25	$3.50	$5	$7	$15	$30

MS-63	MS-64	MS-64FB	MS-65	MS-65FB	MS-66	MS-66FB
$60	$100	$140	$150	$385	$310	$800

Certified Populations

Fair	AG-2	G-4	VG-8	F-12	VF-20	EF-40	AU-50	MS-60
0	2	1	2	2	3	6	25	0

MS-61	MS-62	MS-63	MS-64	MS-65	MS-66	MS-67	MS-68	MS-69
11	32	66	182	130	45	8	0	0

1927-D Mercury Dime

Circulation-strike mintage:
4,812,000

Key to Collecting. 1927-D dimes are common in worn grades and easily enough found in Mint State. Striking is often irregular, and Full Bands coins, which are rare, and all others need to be examined carefully. In this era the Denver Mint spaced its dies too far apart on many different issues across various denominations (with Buffalo nickels being the most egregious).

Market Values • Circulation Strikes

G-4	VG-8	F-12	VF-20	EF-40	AU-50	MS-60
$3.50	$5.50	$8	$25	$80	$100	$200
MS-63	MS-64	MS-64FB	MS-65	MS-65FB	MS-66	MS-66FB
$400	$500	$2,300	$1,200	$8,000	$2,600	$15,000

Certified Populations

Fair	AG-2	G-4	VG-8	F-12	VF-20	EF-40	AU-50	MS-60
0	0	2	0	1	8	8	58	0
MS-61	MS-62	MS-63	MS-64	MS-65	MS-66	MS-67	MS-68	MS-69
13	38	40	57	25	13	0	0	0

1927-S Mercury Dime

Circulation-strike mintage:
4,770,000

Key to Collecting. The 1927-S is common in well-worn grades. Mint State coins are easy to find and are often fairly well struck except for the central bands on the reverse. Full Bands coins are rare.

Market Values • Circulation Strikes

G-4	VG-8	F-12	VF-20	EF-40	AU-50	MS-60
$3.25	$4	$6	$12	$28	$50	$275

MS-63	MS-64	MS-64FB	MS-65	MS-65FB	MS-66	MS-66FB
$550	$700	$2,300	$1,400	$7,500	$2,350	$17,500

Certified Populations

Fair	AG-2	G-4	VG-8	F-12	VF-20	EF-40	AU-50	MS-60
0	0	1	2	0	6	2	31	1

MS-61	MS-62	MS-63	MS-64	MS-65	MS-66	MS-67	MS-68	MS-69
14	19	34	62	35	8	1	0	0

1928 Mercury Dime

Circulation-strike mintage:
19,480,000

Key to Collecting. Dimes of this issue are common in all grades including Mint State. Scattered rolls were in the marketplace in the 1950s. The striking is usually decent. Full Bands coins are in the minority but are easily enough found.

Market Values • Circulation Strikes

G-4	VG-8	F-12	VF-20	EF-40	AU-50	MS-60
$3	$3.25	$3.50	$5	$7	$18	$30

MS-63	MS-64	MS-64FB	MS-65	MS-65FB	MS-66	MS-66FB
$55	$70	$100	$130	$380	$350	$600

Certified Populations

Fair	AG-2	G-4	VG-8	F-12	VF-20	EF-40	AU-50	MS-60
0	0	0	1	0	0	1	21	0

MS-61	MS-62	MS-63	MS-64	MS-65	MS-66	MS-67	MS-68	MS-69
15	25	50	134	136	41	8	0	0

1928-D Mercury Dime

Circulation-strike mintage:
4,161,000

Key to Collecting. 1928-D dimes are common in worn grades. In Mint State there are enough to easily satisfy collector demand. Striking sharpness is often irregular. Full Bands coins are rare, and often have weakness in other areas or have minimal separation of the two central bands. Cherrypicking is recommended. You are the winner if you do this, for, as noted, 90% or more of the buyers in the marketplace do not go beyond reading labels on professionally graded holders.

Market Values • Circulation Strikes

G-4	VG-8	F-12	VF-20	EF-40	AU-50	MS-60
$4	$5	$8	$20	$50	$95	$175
MS-63	MS-64	MS-64FB	MS-65	MS-65FB	MS-66	MS-66FB
$360	$435	$1,150	$850	$2,850	$1,550	$5,500

Certified Populations

Fair	AG-2	G-4	VG-8	F-12	VF-20	EF-40	AU-50	MS-60
0	0	1	2	3	4	9	32	0
MS-61	MS-62	MS-63	MS-64	MS-65	MS-66	MS-67	MS-68	MS-69
4	29	41	87	30	18	9	0	0

1928-S Mercury Dime

Circulation-strike mintage:
7,400,000

Key to Collecting. 1928-S dimes are common in any and all grades up through MS-64. In MS-65 they are slightly scarce, and Full Bands coins are elusive. Striking is usually quite good.

Small S mintmark: Most 1928-S dimes have a small mintmark as used since 1916. These are common in all grades. Full Bands coins are rare.

Large S mintmark: However, about 20% of the S mintmarks are larger and heavier, with much of the center filled in. This style was an anomaly and was not used elsewhere in the series. These command a price about twice that of the Small S variety. Full Bands coins are very rare. (Fivaz-Stanton-10-1928S-501)

Market Values • Circulation Strikes

G-4	VG-8	F-12	VF-20	EF-40	AU-50	MS-60
$3	$3.25	$4	$6	$16	$45	$150

MS-63	MS-64	MS-64FB	MS-65	MS-65FB	MS-66	MS-66FB
$320	$325	$635	$400	$2,100	$550	$2,950

Certified Populations

Fair	AG-2	G-4	VG-8	F-12	VF-20	EF-40	AU-50	MS-60
0	0	0	0	2	0	2	21	1

MS-61	MS-62	MS-63	MS-64	MS-65	MS-66	MS-67	MS-68	MS-69
7	36	43	98	88	49	8	0	0

1929 Mercury Dime

Circulation-strike mintage:
25,970,000

Key to Collecting. 1929 dimes were among the coins made available for face value plus postage from the Treasury Department in 1932. These are common in all grades. Most are well struck.

Market Values • Circulation Strikes

G-4	VG-8	F-12	VF-20	EF-40	AU-50	MS-60
$3	$3.25	$3.50	$5	$6	$12	$22

MS-63	MS-64	MS-64FB	MS-65	MS-65FB	MS-66	MS-66FB
$35	$40	$55	$75	$180	$115	$325

Certified Populations

Fair	AG-2	G-4	VG-8	F-12	VF-20	EF-40	AU-50	MS-60
0	0	0	2	0	0	1	26	0

MS-61	MS-62	MS-63	MS-64	MS-65	MS-66	MS-67	MS-68	MS-69
11	37	72	203	287	164	29	1	0

1929-D Mercury Dime

Circulation-strike mintage:
5,034,000

Key to Collecting. 1929-D dimes were among the coins made available for face value plus postage from the Treasury Department in 1932. These are common in all grades. Full Bands coins are a small percentage of surviving Mint State pieces but are easy to find.

Market Values • Circulation Strikes

G-4	VG-8	F-12	VF-20	EF-40	AU-50	MS-60
$3	$3.50	$5	$8	$15	$24	$30

MS-63	MS-64	MS-64FB	MS-65	MS-65FB	MS-66	MS-66FB
$36	$42	$70	$75	$225	$130	$460

Certified Populations

Fair	AG-2	G-4	VG-8	F-12	VF-20	EF-40	AU-50	MS-60
0	0	1	0	0	2	3	10	0

MS-61	MS-62	MS-63	MS-64	MS-65	MS-66	MS-67	MS-68	MS-69
5	22	84	447	440	143	12	2	0

1929-S Mercury Dime

Circulation-strike mintage:
4,770,000

Key to Collecting. 1929-S dimes were among the coins made available for face value plus postage from the Treasury Department in 1932. These are common in all grades. Full Bands coins make up a small percentage of surviving Mint State pieces.

Market Values • Circulation Strikes

G-4	VG-8	F-12	VF-20	EF-40	AU-50	MS-60
$3	$3.25	$3.75	$5	$10	$20	$35

MS-63	MS-64	MS-64FB	MS-65	MS-65FB	MS-66	MS-66FB
$45	$70	$140	$125	$500	$300	$800

Certified Populations

Fair	AG-2	G-4	VG-8	F-12	VF-20	EF-40	AU-50	MS-60
0	0	0	0	3	2	1	21	0

MS-61	MS-62	MS-63	MS-64	MS-65	MS-66	MS-67	MS-68	MS-69
4	15	35	99	105	70	19	1	0

1930 Mercury Dime

Circulation-strike mintage:
6,770,000

Key to Collecting. 1930 dimes were among the coins made available for face value plus postage from the Treasury Department in 1932. Examples are common in all grades. Full Bands coins are much scarcer than typical strikes.

Market Values • Circulation Strikes

G-4	VG-8	F-12	VF-20	EF-40	AU-50	MS-60
$3	$3.25	$3.50	$5	$8	$16	$30

MS-63	MS-64	MS-64FB	MS-65	MS-65FB	MS-66	MS-66FB
$50	$55	$145	$125	$450	$225	$900

Certified Populations

Fair	AG-2	G-4	VG-8	F-12	VF-20	EF-40	AU-50	MS-60
0	0	0	0	1	0	3	24	0

MS-61	MS-62	MS-63	MS-64	MS-65	MS-66	MS-67	MS-68	MS-69
8	32	35	129	115	54	5	0	0

1930-S Mercury Dime

Circulation-strike mintage:
1,843,000

Key to Collecting. 1930-S dimes were among the coins made available for face value plus postage from the Treasury Department in 1932. Despite this, Mint State coins are elusive in comparison to other dates of the early 1930s, including the lower-mintage dimes of 1931-D and S. Full Bands coins are elusive.

Market Values • Circulation Strikes

G-4	VG-8	F-12	VF-20	EF-40	AU-50	MS-60
$3	$4	$5	$7	$15	$45	$80

MS-63	MS-64	MS-64FB	MS-65	MS-65FB	MS-66	MS-66FB
$150	$175	$250	$210	$700	$350	$1,550

Certified Populations

Fair	AG-2	G-4	VG-8	F-12	VF-20	EF-40	AU-50	MS-60
0	0	0	0	1	3	1	17	0

MS-61	MS-62	MS-63	MS-64	MS-65	MS-66	MS-67	MS-68	MS-69
6	17	33	70	74	51	7	0	0

1931 Mercury Dime

Circulation-strike mintage:
3,150,000

Key to Collecting. 1931 dimes were among the coins the Treasury Department made available for face value plus postage in 1932. These are common in all grades today, although Full Bands coins represent only a small percentage of Mint State pieces.

Market Values • Circulation Strikes

G-4	VG-8	F-12	VF-20	EF-40	AU-50	MS-60
$3	$3.10	$4	$6	$10	$22	$35

MS-63	MS-64	MS-64FB	MS-65	MS-65FB	MS-66	MS-66FB
$70	$85	$235	$150	$675	$260	$1,000

Certified Populations

Fair	AG-2	G-4	VG-8	F-12	VF-20	EF-40	AU-50	MS-60
0	0	0	1	0	2	1	27	0

MS-61	MS-62	MS-63	MS-64	MS-65	MS-66	MS-67	MS-68	MS-69
10	23	51	134	135	55	4	0	0

1931-D Mercury Dime

Circulation-strike mintage:
1,260,000

Key to Collecting. 1931-D dimes were among the coins made available for face value plus postage from the Treasury Department in 1932. These seem to have been popular, for rolls were seen with frequency as late as the 1950s. Beginning with the vast expansion of the hobby in 1960 most if not all rolls were broken up for sale of individual pieces. Most are well struck, and Full Bands coins are not hard to find.

Market Values • Circulation Strikes

G-4	VG-8	F-12	VF-20	EF-40	AU-50	MS-60
$8	$9	$12	$20	$35	$60	$90

MS-63	MS-64	MS-64FB	MS-65	MS-65FB	MS-66	MS-66FB
$140	$165	$190	$280	$400	$380	$600

Certified Populations

Fair	AG-2	G-4	VG-8	F-12	VF-20	EF-40	AU-50	MS-60
0	0	0	2	2	19	6	19	0

MS-61	MS-62	MS-63	MS-64	MS-65	MS-66	MS-67	MS-68	MS-69
1	11	29	139	213	85	17	0	0

1931-S Mercury Dime

Circulation-strike mintage:
1,800,000

Key to Collecting. 1931-S dimes were among the coins made available for face value plus postage from the Treasury Department in 1932. Rolls of 1931-S dimes were seen with frequency as late as the 1950s, indicating their popularity at the time, but somewhat fewer rolls seem to have been set aside than of the 1931-D. Full Bands coins are scarce and represent only a small percentage of surviving Mint State pieces.

Market Values • Circulation Strikes

G-4	VG-8	F-12	VF-20	EF-40	AU-50	MS-60
$4	$5	$6	$10	$16	$45	$90
MS-63	MS-64	MS-64FB	MS-65	MS-65FB	MS-66	MS-66FB
$150	$180	$800	$300	$2,200	$425	$3,000

Certified Populations

Fair	AG-2	G-4	VG-8	F-12	VF-20	EF-40	AU-50	MS-60
0	0	1	6	4	14	10	25	0
MS-61	MS-62	MS-63	MS-64	MS-65	MS-66	MS-67	MS-68	MS-69
3	24	40	97	102	63	7	0	0

1934 Mercury Dime

Circulation-strike mintage:
24,080,000

Key to Collecting. Beginning in 1934 and continuing to the end of the series in 1945 collectors, dealers, and investors set aside large numbers of 50-coin bank-wrapped rolls of Mercury dimes, the only exception being 1934-D (see next listing). This was the start of an era of widespread interest in coins, inspired by Wayte Raymond's National albums. These coins were traded as rolls—without being opened for inspection. No one had heard of Full Bands, and there were no different levels of Mint State. Most of the earlier rolls of the 1940s were broken up beginning with the great coin-collecting boom of 1960. Later rolls of the 1940s continued to be traded as such and were listed in the *Coin Dealer Newsletter* (a wholesale coin-price guide) and elsewhere. Today, most such rolls are long gone, after having been opened and inspected and the higher-grade and Full Bands coins sold separately.

Most Mint State 1934 dimes are well struck, but on some the 4 in the date is light. Many have Full Bands. Population reports are of very little use in comparing the availability of regular Mint State coins with those with FB, as the FB coins are submitted to the grading services in larger quantities (and more frequently) due to their significant value. This point is little understood by investors and casual buyers.

Countless millions of worn Mercury dimes of the 1930s and 1940s were melted in the late 1970s during the great silver speculation that resulted in the metal reaching an all-time high of $50.35 per ounce on Comex on January 18, 1980, giving a silver dime the melt-down value of $3.64.

Market Values • Circulation Strikes

F-12	VF-20	EF-40	AU-50	MS-60	MS-63	MS-64FB
$3	$3.10	$3.50	$16	$25	$35	$40

MS-65	MS-65FB	MS-66	MS-66FB	MS-67	MS-67FB
$50	$140	$65	$220	$260	$500

Certified Populations

Fair	AG-2	G-4	VG-8	F-12	VF-20	EF-40	AU-50	MS-60
0	0	1	1	1	1	1	26	0

MS-61	MS-62	MS-63	MS-64	MS-65	MS-66	MS-67	MS-68	MS-69
7	28	49	184	268	228	92	9	0

1934-D Mercury Dime

Circulation-strike mintage:
6,772,000

Notes. Large and small mintmarks appear on 1934-D dimes. The small mintmarks end the style used for many years, and the large mintmarks introduce the size continued through 1945.

Key to Collecting. This is the one mintmarked variety of Mercury dimes after 1931 that was not available in roll quantities in the 1950s, although single pieces were common enough. Most are fairly well struck and very attractive. Those with Full Bands are in the minority, however, and command a strong premium.

See next page for chart.

Market Values • Circulation Strikes

F-12	VF-20	EF-40	AU-50	MS-60	MS-63	MS-64
$3	$3.10	$8	$33	$50	$60	$70

MS-64FB	MS-65	MS-65FB	MS-66	MS-66FB	MS-67	MS-67FB
$120	$85	$325	$230	$750	$465	$3,000

Certified Populations

Fair	AG-2	G-4	VG-8	F-12	VF-20	EF-40	AU-50	MS-60
0	0	0	0	1	2	0	26	1

MS-61	MS-62	MS-63	MS-64	MS-65	MS-66	MS-67	MS-68	MS-69
3	14	25	172	259	127	24	1	0

1935 Mercury Dime

Circulation-strike mintage:
58,830,000

Key to Collecting. 1935 Mercury dimes are common in all grades. Full Bands coins are in the minority among surviving Mint State pieces but are common on an absolute basis.

Market Values • Circulation Strikes

F-12	VF-20	EF-40	AU-50	MS-60	MS-63	MS-64
$3	$3.10	$3.25	$7	$10	$15	$20

MS-64FB	MS-65	MS-65FB	MS-66	MS-66FB	MS-67	MS-67FB
$30	$35	$75	$60	$120	$110	$450

Certified Populations

Fair	AG-2	G-4	VG-8	F-12	VF-20	EF-40	AU-50	MS-60
0	0	0	0	1	2	2	42	1

MS-61	MS-62	MS-63	MS-64	MS-65	MS-66	MS-67	MS-68	MS-69
7	26	30	142	371	538	222	2	0

1935-D Mercury Dime

Circulation-strike mintage:
10,477,000

Key to Collecting. 1935-D dimes are common in all grades. Full Bands coins represent a small percentage of Mint State coins and sell at a particularly sharp premium.

Market Values • Circulation Strikes

F-12	VF-20	EF-40	AU-50	MS-60	MS-63	MS-64
$3	$3.10	$8	$26	$35	$50	$60
MS-64FB	MS-65	MS-65FB	MS-66	MS-66FB	MS-67	MS-67FB
$180	$90	$525	$325	$800	$500	$3,500

Certified Populations

Fair	AG-2	G-4	VG-8	F-12	VF-20	EF-40	AU-50	MS-60
0	0	0	1	1	0	2	25	0
MS-61	MS-62	MS-63	MS-64	MS-65	MS-66	MS-67	MS-68	MS-69
6	17	36	125	158	88	12	1	0

1935-S Mercury Dime

Circulation-strike mintage:
15,840,000

Key to Collecting. 1935-S dimes are common in all grades. Full Bands coins are rare in comparison to typical strikes. Cherrypicking is advised as most FB coins are not sharply delineated and the bands can be somewhat flat.

See next page for chart.

113

Market Values • Circulation Strikes

F-12	VF-20	EF-40	AU-50	MS-60	MS-63	MS-64
$3	$3.10	$5	$16	$22	$30	$35
MS-64FB	MS-65	MS-65FB	MS-66	MS-66FB	MS-67	MS-67FB
$140	$40	$350	$80	$585	$300	$1,000

Certified Populations

Fair	AG-2	G-4	VG-8	F-12	VF-20	EF-40	AU-50	MS-60
0	0	0	0	0	1	0	10	0
MS-61	MS-62	MS-63	MS-64	MS-65	MS-66	MS-67	MS-68	MS-69
4	10	23	103	184	199	55	0	0

1936 Mercury Dime

Circulation Strike

Proof

Circulation-strike mintage:
87,500,000

Proof mintage:
4,130

Notes. This is the first year that Proofs were made in the Mercury dime series. Production of Proofs continued in succeeding years through 1942.

Key to Collecting. Circulation-strike 1936 dimes are common in all grades. Full Bands coins are easy to find, but sell for a premium. Proofs are readily available. Because of the lower mintage this is the scarcest Proof date.

Market Values • Circulation Strikes and Proof Strikes

F-12	VF-20	EF-40	AU-50	MS-60	MS-63	MS-64	MS-64FB	MS-65
$3	$3.10	$3.50	$7	$10	$18	$22	$30	$30
MS-65FB	MS-66	MS-66FB	MS-67	MS-67FB	PF-64	PF-65	PF-66	PF-67
$90	$48	$120	$140	$275	$1,000	$1,200	$1,750	$4,500

Certified Populations

Fair	AG-2	G-4	VG-8	F-12	VF-20	EF-40	AU-50	MS-60	MS-61	MS-62	MS-63	MS-64	MS-65
0	0	1	1	2	1	4	41	0	7	19	24	121	371
MS-61	MS-62	MS-63	MS-64	MS-65	MS-66	MS-67	MS-68	MS-69	PF-65	PF-66	PF-67	PF-68	PF-69
6	10	52	165	514	668	242	10	0	489	660	234	43	1

1936-D Mercury Dime

Circulation-strike mintage:
16,132,000

Key to Collecting. 1936-D dimes are common in all grades. Most are fairly well struck. The surfaces vary in quality, and deeply frosty coins are in the minority. Full Bands coins are rare in comparison to regular strikes, but enough are around that finding one is easy.

Market Values • Circulation Strikes

F-12	VF-20	EF-40	AU-50	MS-60	MS-63	MS-64
$3	$3.60	$6	$16	$25	$40	$50

MS-64FB	MS-65	MS-65FB	MS-66	MS-66FB	MS-67	MS-67FB
$120	$55	$275	$80	$350	$325	$850

Certified Populations

Fair	AG-2	G-4	VG-8	F-12	VF-20	EF-40	AU-50	MS-60
0	0	1	0	1	1	2	32	0

MS-61	MS-62	MS-63	MS-64	MS-65	MS-66	MS-67	MS-68	MS-69
11	17	20	119	171	133	52	1	0

1936-S Mercury Dime

Circulation-strike mintage:
9,210,000

Key to Collecting. 1936-S dimes are common in all grades. Most are fairly well struck. Full Bands coins are scarce in comparison to regular strikes, but are common in an absolute sense.

See next page for chart.

Market Values • Circulation Strikes

F-12	VF-20	EF-40	AU-50	MS-60	MS-63	MS-64
$3	$3.10	$3.50	$13	$23	$30	$32

MS-64FB	MS-65	MS-65FB	MS-66	MS-66FB	MS-67	MS-67FB
$40	$35	$95	$55	$165	$190	$700

Certified Populations

Fair	AG-2	G-4	VG-8	F-12	VF-20	EF-40	AU-50	MS-60
0	0	0	0	0	0	0	5	0

MS-61	MS-62	MS-63	MS-64	MS-65	MS-66	MS-67	MS-68	MS-69
3	4	13	77	370	426	64	1	0

1937 Mercury Dime

Circulation Strike

Proof

Circulation-strike mintage:
56,860,000

Proof mintage:
5,756

Key to Collecting. Circulation-strike 1937 dimes are common in all grades. Full Bands coins are easy to find, but sell for a premium. Proofs are readily available. Because of the mintage quantity this is the second-scarcest Proof date.

Market Values • Circulation Strikes and Proof Strikes

F-12	VF-20	EF-40	AU-50	MS-60	MS-63	MS-64	MS-64FB	MS-65
$3	$3.10	$3.25	$7	$10	$15	$20	$30	$30

MS-65FB	MS-66	MS-66FB	MS-67	MS-67FB	PF-64	PF-65	PF-66	PF-67
$60	$40	$85	$50	$500	$450	$600	$950	$1,400

Certified Populations

Fair	AG-2	G-4	VG-8	F-12	VF-20	EF-40	AU-50	MS-60	MS-61	MS-62	MS-63	MS-64	MS-65
0	1	0	1	1	4	2	33	0	10	16	42	226	795

MS-66	MS-67	MS-68	MS-69	PF-60	PF-61	PF-62	PF-63	PF-64	PF-65	PF-66	PF-67	PF-68	PF-69
1,734	956	31	0	3	5	14	48	214	304	408	193	38	0

1937-D Mercury Dime

Circulation-strike mintage:
14,146,000

Key to Collecting. 1937-D dimes are common in all grades. Most are fairly well struck. Full Bands coins are common in an absolute sense.

Market Values • Circulation Strikes

F-12	VF-20	EF-40	AU-50	MS-60	MS-63	MS-64
$3	$3.10	$4	$12	$21	$30	$33

MS-64FB	MS-65	MS-65FB	MS-66	MS-66FB	MS-67	MS-67FB
$38	$45	$100	$85	$180	$120	$400

Certified Populations

Fair	AG-2	G-4	VG-8	F-12	VF-20	EF-40	AU-50	MS-60
0	0	0	0	1	2	0	26	1

MS-61	MS-62	MS-63	MS-64	MS-65	MS-66	MS-67	MS-68	MS-69
3	14	25	172	259	127	24	1	0

1937-S Mercury Dime

Circulation-strike mintage:
9,740,000

Key to Collecting. 1937-S dimes are common in all grades. Most are fairly well struck. Full Bands coins are scarce in comparison to regular strikes, but are common in an absolute sense. Many are FB by minimum definition. Cherrypicking is recommended to acquire a really sharp coin. This will cost no more.

See next page for chart.

Market Values • Circulation Strikes

F-12	VF-20	EF-40	AU-50	MS-60	MS-63	MS-64
$3	$3.10	$3.50	$12	$20	$30	$35

MS-64FB	MS-65	MS-65FB	MS-66	MS-66FB	MS-67	MS-67FB
$70	$40	$185	$80	$230	$190	$1,000

Certified Populations

Fair	AG-2	G-4	VG-8	F-12	VF-20	EF-40	AU-50	MS-60
0	0	0	0	0	2	0	14	0

MS-61	MS-62	MS-63	MS-64	MS-65	MS-66	MS-67	MS-68	MS-69
1	7	17	86	204	403	183	3	0

1938 Mercury Dime

Circulation Strike

Proof

Circulation-strike mintage:
22,190,000

Proof mintage:
8,728

Key to Collecting. Circulation-strike 1938 dimes are common in all grades. Full Bands coins are easy to find, but sell for a premium. Proofs are readily available. Because of the mintage this is the third-scarcest Proof date.

Market Values • Circulation Strikes and Proof Strikes

F-12	VF-20	EF-40	AU-50	MS-60	MS-63	MS-64	MS-64FB	MS-65
$3	$3.10	$3.25	$7	$10	$15	$20	$30	$30

MS-65FB	MS-66	MS-66FB	MS-67	MS-67FB	PF-64	PF-65	PF-66	PF-67
$85	$55	$110	$65	$600	$350	$550	$750	$1,100

Certified Populations

Fair	AG-2	G-4	VG-8	F-12	VF-20	EF-40	AU-50	MS-60	MS-61	MS-62	MS-63	MS-64	MS-65
0	0	0	1	1	0	2	17	1	7	19	24	121	371

MS-66	MS-67	MS-68	MS-69	PF-60	PF-61	PF-62	PF-63	PF-64	PF-65	PF-66	PF-67	PF-68	PF-69
594	354	15	0	1	7	19	61	260	489	660	234	43	1

1938-D Mercury Dime

Circulation-strike mintage:
5,537,000

Notes. The 1938-D dime has the lowest mintage of any circulation-strike date and mintmark from 1934 to 1945 inclusive.

Key to Collecting. Unlike the situation for the slightly higher-mintage 1934-D, 1938-D dimes were saved to the extent of hundreds (or more) of rolls and are common in all grades today. Most are fairly well struck. Full Bands coins are common in an absolute sense.

Market Values • Circulation Strikes

F-12	VF-20	EF-40	AU-50	MS-60	MS-63	MS-64
$3	$3.20	$4	$11	$18	$25	$28

MS-64FB	MS-65	MS-65FB	MS-66	MS-66FB	MS-67	MS-67FB
$32	$35	$65	$75	$120	$235	$300

Certified Populations

Fair	AG-2	G-4	VG-8	F-12	VF-20	EF-40	AU-50	MS-60
0	0	0	0	0	1	1	14	0

MS-61	MS-62	MS-63	MS-64	MS-65	MS-66	MS-67	MS-68	MS-69
1	4	18	136	506	771	214	7	0

1938-S Mercury Dime

Circulation-strike mintage:
8,090,000

Key to Collecting. 1938-S dimes are common in all grades. As is true of all regular dates and mint issues of the decade, millions were melted during the silver speculation of the late 1970s. Mint State coins are common and are usually quite attractive. Full Band dimes are much scarcer than regular strikes, but there are enough around that finding one will not be difficult.

See next page for chart.

Market Values • Circulation Strikes

F-12	VF-20	EF-40	AU-50	MS-60	MS-63	MS-64
$3	$3.10	$3.50	$12	$20	$28	$35

MS-64FB	MS-65	MS-65FB	MS-66	MS-66FB	MS-67	MS-67FB
$40	$42	$160	$80	$230	$275	$500

Certified Populations

Fair	AG-2	G-4	VG-8	F-12	VF-20	EF-40	AU-50	MS-60
0	0	0	0	0	2	1	21	0

MS-61	MS-62	MS-63	MS-64	MS-65	MS-66	MS-67	MS-68	MS-69
1	14	19	129	236	366	144	11	0

1939 Mercury Dime

Circulation Strike

Proof

Circulation-strike mintage:
67,740,000

Proof mintage:
9,321

Key to Collecting. Circulation-strike 1939 dimes are common in all grades. Full Bands coins are easy to find but are very scarce in comparison to typical strikes. Proofs are readily available.

Market Values • Circulation Strikes and Proof Strikes

F-12	VF-20	EF-40	AU-50	MS-60	MS-63	MS-64	MS-64FB	MS-65
$3	$3.10	$3.25	$6	$8	$12	$20	$40	$26

MS-65FB	MS-66	MS-66FB	MS-67	MS-67FB	PF-64	PF-65	PF-66	PF-67
$180	$40	$225	$50	$360	$250	$275	$600	$750

Certified Populations

Fair	AG-2	G-4	VG-8	F-12	VF-20	EF-40	AU-50	MS-60	MS-61	MS-62	MS-63	MS-64	MS-65
0	0	0	0	1	4	3	45	0	8	30	30	151	471

MS-66	MS-67	MS-68	MS-69	PF-60	PF-61	PF-62	PF-63	PF-64	PF-65	PF-66	PF-67	PF-68	PF-69
1,173	1,069	93	0	0	3	17	37	144	386	823	472	78	0

1939-D Mercury Dime

Circulation-strike mintage:
24,394,000

Key to Collecting. 1939-D dimes are common in all grades. Most are sharply struck. This is one variety for which Full Bands coins command only a modest premium.

Market Values • Circulation Strikes

F-12	VF-20	EF-40	AU-50	MS-60	MS-63	MS-64
$3	$3.10	$3.25	$6	$8	$12	$28

MS-64FB	MS-65	MS-65FB	MS-66	MS-66FB	MS-67	MS-67FB
$30	$32	$55	$60	$85	$110	$200

Certified Populations

Fair	AG-2	G-4	VG-8	F-12	VF-20	EF-40	AU-50	MS-60
0	0	0	0	0	1	0	30	0

MS-61	MS-62	MS-63	MS-64	MS-65	MS-66	MS-67	MS-68	MS-69
9	16	40	178	746	1,399	807	38	3

1939-S Mercury Dime

Circulation-strike mintage:
10,540,000

Key to Collecting. 1939-S dimes are common in all grades. Full Bands coins represent a small percentage of Mint State coins and sell at a particularly sharp multiplier over a typically struck coin, quite a contrast to the 1939-D.

See next page for chart.

Market Values • Circulation Strikes

F-12	VF-20	EF-40	AU-50	MS-60	MS-63	MS-64
$3	$3.10	$4	$13	$23	$30	$35

MS-64FB	MS-65	MS-65FB	MS-66	MS-66FB	MS-67	MS-67FB
$200	$42	$725	$110	$950	$210	$2,500

Certified Populations

Fair	AG-2	G-4	VG-8	F-12	VF-20	EF-40	AU-50	MS-60
0	0	0	1	1	1	0	16	1

MS-61	MS-62	MS-63	MS-64	MS-65	MS-66	MS-67	MS-68	MS-69
1	10	19	97	183	749	138	2	0

1940 Mercury Dime

Circulation Strike

Circulation-strike mintage:
65,350,000

Proof mintage:
11,827

Proof

Key to Collecting. Circulation-strike 1940 dimes are common in all grades. Most are well struck. Full Bands coins are common, but sell at a premium, partly due to the cost of certifying them. Proofs are readily available.

Market Values • Circulation Strikes and Proof Strikes

F-12	VF-20	EF-40	AU-50	MS-60	MS-63	MS-64	MS-64FB	MS-65
$3	$3.10	$3.25	$5	$7	$12	$20	$25	$30

MS-65FB	MS-66	MS-66FB	MS-67	MS-67FB	PF-64	PF-65	PF-66	PF-67
$45	$70	$65	$220	$185	$250	$350	$600	$1,100

Certified Populations

Fair	AG-2	G-4	VG-8	F-12	VF-20	EF-40	AU-50	MS-60	MS-61	MS-62	MS-63	MS-64	MS-65
0	0	1	0	1	2	1	42	0	7	21	29	138	712

MS-66	MS-67	MS-68	MS-69	PF-60	PF-61	PF-62	PF-63	PF-64	PF-65	PF-66	PF-67	PF-68	PF-69
1,262	881	23	0	0	5	17	62	277	496	896	350	46	2

1940-D Mercury Dime

Circulation-strike mintage:
21,198,000

Key to Collecting. 1940-D dimes are common in all grades. Most are sharply struck with at least partial separation of the central bands. Full Bands coins are common.

Market Values • Circulation Strikes

F-12	VF-20	EF-40	AU-50	MS-60	MS-63	MS-64
$3	$3.10	$3.25	$5	$7	$14	$21

MS-64FB	MS-65	MS-65FB	MS-66	MS-66FB	MS-67	MS-67FB
$26	$35	$50	$50	$65	$80	$180

Certified Populations

Fair	AG-2	G-4	VG-8	F-12	VF-20	EF-40	AU-50	MS-60
0	0	0	0	2	2	2	20	0

MS-61	MS-62	MS-63	MS-64	MS-65	MS-66	MS-67	MS-68	MS-69
3	12	24	117	648	1,080	378	8	0

1940-S Mercury Dime

Circulation-strike mintage:
21,560,000

Key to Collecting. 1940-S dimes are common in all grades. Among Mint State coins, those with Full Bands are much scarcer than normal strikes, and they command a sharp premium.

See next page for chart.

Market Values • Circulation Strikes

F-12	VF-20	EF-40	AU-50	MS-60	MS-63	MS-64
$3	$3.10	$3.25	$6	$8	$15	$20

MS-64FB	MS-65	MS-65FB	MS-66	MS-66FB	MS-67	MS-67FB
$30	$35	$100	$40	$140	$55	$500

Certified Populations

Fair	AG-2	G-4	VG-8	F-12	VF-20	EF-40	AU-50	MS-60
0	0	0	0	0	1	2	20	0

MS-61	MS-62	MS-63	MS-64	MS-65	MS-66	MS-67	MS-68	MS-69
3	15	23	138	590	1,055	447	11	0

1941 Mercury Dime

Circulation Strike

Proof

Circulation-strike mintage:
175,090,000

Proof mintage:
16,557

Key to Collecting. Circulation-strike 1941 dimes are common in all grades. Most are well struck. Full Bands coins are common, but sell at a slight premium, partly due to the cost of certifying them. Proofs are readily available.

Market Values • Circulation Strikes and Proof Strikes

F-12	VF-20	EF-40	AU-50	MS-60	MS-63	MS-64	MS-64FB	MS-65
$3	$3.10	$3.25	$5	$7	$12	$19	$25	$30

MS-65FB	MS-66	MS-66FB	MS-67	MS-67FB	PF-64	PF-65	PF-66	PF-67
$50	$45	$55	$60	$175	$185	$225	$350	$575

Certified Populations

Fair	AG-2	G-4	VG-8	F-12	VF-20	EF-40	AU-50	MS-60	MS-61	MS-62	MS-63	MS-64	MS-65
0	0	0	1	6	7	4	106	2	21	37	60	299	1,124

MS-66	MS-67	MS-68	MS-69	PF-60	PF-61	PF-62	PF-63	PF-64	PF-65	PF-66	PF-67	PF-68	PF-69
1,569	868	7	0	3	7	24	77	399	740	1,019	416	58	0

1941-D Mercury Dime

Circulation-strike mintage:
45,634,000

Key to Collecting. 1941-D dimes are common in all grades. Among Mint State coins, those with Full Bands are quite common.

Market Values • Circulation Strikes

F-12	VF-20	EF-40	AU-50	MS-60	MS-63	MS-64
$3	$3.10	$3.25	$6	$8	$14	$20

MS-64FB	MS-65	MS-65FB	MS-66	MS-66FB	MS-67	MS-67FB
$25	$25	$50	$32	$55	$60	$175

Certified Populations

Fair	AG-2	G-4	VG-8	F-12	VF-20	EF-40	AU-50	MS-60
0	0	0	0	3	5	4	46	0

MS-61	MS-62	MS-63	MS-64	MS-65	MS-66	MS-67	MS-68	MS-69
11	24	40	210	934	1,280	512	5	0

1941-S Mercury Dime

Circulation-strike mintage:
43,090,000

Key to Collecting. 1941-S dimes are common in all grades. Among Mint State coins, examples with Full Bands are quite common.

Small S   Large S

See next page for chart.

Small S mintmark: The vast majority of 1941-S dimes have a small mintmark—the standard size for dimes dating back to 1916. These are readily available in all grades. Full Bands coins are common.

Large S mintmark: The large or "Trumpet Tail" S mintmark is rare. The *Cherrypickers' Guide to Rare Die Varieties* notes that there are several dies known for the 1941-S Large S dime, including one that is repunched. (FS-10-1941S-511)

Market Values • Circulation Strikes

F-12	VF-20	EF-40	AU-50	MS-60	MS-63	MS-64
$3	$3.10	$3.25	$5	$7	$12	$19

MS-64FB	MS-65	MS-65FB	MS-66	MS-66FB	MS-67	MS-67FB
$24	$30	$50	$38	$60	$65	$175

Certified Populations

Fair	AG-2	G-4	VG-8	F-12	VF-20	EF-40	AU-50	MS-60
0	0	0	0	1	1	3	41	1

MS-61	MS-62	MS-63	MS-64	MS-65	MS-66	MS-67	MS-68	MS-69
8	21	27	216	1,113	2,033	773	24	0

1942/1 Mercury Dime

Mintage:
**small part of the 1942
circulation-strike mintage**

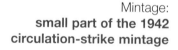

Notes. The 1942/1 overdate was made by taking a 1941 working die and overpunching it with a 1942 master die. The result was a 1942 date with traces of 1941 under it. Many if not most seem to have been released in New York City and towns and cities north of it. The first published mention was in the *Numismatic Scrapbook Magazine*, March 1943:

> Recently I came across a 1942 dime (I look at every coin I touch) that would pass as brilliant Uncirculated, and on close examination it turned out to be 1942 over 1942. Have you heard or seen anything of this dime or can you tell me where I might get some information about it? Arnold Cohn, Kingston, N.Y.

News spread rapidly, and soon the coins were worth several dollars each. Subway-token sellers in kiosks learned of them and started looking. Several would become professional numismatists, including M.L. Kaplan, Herb Tobias, and, less well known, Morris Moscow.

The find caused quite a stir among collectors. Seeking to learn more about the curious coin, Stuart Mosher, editor of *The Numismatist*, wrote to the Mint and received this reply:

Treasury Department

Washington 25, D.C.

June 7, 1946

Dear Mr. Mosher:

Your letter of recent date, addressed to the superintendent of the Mint at Philadelphia, has been referred to this office for attention. You inquired regarding an "overdated" ten-cent piece and enclosed a photograph thereof.

Since it appears that several like specimens have been found, it may be assumed that they were made from an imperfect die, which under the extreme pressure of war work and lack of experienced personnel, escaped detection.

The dime under consideration, with a date of 1942 over 1941, was not re-punched or re-engraved. In September of each year the engraving of the numerals in the new master die for the following year is started. From this master die a working die "hub" is drawn. This is retouched if necessary, and then hardened. This hub is used to fabricate all the working (coinage) dies for that year. Therefore, during the months of September, October, November, and December the Engraving Department is working on dies for the current year's coinage and, at the same time, preparing those for the following year. Approximately one thousand dies with new date must be ready by January 1st of each year. During that period when utmost vigilance was required to keep the dies segregated by respective years, a die may have been given one blow with a 1941 hub and then finished with a 1942 hub.

All dies are usually inspected by a number of skilled workmen before they are delivered. Due to the heavy demand for coins the Engraving Department had necessarily streamlined its operations and such an imperfect die apparently escaped attention.

Very truly yours,
Nellie Tayloe Ross
Director of the Mint

See next page for chart.

Key to Collecting. Editor Mosher, in reply to a reader's question, commented on the overdate in the September 1947 issue and picked up the subject again:

> While the 1942 over 1941 dime is not rare at this time, it is difficult to obtain in Uncirculated condition. As far as we know all the pieces in the hands of collectors were found in circulation. When they were discovered an alert employee employed by the New York Independent Subway System was able to locate over 1,000 of them. This same collector reports that they are rarely found in circulation today, and when they are they are badly worn.

It is likely that several presses were coining dimes on a given day or days in 1942, and the output of each was mixed together and then bagged. However, *Walter Breen's Complete Encyclopedia of U.S. and Colonial Coins*, 1988, stated, "Uncs. are from 4 rolls discovered in 1954." It seems unlikely that a roll would contain dimes from only one pair of dies, but who knows?

The 1942/1 dime was listed in the first edition of *A Guide Book of United States Coins*, 1946, with a cover date of 1947, priced in Fine at $4.50.

Today, examples are easily enough obtained in grades through EF and AU, but they make up a tiny fraction of the 1942 dimes in existence. Most are fairly well struck. Mint State coins are scarce, and if MS-64 or higher are rare in comparison to the demand for them. Full Bands coins are in the minority and command a strong premium when found.

Market Values • Circulation Strikes

F-12	VF-20	EF-40	AU-50	MS-60	MS-63	MS-64
$625	$800	$1,000	$1,750	$2,500	$4,500	$9,000

MS-64FB	MS-65	MS-65FB	MS-66	MS-66FB	MS-67	MS-67FB
$12,500	$15,000	$37,500	$20,000	$60,000	—	—

Certified Populations

Fair	AG-2	G-4	VG-8	F-12	VF-20	EF-40	AU-50	MS-60
0	1	3	21	93	508	397	448	1

MS-61	MS-62	MS-63	MS-64	MS-65	MS-66	MS-67	MS-68	MS-69
28	36	16	17	7	6	0	1	0

1942 Mercury Dime

Circulation-strike mintage:
205,410,000

Proof mintage:
22,329

Circulation Strike

Key to Collecting. Circulation-strike 1942 dimes are common in all grades as might be expected from the record mintage, the highest up to that point, although 1944 would be even higher. Most are well struck. Full Bands coins are common. Proofs are readily available. This is the last year that Proof Mercury dimes were struck.

Proof

Market Values • Circulation Strikes and Proof Strikes

F-12	VF-20	EF-40	AU-50	MS-60	MS-63	MS-64	MS-64FB	MS-65
$2.25	$3.10	$3.25	$4.50	$6	$12	$19	$25	$30
MS-65FB	**MS-66**	**MS-66FB**	**MS-67**	**MS-67FB**	**PF-64**	**PF-65**	**PF-66**	**PF-67**
$50	$45	$60	$55	$475	$185	$225	$350	$575

Certified Populations

Fair	AG-2	G-4	VG-8	F-12	VF-20	EF-40	AU-50	MS-60	MS-61	MS-62	MS-63	MS-64	MS-65
0	1	0	4	9	22	15	108	0	15	30	48	285	1,132
MS-66	**MS-67**	**MS-68**	**MS-69**	**PF-60**	**PF-61**	**PF-62**	**PF-63**	**PF-64**	**PF-65**	**PF-66**	**PF-67**	**PF-68**	**PF-69**
1,982	1,061	12	0	1	0	20	91	497	1,002	1,504	799	140	1

1942/1-D Mercury Dime

Mintage:
small part of the 1942-D circulation-strike mintage

See next page for chart.

Notes. Unlike the situation for the Philadelphia Mint overdate, the 1942/1-D was unknown to collectors until years after the pieces were struck. The motto IN GOD WE TRUST is ever so slightly doubled. In an autobiographical article Delmar K. Romines stated:

I became involved in varieties and errors at the age of nine in 1944. Discovered the first 1943/2-P Jefferson in 1948, the first 1944-D/S Lincoln around 1949, and the first 1942/1-D dime around the same time. About 50% of all known double hubbed die coins through the fifty cent pieces were discovered by me.[8]

That may have been the case, but the variety was not generally known until many years later. Interest was slow in developing, as nearly all known examples were well worn, and the overdate feature was not as distinct as on the Philadelphia coins.

Key to Collecting. The variety was first listed in the *Guide Book of United States Coins* in the 25th edition (published in 1971 with a 1972 cover date), without pricing, and with pricing first in the 27th edition (1974 cover date), Fine $150, VF $200. Collector demand for the variety increased dramatically. Several Mint State coins came on the market and brought surprisingly high prices. In August 1981 one with Full Bands sold for a remarkable $12,000 at the American Numismatic Association convention auction in New Orleans. In December of the same year another brought $9,000. This was in the era before third-party certification of coins in holders, and in retrospect it is difficult to compare prices, as quality varied. In the years since that time the 1942/1-D has been recognized as the most valuable Mercury dime in Mint State.

Today 1942/1-D dimes range from scarce to rare in all grades. After this variety gained notice in the mid-1970s interest in it became very strong. By that time Mercury dimes were no longer in circulation. Sorting through accumulations of worn coins yielded hundreds in grades from VG to VF or so. Mint State coins survived by chance, and a few were found mixed in with other dimes in bank-wrapped rolls. Such coins always create a lot of attention when sold at auction. Full Bands coins are in the minority and command a strong premium when found.

Market Values • Circulation Strikes

F-12	VF-20	EF-40	AU-50	MS-60	MS-63	MS-64
$675	$850	$1,100	$1,850	$2,600	$4,750	$6,700
MS-64FB	MS-65	MS-65FB	MS-66	MS-66FB	MS-67	MS-67FB
$11,500	$9,500	$30,000	$12,000	$37,500	—	—

Certified Populations

Fair	AG-2	G-4	VG-8	F-12	VF-20	EF-40	AU-50	MS-60
0	4	5	35	98	317	173	197	2
MS-61	MS-62	MS-63	MS-64	MS-65	MS-66	MS-67	MS-68	MS-69
7	25	12	27	13	5	3	0	0

1942-D Mercury Dime

Circulation-strike mintage:
60,740,000

Key to Collecting. 1942-D dimes are common in all grades. Many were melted in the 1970s. Mint State coins are common, and Full Bands coins are easily found among them.

Market Values • Circulation Strikes

F-12	VF-20	EF-40	AU-50	MS-60	MS-63	MS-64
$3	$3.10	$3.25	$4.50	$6	$12	$20
MS-64FB	MS-65	MS-65FB	MS-66	MS-66FB	MS-67	MS-67FB
$25	$28	$48	$45	$55	$75	$180

Certified Populations

Fair	AG-2	G-4	VG-8	F-12	VF-20	EF-40	AU-50	MS-60
0	0	9	8	11	34	26	94	1
MS-61	MS-62	MS-63	MS-64	MS-65	MS-66	MS-67	MS-68	MS-69
9	25	11	213	815	1,808	957	25	0

1942-S Mercury Dime

Circulation-strike mintage:
49,300,000

Key to Collecting. All examples seen have a large S mintmark, although Walter H. Breen stated that 1 in 10 has a small mintmark. David W. Lange, who has probably studied Mercury dimes more carefully than anyone, does not list a Small S variety.

1942-S dimes are common in all grades. Among Mint State coins, those with Full Bands are much scarcer than ordinary strikes.

See next page for chart.

Market Values • Circulation Strikes

F-12	VF-20	EF-40	AU-50	MS-60	MS-63	MS-64
$3	$3.10	$3.25	$6	$8	$20	$25

MS-64FB	MS-65	MS-65FB	MS-66	MS-66FB	MS-67	MS-67FB
$30	$35	$150	$50	$225	$125	$650

Certified Populations

Fair	AG-2	G-4	VG-8	F-12	VF-20	EF-40	AU-50	MS-60
0	0	0	1	2	8	5	31	0

MS-61	MS-62	MS-63	MS-64	MS-65	MS-66	MS-67	MS-68	MS-69
3	15	29	130	408	746	291	5	0

1943 Mercury Dime

Circulation-strike mintage:
191,710,000

Key to Collecting. As might be expected from its immense mintage, 1943 dimes are easily available in any grade desired. Full Bands coins are common.

Market Values • Circulation Strikes

F-12	VF-20	EF-40	AU-50	MS-60	MS-63	MS-64
$3	$3.10	$3.25	$4.50	$6	$12	$19

MS-64FB	MS-65	MS-65FB	MS-66	MS-66FB	MS-67	MS-67FB
$24	$27	$55	$35	$60	$45	$300

Certified Populations

Fair	AG-2	G-4	VG-8	F-12	VF-20	EF-40	AU-50	MS-60
0	0	0	2	2	9	6	95	0

MS-61	MS-62	MS-63	MS-64	MS-65	MS-66	MS-67	MS-68	MS-69
14	48	64	285	1,132	1,959	997	12	0

1943-D Mercury Dime

Circulation-strike mintage:
71,949,000

Key to Collecting. 1943-D dimes are very common and are easily found in any grade desired. Full Bands coins are plentiful.

Market Values • Circulation Strikes

F-12	VF-20	EF-40	AU-50	MS-60	MS-63	MS-64
$3	$3.10	$3.25	$4.50	$6	$15	$20

MS-64FB	MS-65	MS-65FB	MS-66	MS-66FB	MS-67	MS-67FB
$25	$30	$50	$45	$55	$65	$130

Certified Populations

Fair	AG-2	G-4	VG-8	F-12	VF-20	EF-40	AU-50	MS-60
0	0	0	0	1	1	3	55	0

MS-61	MS-62	MS-63	MS-64	MS-65	MS-66	MS-67	MS-68	MS-69
14	24	44	333	1,686	2,400	785	19	0

1943-S Mercury Dime

Circulation-strike mintage:
60,400,000

Key to Collecting. 1943-S dimes as a date and mintmark are very common. The S mintmark on most examples has prominent serifs.

See next page for chart.

Market Values • Circulation Strikes

F-12	VF-20	EF-40	AU-50	MS-60	MS-63	MS-64
$3	$3.10	$3.25	$5	$7	$16	$20

MS-64FB	MS-65	MS-65FB	MS-66	MS-66FB	MS-67	MS-67FB
$25	$30	$70	$40	$80	$55	$175

Certified Populations

Fair	AG-2	G-4	VG-8	F-12	VF-20	EF-40	AU-50	MS-60
0	0	0	0	0	4	5	27	0

MS-61	MS-62	MS-63	MS-64	MS-65	MS-66	MS-67	MS-68	MS-69
3	9	23	138	545	1,512	861	15	0

1944 Mercury Dime

Circulation-strike mintage:
231,410,000

Key to Collecting. As might be expected from the all-time-high mintage figure, 1944 dimes are extremely common. Mint State coins are plentiful. Full Bands coins are easily found as well, but are scarcer than regular strikes and command a multiple premium.

Market Values • Circulation Strikes

F-12	VF-20	EF-40	AU-50	MS-60	MS-63	MS-64
$3	$3.10	$3.25	$4.50	$6	$12	$18

MS-64FB	MS-65	MS-65FB	MS-66	MS-66FB	MS-67	MS-67FB
$24	$25	$80	$45	$165	$50	$850

Certified Populations

Fair	AG-2	G-4	VG-8	F-12	VF-20	EF-40	AU-50	MS-60
0	0	0	0	5	7	10	71	0

MS-61	MS-62	MS-63	MS-64	MS-65	MS-66	MS-67	MS-68	MS-69
9	53	66	309	1,383	2,612	871	4	0

1944-D Mercury Dime

Circulation-strike mintage:
62,224,000

Key to Collecting. 1944-D dimes are very common in all grades. Most are very well struck. Full Bands coins are easily to find.

Market Values • Circulation Strikes

F-12	VF-20	EF-40	AU-50	MS-60	MS-63	MS-64
$3	$3.10	$3.25	$5	$7	$15	$20

MS-64FB	MS-65	MS-65FB	MS-66	MS-66FB	MS-67	MS-67FB
$25	$30	$50	$48	$55	$55	$300

Certified Populations

Fair	AG-2	G-4	VG-8	F-12	VF-20	EF-40	AU-50	MS-60
0	0	0	0	2	2	0	38	0

MS-61	MS-62	MS-63	MS-64	MS-65	MS-66	MS-67	MS-68	MS-69
11	27	43	348	1,411	3,561	1,555	24	0

1944-S Mercury Dime

Circulation-strike mintage:
49,490,000

Key to Collecting. 1944-S dimes are very common in all grades. Most are very well struck. Full Bands coins are easily to find, but are less often seen than are regular strikes.

See next page for chart.

Market Values • Circulation Strikes

F-12	VF-20	EF-40	AU-50	MS-60	MS-63	MS-64
$3	$3.10	$3.25	$5	$7	$15	$20

MS-64FB	MS-65	MS-65FB	MS-66	MS-66FB	MS-67	MS-67FB
$25	$30	$55	$50	$75	$60	$180

Certified Populations

Fair	AG-2	G-4	VG-8	F-12	VF-20	EF-40	AU-50	MS-60
0	0	0	1	2	1	1	26	0

MS-61	MS-62	MS-63	MS-64	MS-65	MS-66	MS-67	MS-68	MS-69
4	12	32	214	1,046	2,642	1,085	22	0

1945 Mercury Dime

Circulation-strike mintage:
159,130,000

Key to Collecting. 1945 Philadelphia Mint dimes are very common and can be found in any grade desired. Full Bands dimes are a dramatic exception, are extremely rare, and, in fact, are far rarer than any other FB variety in the series. As such they command an incredible premium.

Market Values • Circulation Strikes

F-12	VF-20	EF-40	AU-50	MS-60	MS-63	MS-64
$3	$3.10	$3.25	$4.50	$6	$12	$20

MS-64FB	MS-65	MS-65FB	MS-66	MS-66FB	MS-67	MS-67FB
$5,250	$28	$10,000	$45	$18,000	$50	$32,000

Certified Populations

Fair	AG-2	G-4	VG-8	F-12	VF-20	EF-40	AU-50	MS-60
0	0	0	1	2	12	5	51	0

MS-61	MS-62	MS-63	MS-64	MS-65	MS-66	MS-67	MS-68	MS-69
6	36	49	331	1,618	2,934	910	5	0

1945-D Mercury Dime

Circulation-strike mintage:
40,245,000

Key to Collecting. Regular die varieties of the 1945-D dime are common in all grades, and Full Bands coins are easily found.

D over horizontal D mintmark: One die has the D mintmark erroneously punched horizontally, and then corrected with a second punching in the correct vertical position. This variety is little known but is far rarer than a regular 1945-D. Examples sell for many multiples of a regular coin. (FS-10-1945D-506)

Market Values • Circulation Strikes

F-12	VF-20	EF-40	AU-50	MS-60	MS-63	MS-64
$3	$3.10	$3.25	$4.50	$6	$12	$19
MS-64FB	**MS-65**	**MS-65FB**	**MS-66**	**MS-66FB**	**MS-67**	**MS-67FB**
$24	$26	$45	$50	$65	$75	$190

Certified Populations

Fair	AG-2	G-4	VG-8	F-12	VF-20	EF-40	AU-50	MS-60
0	0	0	0	0	4	2	25	0
MS-61	**MS-62**	**MS-63**	**MS-64**	**MS-65**	**MS-66**	**MS-67**	**MS-68**	**MS-69**
4	15	24	285	1,807	3,407	1,028	20	0

1945-S Mercury Dime

Circulation-strike mintage:
41,920,000

Key to Collecting. Regular die varieties of the 1945-D dime are common in all grades. Full Bands coins are in the minority among Mint State coins and sell for several multiples of the prices of regular strikes.

"Micro S" mintmark: One or more reverse dies had a slightly smaller S mintmark. While hardly microscopic, this variety is popularly known as the "Micro S" and is listed in *A Guide Book of United States Coins.* Accordingly, strong demand has been built for it, and today the variety is widely collected. (FS-10-1945S-512)

S over horizontal S mintmark: The S mintmark was first punched into the die in a horizontal position and then corrected. Examples sell for many multiples of a regular coin's price. (FS-10-1945S-011)

S over D mintmark: This variety has not been confirmed. Traces of a letter, possibly a D, can be seen beneath the S. (FS-10-1945S-011)

Market Values • Circulation Strikes

F-12	VF-20	EF-40	AU-50	MS-60	MS-63	MS-64
$3	$3.10	$3.25	$4.50	$6	$12	$20

MS-64FB	MS-65	MS-65FB	MS-66	MS-66FB	MS-67	MS-67FB
$28	$30	$125	$40	$165	$60	$640

Certified Populations

Fair	AG-2	G-4	VG-8	F-12	VF-20	EF-40	AU-50	MS-60
0	0	0	0	1	3	0	30	0

MS-61	MS-62	MS-63	MS-64	MS-65	MS-66	MS-67	MS-68	MS-69
4	12	22	212	1,100	2,804	1,190	390	3

Whitman Publishing Offers books for every collector.

The best way to enjoy your hobby (and profit from your investment) is to learn as much as possible, from recognized experts in the field. Whether you collect classic U.S. coins, world coins, ancients, medals, tokens, or paper money, Whitman Publishing has the perfect books to add to your library. **The guide books pictured above are just a few from the Bowers Series. The entire Whitman catalog is online at Whitman.com.**

Books in the Bowers Series include:

- *A Guide Book of Half Cents and Large Cents (Q. David Bowers)*
- *A Guide Book of Flying Eagle and Indian Head Cents (Rick Snow)*
- *A Guide Book of Lincoln Cents (Bowers)*
- *A Guide Book of Shield and Liberty Head Nickels (Bowers)*
- *A Guide Book of Buffalo and Jefferson Nickels (Bowers)*
- *A Guide Book of Mercury Dimes, Standing Liberty Quarters, and Liberty Walking Half Dollars (Bowers)*
- *A Guide Book of Washington and State Quarters (Bowers)*
- *A Guide Book of Franklin and Kennedy Half Dollars (Rick Tomaska)*
- *A Guide Book of Morgan Silver Dollars*
- *A Guide Book of Peace Dollars (Roger W. Burdette)*
- *A Guide Book of Gold Dollars (Bowers)*
- *A Guide Book of Double Eagle Gold Coins (Bowers)*
- *A Guide Book of United States Type Coins (Bowers)*
- *A Guide Book of Modern United States Proof Coin Sets (David W. Lange)*
- *A Guide Book of United States Tokens and Medals (Katherine Jaeger)*
- *A Guide Book of the Official Red Book of United States Coins (Frank J. Colletti)*
- *A Guide Book of Civil War Tokens (Bowers)*
- *A Guide Book of Hard Times Tokens (Bowers)*
- *A Guide Book of Barber Silver Coins (Bowers)*

Whitman Publishing books, folders, albums, and other hobby products are available online, and at local hobby retailers, coin shops, and book stores nationwide.
For information, call toll free, 1-866-546-2995,
or email customerservice@Whitman.com

Standing Liberty Quarters, 1916–1930

The design adopted in 1916 and struck for circulation to the extent of 52,000 coins.

The Design of the New Quarter

Of the three new silver coin designs of 1916, arrangements concerning Hermon A. MacNeil's Standing Liberty quarter were the most complex. Most numismatists agree that the sculptor's original design was more beautiful than its modification done by the Engraving Department at the Mint without MacNeil's knowledge or consent.

The end result, nonetheless, was a quarter dollar that numismatists have admired since it was first made. An excellent study of these coins can be found in J.H. Cline's *Standing Liberty Quarters*, which has appeared in multiple editions over the years.

Of the three new designs for 1916, Standing Liberty quarters were made for the shortest time—only until 1930, and with no coinage in 1922. Today a collection of such pieces is beautiful to behold.

Thus begins the story of the series.

MacNeil and His Ideal Design

Roger W. Burdette, as guest cataloger for Stack's Bowers Galleries offering in the Minot Sale, 1988, of a plaster model by Hermon MacNeil of his ideal obverse for the 1916 quarter, gave this commentary:

> On seeing this spectacular piece for the first time the reaction is, "Wow! So that's what a Standing Liberty quarter is supposed to look like!" But after a moment, the eye is drawn to two playful

Plaster model by Hermon A. MacNeil showing his ideal design with for the Standing Liberty quarter. Much to his dismay the dolphins, wreath, IN GOD WE TRUST on the ribbon, and certain other features were changed at the Mint without his consultation.

141

dolphins aside Liberty's feet, then to the motto IN GOD WE TRUST draped across Miss Liberty, to sprigs of laurel and last, the missing olive branch. What kind of Standing Liberty quarter is this? The truth is *this* is what Hermon MacNeil had intended his new quarter to look like.

In May 1916 MacNeil submitted his first design models for the new quarter. This first obverse looked much like the regular quarters dated 1916 and familiar to collectors. But over the next weeks MacNeil became increasingly dissatisfied with his work. With changes in mind, MacNeil requested permission from Mint Director Robert Woolley to revise the obverse. The sculptor said he wanted:

1. To bring the head of the figure a trifle lower so as not to appear to be holding up the rim of the coin.

2. To prevent the figure appearing "bowlegged."

3. To minimize the sagging of the covering of the shield by having it pulled up a little tighter.

I should also like to see the letters of the word Liberty slightly smaller.

Since Adolph Weinman, who was designing the new dime and half dollar, had already been given permission to change his original compositions, Woolley agreed.

During July and August 1916 Hermon MacNeil radically rearranged and modified the elements of his obverse design. Except for the names given to parts of the design, nearly everything was changed. The overall relief was made more pronounced, and drapery softened. Starting with the border, the original dot-dot-dash pattern was replaced with a cable or chain surrounding the central elements. The portal walls through which Liberty steps were plain—unadorned with either motto or detail. On the upper step at the base of the wall are two dolphins, one on each side of Liberty's feet. The dolphins represent the Atlantic and Pacific oceans much as they did on the 1915 Panama-Pacific International Exposition gold dollar designed by Charles Keck or Robert Aitken's $50 gold piece. Above each dolphin's tail is a laurel branch symbolic of civil triumph; at the upper rim is the word LIBERTY in letters somewhat smaller and much sharper than on the first obverse.

The figure of Liberty differs completely from that on the first design, although she is still semi-nude. She now wears cross-laced sandals in the ancient Roman style and carries a shield embossed with an eagle. The shield covering is also more closely fit and less baggy. A long sash or ribbon engraved IN GOD WE TRUST connects the shield and her outstretched right hand ending near the laurel branch. There is no olive branch of peace, the whole new design being more militant and actively protective.

Treasury Secretary McAdoo approved the design on August 19, and asked MacNeil to provide a photograph showing the proposed location of the artist's monogram or initial. (This photo still exists.) This was done and the new Mint Director, F. J. H. von Engelken, replied on September 1, "Placing of signature under head of dolphin on right of Quarter Dollar approved. You are at liberty to use either the letter 'M' alone, or that monogram of two letters."

MacNeil was asked to expedite delivery of bronze casts and these were scheduled for delivery on September 9. From this point forward the mint should have made reductions and struck a few pattern pieces for von Engelken and others to examine. But from here to the end of the year official records are silent. No pattern coins are known.

In October 1916 MacNeil offered to help finalize the quarter designs, but the Mint decided that "it was deemed inexpedient to authorize Mr. MacNeil to come to Philadelphia."

The Mint engravers had scrapped the sculptor's original reverse design, replacing the two olive branches in front and behind the eagle, with a total of 13 small stars. The flying eagle remained low on the coin as if it were just rising skyward. This Mint concoction was used on both 1916 and 1917 Type I (also known as *Variety 1*) quarters.

As 1917 opened Mint director von Engelken was eager to release the newly designed quarters. A small quantity of coins dated 1916 had been struck to mark the official release year, but a revised, more detailed obverse created by the Mint's engraving department graced the 1917 coins.

Despite radical changes, MacNeil's Liberty on the new quarter is indeed a beautiful piece of work. The idea conceived by the artist is highly expressive of national sentiment.

Dora Doscher as Miss Liberty

The Numismatist, April 1917, included this:

The Girl on the Quarter

From a recent newspaper article by Marguerite Norse we extract the following facts regarding Miss Dora Doscher, who posed for Mr. Hermon A. MacNeil while designing the female figure that appears on our new quarter dollar, and who is now referred to by her friends as "the Girl on the Quarter":

Miss Doscher is 22 years of age, and is 5 feet 4½ inches in height. Through her own efforts she has developed from a half invalid child to a most perfect type of American womanhood. Her days are spent in artistic and intellectual pursuits. She is a lecturer, scenario writer, and trained nurse. At the first intimation of war she enrolled in the Red Cross service and stood from that day ready for a moment's call. She presents an attractive appearance in the Red Cross uniform.

The measurements from which the late Karl Bitter modeled the figure surmounting the Pulitzer Memorial Fountain that stands in the Plaza in New York City were taken from Miss Doscher. Mr. Bitter's *Diana* that stands in the Metropolitan Museum of Art was modeled from the "coin girl."

The figure comes down a flight of steps in an attitude of welcome to the world. In one extended hand she holds a laurel branch of peace, on the left arm she carries a shield. Though she offers peace first she is prepared to defend her honor and her rights. The design suggests a step forward in civilization, protection, and defense with peace as the ultimate goal.

Dora Doscher was born on January 24, 1882, making her more than the 22 years of age quoted above. (It was common for models, actresses, and others to state that they were younger than they really were.) She would later take the stage name and, for writing advice columns and other articles, the nom de plume of *Doris Doree*.

Doscher modeled for Karl Bitter's *Fountain of Abundance*, completed by Isidore Konti and Karl Gruppe, placed in the Pulitzer Fountain in front of the Plaza Hotel in New York City in 1915. Beginning in 1917 she acted in several silent films, most notably *Birth of a Race*, produced in Tampa by the Photoplay Corporation in cooperation with the Selig Polyscope Company and said to have cost a million dollars to produce. In this film she took the part of Eve in the Garden of Eden.[1]

In interviews she stated she modeled as *Columbia* on the quarter. Later, she wrote many articles on various subjects including beauty, sports, health, dieting, and food and gained national recognition. She gave advice to newspaper readers, such as in "Win Back Your Husband's Love." She became "beauty specialist" at the New York *Evening World*. In July 1930 she married Dr. William H. Baum. Dora died on March 9, 1970, at the age of 88.

A few years later, the Associated Press distributed the following obituary that identified a different model for the coin, and it was published nationwide on Saturday, January 6, 1973:

The "Liberty Girl"

Newburgh, N.Y. (AP). Irene MacDowell, who posed for a U.S. coin and earned the nickname "the Liberty Girl" during the 1920s has died in nearby New Windsor at 92.

Mrs. McDowell, who died on Wednesday, posed for sculptor Hermon MacNeil for the design of the Liberty quarter minted in the millions between 1916 and 1932. Its successor was the Washington quarter.

As Miss Liberty the one-time Broadway actress was pictured in a flowing gown descending a staircase and holding a laurel branch and shield.

Mrs. MacDowell was quoted in a recent interview as saying she had only one or two of the Liberty quarters remaining in her possession, and that those copies were faded. She subsequently was deluged with gifts of the quarters from across the nation.

She is survived by her husband George and a daughter. Funeral arrangements were incomplete.

Errors concerning Doscher were amplified by later comments made by Dr. Baum, giving distorted and inaccurate information about his wife's career. Picking up on modern comments by MacDowell and believing them, the author of *Walter Breen's Complete Encyclopedia of U.S. and Colonial Coinage*, 1988, commented in part:

> Mrs. MacDowell's name had remained a secret because her husband (one of MacNeil's tennis partners) disapproved. Photographic evidence indicates a composite portrait, but beyond doubt Irene MacDowell was the principal model.

Not a shred of historical evidence supports the notion that MacDowell was the only or the main model. To believe this one has to wonder why during the lifetimes of both Hermon MacNeil and Doris Doscher neither of them mentioned MacDowell as a model.

Design Modifications

MacNeil was not satisfied with the Engraving Department's alteration of his ideal design, and in 1917 met with them to make some changes. The next *Report of the Commission of Fine Arts* included this:

Designs for Silver Coinage

The Commission had the privilege of advising the director of the Mint in regard to the subsidiary silver coinage, which is subject to change of design every 25 years. The Commission suggested that no form of art is so universal and therefore of such wide influence as is the silver coinage, and therefore no pains should be spared to make it as artistic as the talents of American artists and the capabilities of our mint permit.

After submission of designs, the half-dollar and the dime were entrusted to Adolph A. Weinman and the quarter-dollar to Hermon A. MacNeil. Through misunderstandings the artist's final design for the quarter-dollar was not used, and a bill has been introduced in Congress to permit certain modifications in the coin in order to make it conform entirely to the artist's ideas. The way is thus opened to secure as designers of our coinage artists of proved merit and to have their ideas carried out. The relations between the Mint and the Commission throughout a protracted discussion have been altogether satisfactory.

This resulted in an act, "Modifications of the Designs of the Current Quarter," H.R. 3548, submitted to Congress on June 17, 1917, by Representative William Ashbrook:

The Committee on Coinage, Weights, and Measures, to whom was referred H.R. 3548, providing for the modification of the designs of the current quarter dollar, having had the same under consideration unanimously instructed the chairman to report the bill to the House with the recommendation that the bill be passed.

The object of the bill is set forth in the following letter from the secretary of the Treasury to the chairman of the Committee on Coinage, Weights, and Measures, April 16, 1917:

I have the honor to submit for your consideration a draft of an act to authorize the modification of the designs of the current quarter dollar in accordance with a specimen submitted by Mr. Hermon A. MacNeil, the soultor whose designs were accepted May 23, 1916, for the quarter dollar now being issued.

The modifications proposed are slight, the principal one being that the eagle has been raised and three of the stars placed beneath the eagle. On the reverse the lettering has been rearranged and the collision with the pinions of the wings obviated. These changes, together with a slight concavity, will produce a coin materially improved in artistic merit, and not interfere in any way with its practical use.

I am sorry to have to ask for this change, but since the original dies were made the artist has found that they were not true to the original design and that a great improvement can be made in the artistic value and appearance of the coin by making the slight changes the act contemplates....

The 1917 Type II (also known as Variety 2) quarter, of modified design.

Liberty was encased in a suit of mail, symbolizing military preparedness in view of the World War, a change not mentioned above. The olive branch in her right hand was modified in shape, and a leaf that crossed the L on the Type I coins was removed. On the reverse the stars were rearranged to place three below the eagle. The shield was modified with fewer rivets. Congress approved the modifications on July 9, 1917, "for the purpose of increasing its artistic merit."

In revisionist history years later Walter H. Breen and quite a few others stated that the reason for the change was public outcry concerning the semi-nudity of Miss Liberty. No contemporary articles or documents have been located to reinforce this assertion. At the time nude statues were common in public areas, nude figures were shown on medals during the second decade of the twentieth century, and nudity was even occasionally seen on the movie screen, such as in Thanhouser's 1915 film, *Inspiration*, which featured Audrey Munson (who had posed for sculpture at the 1915 Panama-Pacific International Exposition) without a stitch of clothing.

To further demolish the "obscene" stories two relevant articles are quoted. The first is from *The Numismatist*, November 1917:

Quarter Dollar Design Modified

One of the most noticeable differences in the new dies from which our quarter dollars are now being struck, a description of which appears elsewhere in this issue, is that the upper portion of the figure of Liberty, which was formerly but partly draped, is now clothed in what appears to be a gown of mail....

But we are more than idly interested in this new outfit of Miss Liberty for more than one reason. When the first issue of the quarter dollar was placed in circulation a little less than a year ago the United States was at peace with the world, and this particular denomination was regarded as a "Preparedness" coin. We were officially told that "the design of the 25-cent piece is intended to typify in a measure the awakening interest of the country to its own protection."

The issue from the revised dies occurs at a time when we are at war with Germany. If Liberty's new costume is a gown of mail, is it suggestive of that fact, and is it another instance of where coins are records of history?

An article by Roger W. Burdette as a "Guest Commentary" in *Coin World*, January 5, 2004, gives information on this as well as some of the awkward interactions MacNeil had with the Mint.

Records Show MacNeil Instigator

During the past four years, I have examined thousands of documents on the subject of the Mint Bureau's subsidiary silver coin redesign of 1916 and 1917. Research has involved primary sources in manuscript collections of academic, art, government, and private archives. Of the many documents and newspaper articles dealing with Hermon MacNeil's Standing Liberty quarter dollar, a few address the primary controversy surrounding the coin: the position of the eagle's talons on the reverse. Most correspondence ignores the obverse entirely, or quotes from the May 1916 Treasury Department description. Not one letter or article contemporary with issuance of the coin refers to the obverse design as "obscene," "offensive" or in any way morally inappropriate.

To the best of my knowledge, no article from 1917 has ever been reproduced that describes the obverse in such terms. Further, an event timeline of early 1917 indicates the decision to change the quarter's obverse and reverse designs was not the result of public commentary. Each event has one or more supporting documents drawn from multiple primary sources. There are no known contradicting documents. Principal events for early 1917 were:

January 6, 1917: MacNeil sends $5 to the Philadelphia Mint requesting 20 new quarters.

January 10, 1917: MacNeil receives 20 new design quarters from Superintendent Adam M. Joyce.

January 10, 1917: MacNeil makes an "uninvited" visit to the Philadelphia Mint.

January 10, 1917: Mint Director F.J.H. von Engelken hears about MacNeil's visit from Joyce and orders all mints not to release the new quarters.

January 11, 1917: MacNeil asks ("insists" might be a better word) to change quarter design.

January 11, 1917: MacNeil contacts Charles Moore, chairman of the Commission of Fine Arts.

January 13, 1917: Moore and Commission member Herbert Adams meet with von Engelken in Washington. All agree MacNeil should be allowed to change quarter if basic composition is not altered.

January 17, 1917: Treasury Secretary William Gibbs McAdoo verbally agrees to change.

January 17, 1917: Von Engelken authorizes release of new quarters.

January 22, 1917: MacNeil, McAdoo, and von Engelken hold a conference in Washington. McAdoo agrees to pay expenses and approve MacNeil's models.

January 22, 1917: Von Engelken issues letter to Philadelphia Mint authorizing complete cooperation with MacNeil.

January 23, 1917: MacNeil visits Philadelphia Mint to talk with Joyce and engravers Barber and Morgan.

February 16, 1917: Final models of revised designs are sent to Mint. The timeline clearly shows design changes were requested by MacNeil and approved by von Engelken and McAdoo before any of the coins were available to the public.

Objections to the obverse design—if there were any significant number—were not the reason the design was changed....By the time MacNeil's revisions were complete and patterns approved, the United States was at war with Germany and other Axis Powers and minor adjustments to the quarter's design were irrelevant.

Date Modified in 1925 to Lessen Wear

On the Standing Liberty quarter of 1916 and later years the date was raised on a pedestal or plaque at the bottom. This caused the numbers to wear quickly, often to the extent of being removed entirely. In 1925 a modification was made and the date position was recessed, solving the problem.

Release and Distribution

In contrast to the release of Mercury dimes in October 1916, the new quarters and half dollars, including those dated 1916, were not placed into circulation until after the Treasury authorization of January 17, 1917.

On December 2, 1916, the Treasury had announced:

Issuance of the new [coins] was deferred today by the Treasury Department until the beginning of 1917. The extraordinary demand for small coins is overtaxing the facilities of the mints, and officials believed calls for the new quarter and half dollar coins would swamp the mints if they are issued at this time.

In early 1917 the low-mintage quarters dated 1916 were mixed in with quarters of 1917, resulting in those of 1916 not being showcased as novelties.

Comments and Reviews

The August 1916 issue of *The Numismatist* reprinted a *Boston Herald* article, seemingly taken from viewing sketches or models, which noted in part:

Uncle Sam has some coins coming from his Mint this month that are sure to be coveted by collectors. For the first time since 1892 we are to see new dimes, quarters, and half-dollars, and on each of them is to appear some remainder of our advanced status as a nation. On the 25-cent piece, taking a new pose and gesture, Liberty is to be seen stepping toward the country's gateway, bearing upraised a shield from which the covering is being drawn, and in her right hand the olive branch of peace. This is the coin of the preparedness movement; it indicates, as Secretary McAdoo tells us, that the country is "awakening to its own protection."

The design itself set the precedent of depicting a semi-nude figure on circulating American coinage, although many medals of the time presented images of the human form in various poses....

By the time the first Standing Liberty quarters were released in 1917 the press coverage of the new designs had diminished dramatically. In contrast to countless articles about the Mercury dimes in the popular press after their release in October 1916, the quarter was not deemed particularly newsworthy. Therefore, laudatory comments from the public were few.

A writer for the *Philadelphia Inquirer* did not like the new coin at all. The editorial page on January 16, 1917, had this:

> *A Coin Absolutely Without Merit:* Whatever else the new twenty-five-cent piece may be, it surely is not an artistic coin. The duck or dove or what-is-it that appears on one side and the giant fat lady who guards the other side may have pleased the artist, but one cannot help wondering what he thought he was trying to accomplish.
>
> The old coin was dignified and every way worthy. The new contrivance is absolutely without merit, unless it be told in the way of a token to give away in prize packages of peanuts. The coinage of this monstrosity ought to be stopped. Give us back the head of Liberty and the good old eagle with the shield. They meant something.

The Philadelphia *Public Ledger* weighed in with similar sentiments on the next day, January 17:

> The last coin is out of the government bag and the new silver quarter is at hand and in circulation. While the eagle of the reverse looks very like the eagle of the "white penny" of the late fifties, since it flies with outspread wings, it is not unlike some dove of peace.
>
> The lady of the obverse, on the other hand, seems to be in a quandary as to what she expects. For, while she seems to be walking through an open gateway in a walled balustrade, as if answering the call of "Come into the garden, Maud," she has her face averted from the free, outreaching right hand, which holds an olive branch, and instead is looking steadily toward the left, which holds a shield firmly against her shoulder. There may be no symbolism in this pose, intended or accidental, but the goddess certainly seems to be more expectant of things to defend than concerned about meeting the peace folks half way.
>
> At the same time the designs on the two faces represent an artistic advance, present a proper variation from the fifty-cent designs, and give us a minor silver coinage that is picturesque and developed along the lines of the best numismatic practice abroad, where good coinage standards prevail.

In January 1917 the editor of *The Numismatist* invited readers to send in comments about the new quarter and half dollar, anticipating that many would be received, as had been the case with the dime. This did not happen, and there were only two brief notes published.

Standing Liberty Quarters in Circulation

As noted, the new quarters of 1916 and 1917 both entered circulation in January 1917. The public claimed many as souvenirs, after which the novelty passed.

Mintages continued from 1917 onward at the Philadelphia, Denver, and San Francisco mints, but not all mints in all years. In 1922 no quarters were minted, and in 1921 and 1925 only the Philadelphia Mint struck them. These coins entered circulation and were widely used. Numismatists did not pay much attention to them as the specialty of collecting by dates and mintmarks was not widespread and would not be until the next decade, after the series had ended.

By the mid-1930s, when collecting coins by date and mint became widely popular with the distribution of Wayte Raymond's "National" albums and, somewhat later, Whitman coin holders, most quarters of the 1916 to 1924 years had the dates worn away completely or only faintly discernible. This was dramatically revealed by a survey published in *The Numismatic Scrapbook*, January 1939. A study of 5,000 quarters taken from circulation in Rock Island, Illinois, over a period of 10 months included Barber, Standing Liberty, and Washington issues. The Standing Liberty quarters included these:

Type I

1916: 0

1917-D: 4

1917-S : 1

Type I quarters with dates worn away: Philadelphia, 61; Denver, 11; San Francisco, 7; no date or mint, 6

Type II

1917: 2	1920: 6
1917-D: 0	1920-D: 1
1917-S: 0	1920-S: 2
1918: 2	1921: 0
1918-D: 1	1923: 16
1918-S: 3	1923-S: 0
1919: 1	1924: 7
1919-D: 2	1924-D: 2
1919-S: 0	1924-S: 0

Type II quarters with dates worn away: Philadelphia 790, Denver 226, San Francisco 271; no date or mint: 90

Start of recessed dates:

1925: 129	1928-D: 27
1926: 129	1928-S: 28
1926-D: 19	1929: 86
1926-S: 31	1929-D: 29
1927: 102	1929-S: 9
1927-D: 14	1930: 32
1927-S: 6	1930-S: 15
1928: 62	

It is seen that among Type I quarters and early 1917–1924 Type II quarters with the date on a raised pedestal the vast majority of coins in circulation by 1939 had no dates visible! Accordingly, unlike for the dimes and half dollars of this era, it was virtually impossible to build a collection of early quarters from circulation. Those that were identifiable as to date were mostly only barely so.

Aspects of Striking

A 1917-S Type II quarter certified as MS-68 Full Head, with good details on the head and shield, a nice example overall.

A 1924-S quarter certified as MS-66 Full Head, with the head details not sharp and with missing shield rivets at the lower left. Connoisseurs might want to look further if such a coin is offered.

A Mint State 1927-S quarter with a typical strike—details missing on the head and shield. Most Type II quarters have such weakness. The compensation is that they are much less expensive than coins certified as Full Head.

A 1916 Standing Liberty quarter certified as MS-65 Full Head that on close inspection shows some indistinctness on the head and weakness on the shield. The label on the coin will sell it, but connoisseurs would probably keep looking.

The striking sharpness or lack thereof in the Standing Liberty quarter series has not been carefully studied.

As is the case with Mercury dimes and Liberty Walking half dollars, sharpness of details on Standing Liberty quarters is determined by the spacing of the dies in a coining press. If the dies are positioned closely apart, all details will be struck sharply, but the dies will wear more quickly. If they are spaced farther apart, the features deepest in the dies will not be struck up and will be flat or weak.

On Standing Liberty quarters flatness can occur mainly on the obverse on the head of Miss Liberty, the details in the shield (especially the rivets), the sash above Liberty's waist, and, much less often, the lower part of Liberty and the date. Type I quarters of 1916 usually are indistinct in some areas. Those of 1917 are often very well struck. In contrast, very few Type II quarters have full head and shield details. Scarcely any numismatic attention has been paid to anything except the head!

On the reverse flatness mostly occurs on the eagle but is not particularly noticeable.

If you are a connoisseur you will want to examine both sides carefully and pick a coin that has full details. This can be a reality for those of Type I, especially 1917 (1916 can be a challenge). For Type II the best you can do is come close to full details for some of the varieties for which completely sharp coins do not exist.

That said, the majority of coin buyers are content to have coins labeled Full Head on the holders. A study of such FH coins can be found in J.H. Cline's *Standing Liberty Quarters*. This does not take into consideration weakness in other areas, although sometimes such is mentioned. The 1926-S is a good example. Cline estimates in the fourth edition (2007) that about 50 FH examples exist and adds: "On even the finest 1926-S out there the third and fourth rivets are missing from the outer shield."

As is the case for Mercury dimes, simplicity is the byword for descriptions in the marketplace. A quick fix, but one that does not work well, is the designation Full Head

(FH). On 1917 Type I coins this usually means a sharp head and facial details. On Type II even certified FH coins often have some facial and hair details indistinct. Certified FH quarters can bring great premiums, never mind that other areas of the coin might be weak.

Dramatic examples are provided by the listing of a 1926-D in the sixth *Professional Edition* (2014) of *A Guide Book of United States Coins*. A regular MS-65 was priced at $550 while one with FH was priced at $24,000! A 1927-S was priced at $10,500 and $185,000 respectively. Anyone contemplating buying a Full Head 1927-S for $185,000 might well ask himself or herself: Do I really want to pay the price of a high-performance sports car to get a coin which may not have full facial details and may be weak in other areas?

For a really deluxe specimen of any Standing Liberty quarter, find one that has sharp rivets in the shield, a fairly full head, and sharp details elsewhere. If it is certified as FH be sure your bank account is well fortified. For really excellent *numismatic value for the price paid* find one that has sharp rivets in the shield, some facial details but not a Full Head, and sharp details elsewhere. By cherrypicking these will cost no more than a poorly struck coin.

The Ron Pope Survey

In 2004 numismatist Ron Pope did a study of the sharpness or lack thereof in the Standing Liberty quarter series.[2] While many had so-called Full Heads, his survey revealed that coins with Full Details—including the head, all shield details, the date, and the eagle on the reverse were a different story completely. This and the narrative following tie in nicely with the preceding paragraphs.

This can be a very valuable guide for connoisseurs and anyone else wishing to avoid overpaying for "Full Head" coins that are weak in other features:

1916 (144 were examined) 13% had Full Details	1923-S (107) 2%
1917 Type I (1,042) 76%	1924 (226) 3%
1917-D Type I (284) 67%	1924-D (337) 2%
1917-S Type I (198) 62%	1924-S (189) 0.5%
1917 Type II (259) 15%	1925 (281) 3%
1917-D Type II (161) 2%	1926 (300) 1%
1917-S Type II (162) 4%	1926-D (351) 0%
1918 (221) 5%	1926-S (134) 0%
1918-D (214) 2%	1927 (343) 1%
1918/7-S (108) 0%	1927-D (170) 0%
1918-S (269) 0.4%	1927-S (145) 0%
1919 (238) 8%	1928 (228) 6%
1919-D (121) 2%	1928-D (379) 1%
1919-S (174) 2%	1928-S (318) 0.6%

1920 (532) 3%	1929 (476) 2%
1920-D (107) 4%	1929-D (214) 0.4%
1920-S (266) 0.4%	1929-S (332) 0%
1921 (141) 6%	1930 (1,008) 4%
1923 (413) 3%	1930-S (275) 0.4%

To summarize, the following varieties had no Full Details coins at all: 1918/7-S, 1926-D, 1926-S, 1927-D, 1927-S, and 1929-S. Never mind that all of these can be found in certified holders marked Full Head, some being *common* with such labels.

These varieties had fewer than 1% with Full Details: 1920-S, 1924-S, 1928-S, 1929-S, and 1930-S.

These had just 1% with Full Details: 1918/7-S, 1926, and 1928-D.

For the above it would seem that a good buying strategy—and one that will save a lot of money—is to acquire coins not marked FH but have reasonably good details elsewhere, such as on the shield, as mentioned earlier. This goes against the conventional wisdom that all that counts is the label on a holder.

Grading Standing Liberty Quarters

1917, No Stars. Graded MS-67.

MS-60 to 70 (Mint State)

Obverse: At MS-60 some abrasion and contact marks are evident on the higher areas, which are also the areas most likely to be weakly struck. This includes the rivets on the shield to the left and the central escutcheon on the shield, the head, and the right leg of Miss Liberty. The luster may not be complete in those areas on weakly struck coins, even those certified above MS-65—the *original planchet surface* may be revealed as it was not smoothed out by striking. Accordingly, grading is best done by evaluating abrasion and mint luster as it is observed. Luster may be dull or lifeless at MS-60 to 62 but should have deep frost at MS-63 or better, particularly in the lower-relief areas. At MS-65 or better, it should be full and rich.

Reverse: Striking is usually quite good, permitting observation of luster in all areas. Check the eagle's breast and the surface of the right wing. Luster may be dull or lifeless at MS-60 to 62 but should have deep frost at MS-63 or better, particularly in the lower-relief areas. At MS-65 or better, it should be full and rich.

Illustrated coin: This gorgeous coin has sharply struck details and full luster.

1916. Graded AU-55.

AU-50, 53, 55, 58 (About Uncirculated)

Obverse: Light wear is seen on the figure of Miss Liberty, especially noticeable around her midriff and right knee. The shield shows wear, as does the highest part of the sash where it crosses Miss Liberty's waist. At AU-58 the luster is extensive, but incomplete on the higher areas, although it should be nearly full in the panels of the parapet to the left and right, and in the upper field. At AU-50 and 53, luster is less.

Reverse: Wear is most evident on the eagle's breast, the edges of both wings, and the interior area of the right wing. Luster is nearly complete at AU-58, but at AU-50, half or more is gone.

Illustrated coin: The original luster is still present in some areas of this lightly struck coin.

1927-S. Graded EF-40.

EF-40, 45 (Extremely Fine)

Obverse: Wear is more extensive, with the higher parts of Miss Liberty now without detail and the front of the right leg flat. The shield is worn. On coins dated from 1917 to 1924 the date shows wear at the top (on those of 1925 to 1930, with the date recessed, the numbers are bold). Little or no luster is seen, except perhaps among the letters.

Reverse: The eagle shows more wear, with the surface of the right wing being mostly flat. Little or no luster is evident.

1927-S. Graded VF-20.

VF-20, 30 (Very Fine)

Obverse: Wear is more extensive. The higher-relief areas of Miss Liberty are flat, and the sash crossing her waist is mostly blended into it (some sharply struck pieces being exceptions). The left side of the shield is mostly flat, although its outline can be seen. On quarters dated 1917 to 1924 the top of the date shows more wear.

Reverse: The eagle shows further wear, with the body blending into the wing above it. Much feather detail is gone from the wing to the left (on quarters dated 1925 to 1930; less so for those dated 1917 to 1924). Most detail is gone from the right wing.

1916. Graded F-12.

F-12, 15 (Fine)

Obverse: Miss Liberty is worn nearly flat. Most detail in her gown is gone, except to the left of her leg and below her knee to the right. The stars on the parapet are well worn, with some indistinct. The top of the date is weak. Quarters of the rare 1916 date are slightly weaker than those of 1917 in this and lower grades. On quarters of 1917 to 1924 the top of the date is weak. On those dated 1925 to 1930 the date remains strong.

Reverse: The eagle shows further wear, this being greater on 1925 to 1930 issues than on the earlier dates.

1917, No Stars. Graded VG-8.

VG-8, 10 (Very Good)

Obverse: The obverse is worn further, with fewer details in the skirt, and part of the shield border to the left blended into the standing figure. The date is partially worn away at the top, and quarters from 1917 to 1924 have less detail. Those from 1925 to 1930 retain more detail, and the date is full.

Reverse: The eagle is worn further, with only about a third of the feathers now discernible, these mostly on the wing to the left.

1927. Graded G-6.

G-4, 6 (Good)

Obverse: The wear is more extensive. Most coins have the stars missing, the standing figure flat, and much of the date worn away, although still clearly identifiable. Quarters of 1925 to 1930 show more detail and the date is clear.

Reverse: The eagle is mostly in outline form, with only a few feather details visible. The rim is worn into the letters, and on quarters of 1916 to 1924, E PLURIBUS UNUM is very faint; it is clear on quarters of later dates.

1927. Graded AG-3.

AG-3 (About Good)

Obverse: The obverse is worn nearly smooth, and the date is mostly gone. On some coins just one or two digits are seen. Fortunately, those digits are usually on the right, such as a trace of just a 6, which will identify the coin as a 1916. On quarters of 1925 to 1930 the wear is more extensive than for G-4, but most features are discernible and the date is clear.

Reverse: The eagle is flat, and the border is worn down further. On quarters of 1916 to 1924, E PLURIBUS UNUM is extremely faint or even missing in areas; it remains readable on quarters of later dates.

Being a Smart Buyer

There are enough Standing Liberty quarters in the marketplace that with very little effort the typical or casual collector can easily acquire a full set of dates and mint-marks in MS-64 or MS-65 in a short time—within a day. Quality, however, would be a mixed bag.

My advice is to be a connoisseur. Buy only certified coins, such as from PCGS or NGC, the two leading professional third-party grading services. If you feel that having a so-called FH coin is desirable in view of the great premium often required, then be certain that the coin has full details everywhere else. Keep in mind that on such coins the head details still may be weak for some features. A top-of-the-line FH quarter should have *nearly* full facial sharpness and should have all of the rivets visible. The center of the shield should be distinct as well. Otherwise you are wasting your money, in my opinion.

To reiterate, in my opinion you will get the most value for your money if you ignore FH designations and do your best to buy Standing Liberty quarters that lack this often misleadingly described feature, but are sharp in all other details. The cost is no more.

Eye appeal is another consideration. A certified MS-65 quarter can be dark, stained, ugly, or spotted, in which case I suggest you avoid it. Among Mint State coins look for pieces that have rich frosty mint luster and are brilliant or with light iridescent toning. Most "rainbow" toning is artificial. A curious aspect of thinking for the vast majority of non-savvy buyers is that they consider *any* MS-65 coin, even one with no eye appeal, to be better than, say, a gorgeous MS-63.

Furthermore, over the years there has been a trend with certified coins known as "gradeflation." Many that were graded as MS-64 20 years ago are graded MS-65 or even higher today. In the late 1980s MS-66 and MS-67 grades were few and far between in the population reports published by PCGS and NGC. Today, such grades are very common. As is also true for Mercury dimes and Liberty Walking half dollars, "cracking" coins out of holders and resubmitting them in the hopes of attaining a higher grade has become an industry in itself. Often "low-end" (common-date, less valuable) coins are left in holders and "high-end" (scarcer or rare key dates) coins are resubmitted in hopes of getting a higher grade. The cost of doing this repeated times can be small in comparison to the extra value received when, for example, an MS-65 graduates to become an MS-66.

Not everyone can afford a Mint State 1916, 1918/7-S overdate, 1926-S, or 1927-S quarter. If this includes you, cherrypick nice VF, EF, or AU coins with care, selecting only examples with nice eye appeal.

Take your time. All the coins that meet your particular requirements are in the marketplace, but to find them may take a few weeks or months. Study each coin carefully before making a purchase decision. The thrill of the chase is part of what the art and science of numismatics is all about.

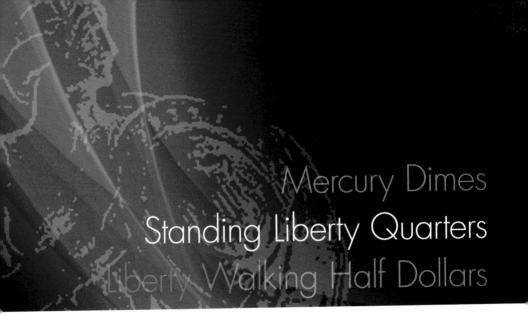

1916 Standing Liberty Quarter

Circulation-strike mintage:
52,000

Notes. The mintage of 52,000 1916 Standing Liberty quarters was released into circulation in January 1917 at the same time 1917-dated coins were distributed. Therefore the 1916 quarters attracted no particular attention. In comparison to the 8,740,000 mintage for Philadelphia 1917 Type I quarters the 1916 is 168 times rarer—another explanation why they are rare.

Key to Collecting. For several numismatic generations the 1916 Standing Liberty quarter has been a celebrated rarity combining a low mintage of just 52,000 coins with first-year-of-issue honors. Today, examples are *very rare* in relation to the demand for them. This is, of course, a wonderful combination of appealing factors for any rarity! Among regular-issue twentieth-century United States coins from cents through silver dollars (excluding commemoratives and unusual varieties such as over-dates), only the 1913-S quarter has a lower mintage, with just 40,000 struck.

As noted above, there was not a great deal of numismatic interest in the 1916 Standing Liberty quarter when it first appeared. It was not until the 1930s, when Wayte Raymond introduced his "National" coin albums that collecting twentieth-century coins by date and mintmark sequence became *wildly* popular. After that time the

See next page for chart.

demand for and price of the 1916 Standing Liberty quarter soared. Today, the offering of an example in any grade draws a lot of interest.

In May 1917 Henry Chapman, one of the few coin dealers who accommodated his clients by providing new issues, advertised: "1916 quarter dollar. New design. Brilliant Uncirculated $1.00." In November 1918 he offered: "25c 1916 new type, Fine 55c, Unc. $1.25." Chapman maintained a store stock of current issues, as did John Zug in Maryland and William K. Pukall in New Jersey. Most other dealers ignored new releases and concentrated on rare coins from the past. In October 1925 John B. Boss, a Philadelphia dealer, advertised: "We have a small stock of 1916 new-type quarters, Unc., which have an auction record of $2.10 each. Price $1 postpaid while they last."

Walter Breen's Encyclopedia of U.S. and Colonial Coins, 1988, states this: "Mint State survivors are mostly from 2 hoards of 100 and 80 specimens dispersed between 1944 and 1976. Nearly all have flat heads; I have seen no true full-head coin in over 30 years." No further information about these "2 hoards" has been found, but the fact is that Mint State coins were widely advertised before then, as cited above.

Reports of 40-coin rolls have appeared in print from time to time. In the *Coin Dealer Newsletter Monthly Supplement*, August 8, 1997, J.H. Cline commented concerning the 1916 recently sold in the Eliasberg Collection sale: "This one was probably purchased by Eliasberg before the breakup of several rolls of 1916s in an estate in the Northeast. I saw one of these rolls in 1953/1954. All were blst white and I believe many were sold by New York dealer Lester Merkin."[3]

In the Ron Pope survey (see above) 144 quarters of 1916 were examined and 13% had Full Details. In general the 1916 coins of a slightly different design than the later ones are weak overall. The most obvious spots to check are the head, the upper-left area of the shield, and the eagle's breast. This weakness precipitated a slight design modification in 1917. This change is generally overlooked, and both 1916 and early 1917 quarters are called Type I. Well-worn coins often have the left side of the date more worn than the right, with the result that on a few just the 6 is visible.

Market Values • Circulation Strikes

G-4	VG-8	F-12	VF-20	EF-40	AU-50	MS-60	MS-63	MS-65	MS-65FH
$2,600	$5,500	$6,750	$7,500	$10,000	$11,500	$15,000	$18,500	$25,000	$35,000

Certified Populations

Fair	AG-2	G-4	VG-8	F-12	VF-20	EF-40	AU-50	MS-60
1	3	73	92	44	57	38	128	4

MS-61	MS-62	MS-63	MS-64	MS-65	MS-66	MS-67	MS-68	MS-69
36	71	90	114	76	23	5	0	0

1917 Type I Standing Liberty Quarter

Circulation-strike mintage:
8,740,000

Notes. Quarters of this design were placed into circulation in early 1917. They did not attract much public attention at the time. However, their novelty was indeed noticed by some citizens, with the result that many were saved.

Key to Collecting. With relatively few exceptions, 1917 Type I quarters from the Philadelphia Mint are extremely well struck, with head details excellently defined, such details consisting of the cheek and facial features of Miss Liberty and, especially, the wreath she wears around her head. The shield details are excellent as well. As such a 1917 is an ideal coin to add to a type set.

In the Ron Pope survey of 1917 Type I quarters 1,042 were examined and 76% had Full Details. No other variety in the series scored so high. As result a Philadelphia Mint coin of this type is an ideal candidate for inclusion in a type set.

Market Values • Circulation Strikes

G-4	VG-8	F-12	VF-20	EF-40	AU-50	MS-60	MS-63	MS-65	MS-65FH
$25	$45	$65	$90	$110	$200	$250	$350	$750	$1,100

Certified Populations

Fair	AG-2	G-4	VG-8	F-12	VF-20	EF-40	AU-50	MS-60
2	3	8	34	80	146	139	770	4

MS-61	MS-62	MS-63	MS-64	MS-65	MS-66	MS-67	MS-68	MS-69
164	737	991	1,814	921	364	74	0	0

1917-D Type I Standing Liberty Quarter

Circulation-strike mintage:
1,509,200

Key to Collecting. In the Ron Pope survey of 1917-D Type I quarters, 284 were examined and 67% had Full Details, the second-highest such in the study. Due to the differences in mintage quantities, the Denver and San Francisco quarters of this type are scarce in comparison to Philadelphia Mint coins.

After the coins were placed in circulation the date wore away quickly and on most was completely gone by the late 1930s, this comment being true of all of the 1916 to 1924 issues, before the date placement area was modified. If the D mintmark is visible, these can still be attributed as 1917-D Type I, as no other Denver coins of the type were made.

Market Values • Circulation Strikes

G-4	VG-8	F-12	VF-20	EF-40	AU-50	MS-60	MS-63	MS-65	MS-65FH
$30	$55	$80	$120	$200	$250	$325	$425	$950	$2,000

Certified Populations

Fair	AG-2	G-4	VG-8	F-12	VF-20	EF-40	AU-50	MS-60
0	0	4	10	18	61	49	290	3

MS-61	MS-62	MS-63	MS-64	MS-65	MS-66	MS-67	MS-68	MS-69
68	191	269	467	254	91	26	2	0

1917-S Type I Standing Liberty Quarter

Circulation-strike mintage:
1,952,000

Key to Collecting. In the Ron Pope survey of 1917-S Type I quarters, 198 were examined and 62% had Full Details. This was a creditable showing even though less than for the quarters of the other two mints. Even though more were coined of the 1917-S, Mint State coins are scarcer than are 1917-D quarters.

Those with the date *gone* can still be attributed if the mintmark is visible, as noted under 1917-D above.

Market Values • Circulation Strikes

G-4	VG-8	F-12	VF-20	EF-40	AU-50	MS-60	MS-63	MS-65	MS-65FH
$40	$70	$110	$150	$210	$285	$350	$475	$1,200	$3,200

Certified Populations

Fair	AG-2	G-4	VG-8	F-12	VF-20	EF-40	AU-50	MS-60
0	0	1	17	45	69	50	160	1

MS-61	MS-62	MS-63	MS-64	MS-65	MS-66	MS-67	MS-68	MS-69
31	133	131	260	116	81	21	0	0

1917 Type II Standing Liberty Quarter

Circulation-strike mintage:
13,880,000

Key to Collecting. In the Ron Pope survey of 1917 Type II quarters 259 were examined and 15% had Full Details.

This initiated an era of generally unsatisfactory strikes for Type II quarters. Among Type II quarters, the 1917 Philadelphia issue is the only one for which more than 10% of existing Mint State coins have Full Details. As such it is a good candidate for a type set.

In November 1918 Henry Chapman offered: "25c 1917 without stars below eagle, Unc. $1, with stars, 75c." Chapman's retail stock was considered the finest in the country at the time, with John Zug, the mail-order dealer based in Bowie, Maryland, being the runner-up.

As is true of all varieties issued before 1925, the date wore away quickly, with the result that by the 1930s only a fraction of the mintage survived with the date visible.

See next page for chart.

Market Values • Circulation Strikes

G-4	VG-8	F-12	VF-20	EF-40	AU-50	MS-60	MS-63	MS-65	MS-65FH
$25	$40	$55	$70	$100	$150	$210	$275	$600	$900

Certified Populations

Fair	AG-2	G-4	VG-8	F-12	VF-20	EF-40	AU-50	MS-60
0	0	0	3	15	31	27	232	0

MS-61	MS-62	MS-63	MS-64	MS-65	MS-66	MS-67	MS-68	MS-69
58	210	243	382	202	78	17	0	0

1917-D Type II Standing Liberty Quarter

Circulation-strike mintage:
6,224,400

Key to Collecting. In the Ron Pope survey of 1917-D Type II quarters, 161 were examined and 2% had Full Details. As such they are far rarer than coins certified with Full Head, the latter being easy to find in the marketplace. Most are somewhat weak on the shield and sash. In circulated grades this issue is far rarer than the mintage indicates as on most coins the date was worn away.

Market Values • Circulation Strikes

G-4	VG-8	F-12	VF-20	EF-40	AU-50	MS-60	MS-63	MS-65	MS-65FH
$45	$55	$85	$110	$150	$210	$260	$350	$1,300	$3,000

Certified Populations

Fair	AG-2	G-4	VG-8	F-12	VF-20	EF-40	AU-50	MS-60
0	0	0	2	12	29	20	182	2

MS-61	MS-62	MS-63	MS-64	MS-65	MS-66	MS-67	MS-68	MS-69
28	102	145	184	72	24	3	0	0

1917-S Type II Standing Liberty Quarter

Circulation-strike mintage:
5,552,000

Key to Collecting. In the Ron Pope survey of 1917-S Type II quarters, 162 were examined and 4% had Full Details. Despite this relatively high (!) score for sharpness, most coins are weak overall and have minimal eye appeal. Circulated coins are far less common than expected as the dates wore away on most.

Market Values • Circulation Strikes

G-4	VG-8	F-12	VF-20	EF-40	AU-50	MS-60	MS-63	MS-65	MS-65FH
$45	$60	$90	$120	$160	$225	$260	$350	$1,100	$3,250

Certified Populations

Fair	AG-2	G-4	VG-8	F-12	VF-20	EF-40	AU-50	MS-60
0	0	0	4	6	16	22	164	1

MS-61	MS-62	MS-63	MS-64	MS-65	MS-66	MS-67	MS-68	MS-69
33	94	130	177	78	28	2	3	0

1918 Standing Liberty Quarter

Circulation-strike mintage:
14,240,000

Key to Collecting. In the Ron Pope survey of 1918 quarters, 221 were examined and 5% had Full Details. Circulated coins are far less common than one might expect, as the dates wore away on most.

See next page for chart.

Market Values • Circulation Strikes

G-4	VG-8	F-12	VF-20	EF-40	AU-50	MS-60	MS-63	MS-65	MS-65FH
$20	$25	$30	$35	$55	$90	$140	$225	$750	$1,650

Certified Populations

Fair	AG-2	G-4	VG-8	F-12	VF-20	EF-40	AU-50	MS-60
0	0	0	1	6	10	15	165	3

MS-61	MS-62	MS-63	MS-64	MS-65	MS-66	MS-67	MS-68	MS-69
28	97	108	240	101	66	6	2	0

1918-D Standing Liberty Quarter

Circulation-strike mintage:
7,380,000

Key to Collecting. In the Ron Pope survey of 1918-D quarters, 214 were examined and 2% had Full Details. Many are weakly struck at the center in addition to the shield and head. Circulated coins are encountered far less frequently than expected because the dates wore away on most.

Market Values • Circulation Strikes

G-4	VG-8	F-12	VF-20	EF-40	AU-50	MS-60	MS-63	MS-65	MS-65FH
$25	$40	$75	$90	$145	$200	$275	$400	$1,300	$4,000

Certified Populations

Fair	AG-2	G-4	VG-8	F-12	VF-20	EF-40	AU-50	MS-60
0	0	1	3	8	27	23	186	1

MS-61	MS-62	MS-63	MS-64	MS-65	MS-66	MS-67	MS-68	MS-69
22	74	97	146	84	20	3	0	0

1918/7-S Standing Liberty Quarter

Circulation-strike mintage:
**small part of the
1918-S circulation-strike
mintage**

Key to Collecting. This variety was not recognized until the 1930s, and even then not much attention was paid to it, as it was omitted from popular coin holders and folders. Even dedicated numismatists were apt to be unaware of its existence. On February 26, 1938, Thomas L. Elder offered this at auction as lot 262: "1918 over '17. Three stars under eagle. Uncirculated. Very rare. First in the sales."

When the overdate finally became widely noticed in the 1940s it was omitted from many "want lists." It came into its own at a later time. Today, examples are widely desired. Such pieces are the key to the series, in Mint State far rarer than any other variety. Nearly all are in circulated grades. In the Ron Pope survey of 1918/7-S quarters 108 were examined and 0%—not a single coin—had Full Details. The few that have been certified as Full Head do not stand up to close scrutiny if other features are studied, such as the lower left of the shield and Liberty's sash and clothing near the center. About a dozen have been certified as FH by PCGS and NGC.

Market Values • Circulation Strikes

G-4	VG-8	F-12	VF-20	EF-40	AU-50	MS-60	MS-63	MS-65	MS-65FH
$1,600	$2,200	$3,600	$5,000	$8,000	$13,000	$19,000	$32,500	$90,000	$250,000

Certified Populations

Fair	AG-2	G-4	VG-8	F-12	VF-20	EF-40	AU-50	MS-60
0	0	7	14	32	78	59	80	0

MS-61	MS-62	MS-63	MS-64	MS-65	MS-66	MS-67	MS-68	MS-69
8	22	11	18	4	2	1	0	0

1918-S Standing Liberty Quarter

Circulation-strike mintage:
11,072,000

Key to Collecting. In the Ron Pope survey of 1918-S quarters, 269 were examined and only 0.4% had Full Details. The lower left of the shield and the sash are points of weakness. Several dozen FH coins have been certified by PCGS and NGC. Circulated coins are far less common than expected, as the dates wore away on most.

Market Values • Circulation Strikes

G-4	VG-8	F-12	VF-20	EF-40	AU-50	MS-60	MS-63	MS-65	MS-65FH
$20	$25	$35	$45	$60	$120	$200	$300	$1,400	$12,000

Certified Populations

Fair	AG-2	G-4	VG-8	F-12	VF-20	EF-40	AU-50	MS-60
0	2	4	25	21	29	35	209	2

MS-61	MS-62	MS-63	MS-64	MS-65	MS-66	MS-67	MS-68	MS-69
27	116	146	200	75	26	8	0	0

1919 Standing Liberty Quarter

Circulation-strike mintage:
11,324,000

Key to Collecting. In the Ron Pope survey of 1919 quarters, 238 were examined and 8% had Full Details, a remarkably high showing with just a few varieties scoring higher. Circulated examples of this date are far less common than might be expected given the mintage, as the numerals of the date wore away on most coins during circulation.

Market Values • Circulation Strikes

G-4	VG-8	F-12	VF-20	EF-40	AU-50	MS-60	MS-63	MS-65	MS-65FH
$35	$45	$60	$80	$100	$135	$185	$250	$600	$1,500

Certified Populations

Fair	AG-2	G-4	VG-8	F-12	VF-20	EF-40	AU-50	MS-60
0	0	2	2	11	13	25	168	1

MS-61	MS-62	MS-63	MS-64	MS-65	MS-66	MS-67	MS-68	MS-69
32	103	144	267	167	101	33	2	2

1919-D Standing Liberty Quarter

Circulation-strike mintage:
1,944,000

Key to Collecting. In the Ron Pope survey of 1919-D quarters, 121 were examined and 2% had Full Details. The lower left of the sash and the central clothing details are points to check. For coins certified as FH, even though other aspects may not be sharp, a huge premium must be paid. Pocket-change circulation wore away the numerals of the date on most 1919-D quarters, with the result that circulated examples are far less common than might be expected.

Market Values • Circulation Strikes

G-4	VG-8	F-12	VF-20	EF-40	AU-50	MS-60	MS-63	MS-65	MS-65FH
$85	$120	$200	$400	$600	$800	$950	$1,500	$3,000	$35,000

Certified Populations

Fair	AG-2	G-4	VG-8	F-12	VF-20	EF-40	AU-50	MS-60
0	0	1	9	35	70	53	103	1

MS-61	MS-62	MS-63	MS-64	MS-65	MS-66	MS-67	MS-68	MS-69
10	36	24	56	34	17	1	0	0

1919-S Standing Liberty Quarter

Circulation-strike mintage:
1,836,000

Key to Collecting. In the Ron Pope survey of 1919-S quarters, 174 were examined and 2% had Full Details. Similar to the 1919-D, coins certified as FH, even though other aspects may not be sharp, a huge premium must be paid. Circulated coins are far less common than expected, as the dates wore away on most during circulation.

Market Values • Circulation Strikes

G-4	VG-8	F-12	VF-20	EF-40	AU-50	MS-60	MS-63	MS-65	MS-65FH
$80	$110	$175	$350	$550	$750	$900	$1,500	$4,000	$30,000

Certified Populations

Fair	AG-2	G-4	VG-8	F-12	VF-20	EF-40	AU-50	MS-60
0	0	0	7	28	76	70	114	0

MS-61	MS-62	MS-63	MS-64	MS-65	MS-66	MS-67	MS-68	MS-69
7	27	33	43	40	20	5	0	0

1920 Standing Liberty Quarter

Circulation-strike mintage:
27,860,000

Key to Collecting. In the Ron Pope survey of 1920 quarters, 532 were examined and 3% had Full Details. The friction of day-to-day commerce wore away the dates of most examples, resulting in circulated examples being far less common than one might expect, given the high mintage.

Market Values • Circulation Strikes

G-4	VG-8	F-12	VF-20	EF-40	AU-50	MS-60	MS-63	MS-65	MS-65FH
$15	$20	$30	$35	$55	$100	$160	$230	$600	$1,500

Certified Populations

Fair	AG-2	G-4	VG-8	F-12	VF-20	EF-40	AU-50	MS-60
0	0	2	2	7	23	33	284	0

MS-61	MS-62	MS-63	MS-64	MS-65	MS-66	MS-67	MS-68	MS-69
49	188	249	483	242	90	29	0	0

1920-D Standing Liberty Quarter

Circulation-strike mintage:
3,586,400

Key to Collecting. In the Ron Pope survey of 1920-D quarters, 107 were examined and 4% had Full Details. This is a good coin to cherrypick for a fairly well struck shield and other features, even though the facial features may be indistinct. Circulated coins are far less common than expected, as the dates wore away on most.

Market Values • Circulation Strikes

G-4	VG-8	F-12	VF-20	EF-40	AU-50	MS-60	MS-63	MS-65	MS-65FH
$50	$60	$80	$120	$165	$225	$350	$800	$2,000	$6,500

Certified Populations

Fair	AG-2	G-4	VG-8	F-12	VF-20	EF-40	AU-50	MS-60
0	0	1	5	9	46	24	77	0

MS-61	MS-62	MS-63	MS-64	MS-65	MS-66	MS-67	MS-68	MS-69
13	34	45	70	35	17	7	0	0

1920-S Standing Liberty Quarter

Circulation-strike mintage:
6,380,000

Key to Collecting. In the Ron Pope survey of 1920-S quarters, 266 were examined and 0.4% had Full Details. As is true of most other varieties in the series, those that have been certified as Full Head do not stand up to close scrutiny if other features such as the lower left of the shield and the clothing details at the center are studied. For coins certified as FH, even though other aspects may not be sharp, an extreme premium must be paid. This is another variety to cherrypick for sharpness other than the head. Years of everyday wear from hand-to-hand circulation slicked down the dates of most 1920-S quarters; one result is that examples in circulated grades are far less common than might be otherwise be expected.

Market Values • Circulation Strikes

G-4	VG-8	F-12	VF-20	EF-40	AU-50	MS-60	MS-63	MS-65	MS-65FH
$20	$25	$35	$50	$65	$140	$270	$750	$2,200	$20,000

Certified Populations

Fair	AG-2	G-4	VG-8	F-12	VF-20	EF-40	AU-50	MS-60
0	0	2	2	8	22	21	139	3

MS-61	MS-62	MS-63	MS-64	MS-65	MS-66	MS-67	MS-68	MS-69
21	64	76	124	47	18	6	0	0

1921 Standing Liberty Quarter

Circulation-strike mintage:
1,916,000

Notes. During the previous year, 1920, production of Standing Liberty quarters occurred at all three mints, and to the extent of over 35 million pieces. In 1921 the nation was in an economic recession, and the quantity of quarters produced took a precipitous fall to just 1,916,000—about 1/20th of what it had been earlier! In the year after that, 1922, no quarter dollars were struck at all.

Key to Collecting. In the Ron Pope survey of 1921 quarters, 141 were examined and 6% had Full Details. The 1921 and 1928 with 6% having Full Details are tied for second in this quality among Type II quarters, with only 1917 higher (with 15%).

Some 1921 Standing Liberty quarters are certified as having a Full Head, but the coins are weak in other areas, at the first digit of the date and to a lesser extent the fourth digit (this being the only variety in the series often seen with this weakness arrangement). Circulated examples of the 1921 quarter are far less common than expected, as everyday commerce wore away the dates on most examples.

Market Values • Circulation Strikes

G-4	VG-8	F-12	VF-20	EF-40	AU-50	MS-60	MS-63	MS-65	MS-65FH
$175	$225	$475	$700	$800	$1,150	$1,600	$2,200	$3,750	$5,500

Certified Populations

Fair	AG-2	G-4	VG-8	F-12	VF-20	EF-40	AU-50	MS-60
0	1	30	88	82	131	74	147	3

MS-61	MS-62	MS-63	MS-64	MS-65	MS-66	MS-67	MS-68	MS-69
13	54	84	158	104	30	2	0	0

1923 Standing Liberty Quarter

Circulation-strike mintage:
9,716,000

Key to Collecting. In the Ron Pope survey of 1923 quarters, 413 were examined and 3% had Full Details. With a mintage close to 10 million, a collector might expect to find many circulated examples; however, day-to-day circulation wore away the dates of many pre-1925 Standing Liberty quarters, resulting in fewer identifiable examples being available than would otherwise be expected.

See next page for chart.

Market Values • Circulation Strikes

G-4	VG-8	F-12	VF-20	EF-40	AU-50	MS-60	MS-63	MS-65	MS-65FH
$15	$20	$30	$38	$55	$100	$170	$240	$600	$4,000

Certified Populations

Fair	AG-2	G-4	VG-8	F-12	VF-20	EF-40	AU-50	MS-60
0	0	6	4	15	19	24	173	0

MS-61	MS-62	MS-63	MS-64	MS-65	MS-66	MS-67	MS-68	MS-69
24	119	188	364	316	188	54	0	0

1923-S Standing Liberty Quarter

Circulation-strike mintage:
1,360,000

Key to Collecting. In the Ron Pope survey of 1923-S quarters, 107 were examined and 2% had Full Details. Most but not all that have been certified as Full Head do not stand up to close scrutiny if other features are studied, although some come close. There are enough such "FH" coins around that the price differential for them is not huge. Circulated coins of 1923-S are far less commonly observed than one might expect, as the dates wore away on most.

Market Values • Circulation Strikes

G-4	VG-8	F-12	VF-20	EF-40	AU-50	MS-60	MS-63	MS-65	MS-65FH
$280	$425	$740	$1,100	$1,500	$2,000	$2,600	$3,400	$5,000	$6,500

Certified Populations

Fair	AG-2	G-4	VG-8	F-12	VF-20	EF-40	AU-50	MS-60
0	6	5	29	40	112	63	158	1

MS-61	MS-62	MS-63	MS-64	MS-65	MS-66	MS-67	MS-68	MS-69
23	36	58	107	68	48	10	0	0

1924 Standing Liberty Quarter

Circulation-strike mintage:
10,920,000

Key to Collecting. In the Ron Pope survey of 1924 quarters 226 were examined and 3% had Full Details. Given its fairly high mintage, today's collector might expect to find many circulated examples of the 1924 quarter. However, the height of the date in the overall design made it one of the first areas to wear away in everyday commerce. As a result, there are fewer circulated 1924 quarters—identifiable by their date, that is—than one might otherwise anticipate.

Market Values • Circulation Strikes

G-4	VG-8	F-12	VF-20	EF-40	AU-50	MS-60	MS-63	MS-65	MS-65FH
$15	$20	$25	$35	$55	$110	$185	$275	$600	$1,500

Certified Populations

Fair	AG-2	G-4	VG-8	F-12	VF-20	EF-40	AU-50	MS-60
0	0	0	0	14	25	18	141	0

MS-61	MS-62	MS-63	MS-64	MS-65	MS-66	MS-67	MS-68	MS-69
28	100	169	313	161	72	31	7	0

1924-D Standing Liberty Quarter

Circulation-strike mintage:
3,112,000

See next page for chart.

Key to Collecting. In the Ron Pope survey of 1924-D quarters, 337 were examined and 2% had Full Details. Those that have been certified as Full Head do not stand up to close scrutiny if other features such as the lower left of the shield and the central clothing details are studied. Circulated coins are far less common than expected, as the dates wore away on most.

Market Values • Circulation Strikes

G-4	VG-8	F-12	VF-20	EF-40	AU-50	MS-60	MS-63	MS-65	MS-65FH
$55	$70	$100	$140	$195	$230	$325	$375	$600	$4,500

Certified Populations

Fair	AG-2	G-4	VG-8	F-12	VF-20	EF-40	AU-50	MS-60
0	0	0	4	11	23	17	96	0

MS-61	MS-62	MS-63	MS-64	MS-65	MS-66	MS-67	MS-68	MS-69
18	57	115	381	466	276	45	2	0

1924-S Standing Liberty Quarter

Circulation-strike mintage:
2,860,000

Key to Collecting. In the Ron Pope survey of 1924-S quarters, 189 were examined and 0.5% had Full Details. This is another variety to cherrypick for sharpness other than the head. With a few years of circulation, the date on many 1924-S quarters wore away to the point of being illegible. As a result, the coin is far less common in circulated grades than one might expect.

Market Values • Circulation Strikes

G-4	VG-8	F-12	VF-20	EF-40	AU-50	MS-60	MS-63	MS-65	MS-65FH
$26	$33	$45	$65	$130	$250	$350	$900	$1,750	$5,500

Certified Populations

Fair	AG-2	G-4	VG-8	F-12	VF-20	EF-40	AU-50	MS-60
0	0	1	2	2	29	20	110	2

MS-61	MS-62	MS-63	MS-64	MS-65	MS-66	MS-67	MS-68	MS-69
21	38	80	147	95	20	6	1	0

1925 Standing Liberty Quarter

Circulation-strike mintage:
12,280,000

Notes. In 1925 Philadelphia was the only mint to strike quarters.

Key to Collecting. In the Ron Pope survey of 1925 quarters, 281 were examined and 3% had Full Details. Beginning with this year the date is in a recessed position. Accordingly, Standing Liberty quarters of this and later years were readily identifiable in circulation when collecting by date and mintmark became popular in the 1930s.

Market Values • Circulation Strikes

G-4	VG-8	F-12	VF-20	EF-40	AU-50	MS-60	MS-63	MS-65	MS-65FH
$7.50	$8	$10	$20	$45	$100	$160	$250	$600	$1,000

Certified Populations

Fair	AG-2	G-4	VG-8	F-12	VF-20	EF-40	AU-50	MS-60
0	2	7	5	5	5	15	161	0

MS-61	MS-62	MS-63	MS-64	MS-65	MS-66	MS-67	MS-68	MS-69
34	135	211	367	162	52	16	0	0

1926 Standing Liberty Quarter

Circulation-strike mintage:
11,316,000

Key to Collecting. In the Ron Pope survey of 1926 quarters, 300 were examined and only 1% had Full Details. This is another variety to cherrypick for sharpness other than the head. There are many attractive coins in the marketplace. Only a few buyers will take the time to examine them for sharpness.

See next page for chart.

Market Values • Circulation Strikes

G-4	VG-8	F-12	VF-20	EF-40	AU-50	MS-60	MS-63	MS-65	MS-65FH
$7.50	$8	$9	$20	$45	$90	$150	$250	$600	$2,000

Certified Populations

Fair	AG-2	G-4	VG-8	F-12	VF-20	EF-40	AU-50	MS-60
0	1	4	2	5	7	16	193	0

MS-61	MS-62	MS-63	MS-64	MS-65	MS-66	MS-67	MS-68	MS-69
40	141	213	373	158	47	6	2	0

1926-D Standing Liberty Quarter

Circulation-strike mintage:
1,716,000

Key to Collecting. Taken as a whole the 1926-D quarter is the least satisfactory of all Standing Liberty issues from the standpoint of striking quality. Dozens of FH quarters have been certified by PCGS and NGC and cost a tremendous premium to buy. In another series the same can be said for 1926-D Buffalo nickels. In the Ron Pope survey of 1926-D quarters, 351 were examined and 0%—not a single coin—had Full Details. On careful study some came quite close. This is a poster example of an issue to cherrypick for sharpness other than in the head.

In October 1937 B. Max Mehl must have had a small hoard, for in *The Numismatic Scrapbook Magazine* he devoted an entire page to this: "I offer a brilliant Mint Uncirculated quarter dollar of 1926, Denver Mint, which is listed for $1.25 to $1.50, for only seventy-five cents!" Bank-wrapped rolls were common in numismatic circles until the coin boom that started in 1960 resulted in the breaking up of quantities of many early coins. The 1926-D was viewed as the most common variety in the series at the Mint State level.

Walter Breen's Complete Encyclopedia of U.S. and Colonial Coins, 1988, included this: "Plentiful in Mint State from bags recovered from banks in the early 1930s. Usually weak at head and drapery; full heads are prohibitively rare." No other record of *bags* of the date has been found.

Market Values • Circulation Strikes

G-4	VG-8	F-12	VF-20	EF-40	AU-50	MS-60	MS-63	MS-65	MS-65FH
$7.50	$10	$22	$40	$80	$140	$180	$250	$550	$24,000

Certified Populations

Fair	AG-2	G-4	VG-8	F-12	VF-20	EF-40	AU-50	MS-60
0	1	3	2	3	5	5	50	0
MS-61	MS-62	MS-63	MS-64	MS-65	MS-66	MS-67	MS-68	MS-69
23	184	607	1,005	268	24	1	0	0

1926-S Standing Liberty Quarter

Circulation-strike mintage:
2,700,000

Key to Collecting. In the Ron Pope survey of 1926-S quarters 134 were examined and 0%—not even one coin—had Full Details. Most fail at the center and the lower left of the shield. This is a poster example of an issue to cherrypick for sharpness other than in the head. Several dozen FH coins have been certified by PCGS and NGC and they sell at many multiples of coins that are not so labeled.

Market Values • Circulation Strikes

G-4	VG-8	F-12	VF-20	EF-40	AU-50	MS-60	MS-63	MS-65	MS-65FH
$7.50	$10	$15	$28	$110	$225	$350	$775	$2,000	$25,000

Certified Populations

Fair	AG-2	G-4	VG-8	F-12	VF-20	EF-40	AU-50	MS-60
0	0	7	5	6	22	26	95	1
MS-61	MS-62	MS-63	MS-64	MS-65	MS-66	MS-67	MS-68	MS-69
13	36	49	96	44	14	2	0	0

1927 Standing Liberty Quarter

Circulation-strike mintage:
11,912,000

Key to Collecting. In the Ron Pope survey of 1927 quarters, 343 were examined and only 1% had Full Details. Striking quality was poor at all three mints this year. This is another variety to cherrypick for sharpness other than in the head, and also for eye appeal. There quite a few around that are *nearly* Full Details and are attractive.

Market Values • Circulation Strikes

G-4	VG-8	F-12	VF-20	EF-40	AU-50	MS-60	MS-63	MS-65	MS-65FH
$7.50	$8	$9	$17	$35	$80	$140	$225	$550	$1,100

Certified Populations

Fair	AG-2	G-4	VG-8	F-12	VF-20	EF-40	AU-50	MS-60
0	4	6	9	7	13	18	259	1

MS-61	MS-62	MS-63	MS-64	MS-65	MS-66	MS-67	MS-68	MS-69
41	190	264	388	154	55	6	0	0

1927-D Standing Liberty Quarter

Circulation-strike mintage:
976,000

Key to Collecting. Bank-wrapped rolls of 1927-D quarters, the second-lowest mintage (after 1927-S) of the later-date 1925 to 1930 issues, were available in the 1950s, but far fewer than for 1926-D. These were always saleable due to their general scarcity among coins found in circulation. In the Ron Pope survey of 1927-D quarters, 170 were examined and 0%—not a single coin—had Full Details. This is still another variety to cherrypick for sharpness other than in the head. More than 100 FH coins have been certified by PCGS and NGC, without regard to shield sharpness and certain other details.

Market Values • Circulation Strikes

G-4	VG-8	F-12	VF-20	EF-40	AU-50	MS-60	MS-63	MS-65	MS-65FH
$15	$20	$30	$75	$150	$220	$270	$310	$600	$3,000

Certified Populations

Fair	AG-2	G-4	VG-8	F-12	VF-20	EF-40	AU-50	MS-60
0	3	7	12	14	19	17	41	0

MS-61	MS-62	MS-63	MS-64	MS-65	MS-66	MS-67	MS-68	MS-69
7	28	123	394	240	42	6	0	0

1927-S Standing Liberty Quarter

Circulation-strike mintage:
396,000

Key to Collecting. The 1927-S has always been a key issue in the series. Even before 1960 Mint State coins were found one at a time, and not often, in the marketplace. No rolls or other groups have been reported. In the Ron Pope survey of 1927-S quarters, 145 were examined and 0%—not a single coin—had Full Details. The usual suspect areas are the shield and the central clothing details. Again, here is a variety to cherrypick for sharpness other than in the head. More than two dozen FH coins have been certified by PCGS and NGC, and these sell for huge premiums.

See next page for chart.

Market Values • Circulation Strikes

G-4	VG-8	F-12	VF-20	EF-40	AU-50	MS-60	MS-63	MS-65	MS-65FH
$40	$50	$130	$350	$1,100	$2,800	$5,000	$7,000	$10,500	$150,000

Certified Populations

Fair	AG-2	G-4	VG-8	F-12	VF-20	EF-40	AU-50	MS-60
0	11	85	174	223	238	113	92	1
MS-61	MS-62	MS-63	MS-64	MS-65	MS-66	MS-67	MS-68	MS-69
7	16	15	56	27	24	4	0	0

1928 Standing Liberty Quarter

Circulation-strike mintage:
6,336,000

Key to Collecting. In the Ron Pope survey of 1928 quarters, 228 were examined and 6% had Full Details. The 1921 and 1928 with 6% having Full Details are tied for second in this quality among Type II quarters, with only 1917 being higher (with 15%).

Market Values • Circulation Strikes

G-4	VG-8	F-12	VF-20	EF-40	AU-50	MS-60	MS-63	MS-65	MS-65FH
$7.50	$8	$9	$17	$40	$80	$140	$225	$550	$1,750

Certified Populations

Fair	AG-2	G-4	VG-8	F-12	VF-20	EF-40	AU-50	MS-60
0	0	4	8	2	9	12	147	0
MS-61	MS-62	MS-63	MS-64	MS-65	MS-66	MS-67	MS-68	MS-69
21	114	149	258	127	52	24	2	0

1928-D Standing Liberty Quarter

Circulation-strike mintage:
1,627,600

Key to Collecting. 1928-D quarters were available at face value plus postage from the Treasury Department at a later time, per a notice received by the American Numismatic Association on April 23, 1932. In the Ron Pope survey of 1928-D quarters, 379 were examined and only 1% had Full Details. This is another variety to cherrypick for sharpness other than in the head, as coins labeled FH are very expensive.

Market Values • Circulation Strikes

G-4	VG-8	F-12	VF-20	EF-40	AU-50	MS-60	MS-63	MS-65	MS-65FH
$7.50	$8	$9	$17	$35	$80	$150	$235	$550	$5,000

Certified Populations

Fair	AG-2	G-4	VG-8	F-12	VF-20	EF-40	AU-50	MS-60
0	0	1	2	4	9	14	75	1

MS-61	MS-62	MS-63	MS-64	MS-65	MS-66	MS-67	MS-68	MS-69
14	59	146	542	437	122	11	0	0

1928-S Standing Liberty Quarter

Circulation-strike mintage:
2,644,000

See next page for chart.

Key to Collecting. 1928-S quarters were available at face value plus postage from the Treasury Department at a later time, per a notice received by the American Numismatic Association on April 23, 1932. In the Ron Pope survey of 1928-S quarters, 318 were examined and 0.6% had Full Details. This is another variety to cherrypick for sharpness other than in the head.

Inverted S mintmark: On some 1928-S quarters the mintmark was punched upside down in the die with the result that it is wider and heavier on top. As these have not been widely noticed they can often be found by cherrypicking. (FS-25-1928S-501)

Market Values • Circulation Strikes

G-4	VG-8	F-12	VF-20	EF-40	AU-50	MS-60	MS-63	MS-65	MS-65FH
$7.50	$8	$9	$22	$40	$90	$140	$235	$550	$900

Certified Populations

Fair	AG-2	G-4	VG-8	F-12	VF-20	EF-40	AU-50	MS-60
0	1	4	3	4	12	18	87	0

MS-61	MS-62	MS-63	MS-64	MS-65	MS-66	MS-67	MS-68	MS-69
18	44	119	323	402	266	58	2	0

1929 Standing Liberty Quarter

Circulation-strike mintage:
11,140,000

Key to Collecting. 1929 quarters were available at face value plus postage from the Treasury Department at a later time, according to a notice received by the American Numismatic Association on April 23, 1932. In the Ron Pope survey of 1929 quarters, 476 were examined and 2% had Full Details.

Market Values • Circulation Strikes

G-4	VG-8	F-12	VF-20	EF-40	AU-50	MS-60	MS-63	MS-65	MS-65FH
$7.50	$8	$9	$17	$35	$80	$140	$225	$525	$800

Certified Populations

Fair	AG-2	G-4	VG-8	F-12	VF-20	EF-40	AU-50	MS-60
0	1	3	7	5	10	21	280	1
MS-61	MS-62	MS-63	MS-64	MS-65	MS-66	MS-67	MS-68	MS-69
52	256	333	512	222	81	14	0	0

1929-D Standing Liberty Quarter

Circulation-strike mintage:
1,358,000

Key to Collecting. In the Ron Pope survey of 1929-D quarters, 214 were examined and 0.4% had Full Details. This is another variety to cherrypick for sharpness other than in the head. Certified FH coins are easy enough to find and cost a great premium over ones that are nearly as nice, but are not so labeled. Striking quality dropped even lower toward the end of the series.

Market Values • Circulation Strikes

G-4	VG-8	F-12	VF-20	EF-40	AU-50	MS-60	MS-63	MS-65	MS-65FH
$7.50	$8	$9	$17	$40	$80	$140	$230	$525	$5,000

Certified Populations

Fair	AG-2	G-4	VG-8	F-12	VF-20	EF-40	AU-50	MS-60
0	0	6	1	3	13	14	186	0
MS-61	MS-62	MS-63	MS-64	MS-65	MS-66	MS-67	MS-68	MS-69
27	114	184	262	113	45	1	0	0

1929-S Standing Liberty Quarter

Circulation-strike mintage:
1,764,000

Key to Collecting. 1929-S quarters were available at face value plus postage from the Treasury Department at a later time, per a notice received by the American Numismatic Association on April 23, 1932.

In the Ron Pope survey of 1929-S quarters, 332 were examined and 0%—not a single coin—had Full Details. This is another variety to cherrypick for sharpness other than in the head. Points to check include details of the shield, the central clothing, and the eagle's breast. In sharp contrast *hundreds* of FH coins have been certified by PCGS and NGC.

Market Values • Circulation Strikes

G-4	VG-8	F-12	VF-20	EF-40	AU-50	MS-60	MS-63	MS-65	MS-65FH
$7.50	$8	$9	$17	$35	$80	$140	$225	$525	$850

Certified Populations

Fair	AG-2	G-4	VG-8	F-12	VF-20	EF-40	AU-50	MS-60
0	1	3	7	10	18	32	146	0

MS-61	MS-62	MS-63	MS-64	MS-65	MS-66	MS-67	MS-68	MS-69
22	97	125	329	309	211	53	1	0

1930 Standing Liberty Quarter

Circulation-strike mintage:
5,632,000

Key to Collecting. A notice received by the American Numismatic Association on April 23, 1932, indicated that 1930 quarters were available at face value plus postage from the Treasury Department. Due to its high mintage the 1930 quarter is very common in Mint State today, nearly all being typical strikes with lightness. In the Ron Pope survey of 1930 quarters, 1,008 were examined and 4% had Full Details.

Market Values • Circulation Strikes

G-4	VG-8	F-12	VF-20	EF-40	AU-50	MS-60	MS-63	MS-65	MS-65FH
$7.50	$8	$9	$17	$35	$80	$140	$225	$525	$800

Certified Populations

Fair	AG-2	G-4	VG-8	F-12	VF-20	EF-40	AU-50	MS-60
0	0	1	8	3	20	44	595	4

MS-61	MS-62	MS-63	MS-64	MS-65	MS-66	MS-67	MS-68	MS-69
89	347	529	981	549	202	37	0	0

1930-S Standing Liberty Quarter

Circulation-strike mintage:
1,556,000

Key to Collecting. 1930-S quarters were available at face value plus postage from the Treasury Department at a later time, per a notice received by the American Numismatic Association on April 23, 1932.

In the Ron Pope survey of 1930-S quarters, 275 were examined and 0.4% had Full Details. *Scott's Catalogue and Encyclopedia of United States Coins*, written by Don Taxay and published in 1971, stated that there was no such thing as a 1930-S quarter dollar with a Full Head. When the book came out, collectors and dealers were surprised to read this. Before long many "Full Head" coins were listed, and today coins certified as FH are common. However, nearly all are lacking in sharpness of some of the other details. Quite a few "almost" coins have lightness at the lower left of the shield and on the eagle's breast.

Market Values • Circulation Strikes

G-4	VG-8	F-12	VF-20	EF-40	AU-50	MS-60	MS-63	MS-65	MS-65FH
$7.50	$8	$9	$17	$35	$80	$140	$225	$525	$800

Certified Populations

Fair	AG-2	G-4	VG-8	F-12	VF-20	EF-40	AU-50	MS-60
0	0	1	7	3	21	14	110	2

MS-61	MS-62	MS-63	MS-64	MS-65	MS-66	MS-67	MS-68	MS-69
14	89	115	240	240	135	48	3	0

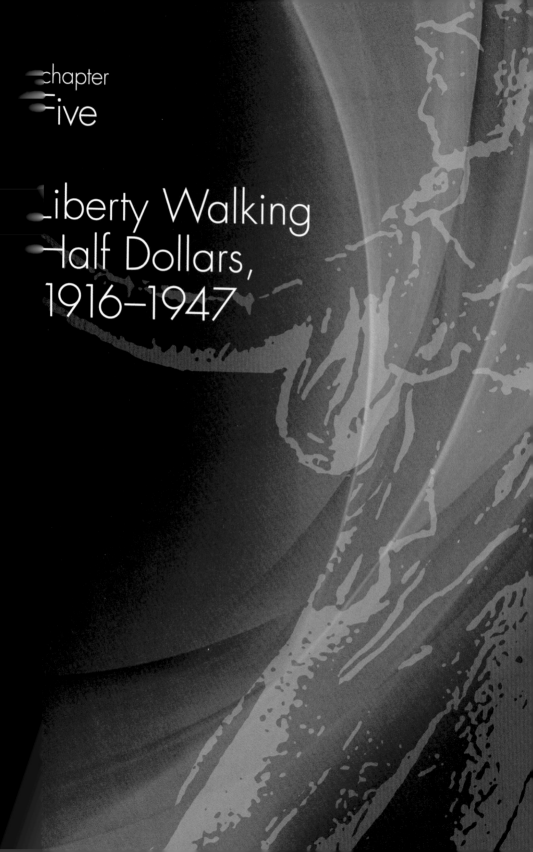

chapter
Five

Liberty Walking
Half Dollars,
1916–1947

The Design of the New Half Dollar

The Liberty Walking half dollar, called by some the Walking Liberty half dollar, is the highest of the three new denominations of 1916. Adolph A. Weinman, who also designed the Mercury dime, created the motif for the new half dollar.

The first coins were struck in 1916 but were not released until the authorization of January 1917. Unlike the Mercury dime that reached circulation in October 1916, the new half dollar received little public notice. The public excitement over new designs for silver coins was mainly concentrated on the dime.

Liberty Walking half dollars were struck at the Philadelphia, Denver, and San Francisco mints in 1916, with the D and S mintmarks on the lower right of the obverse of the branch-mint issues. Partway through 1917 the mintmark position was changed to the reverse. Production continued at all three mints through 1921, after which the half dollars were struck only occasionally until 1933. After that they were made continuously through 1947.

From 1916 through the 1920s collecting Liberty Walking half dollars by date and mint varieties was a specialty for relatively few numismatists. That changed in the 1930s when Wayte Raymond took over the Unique coin albums launched by M.L. Beistle in 1928 and promoted them under the "National" name. When other albums and holders became available interest went into high gear. Many sets were assembled from circulation. By that time earlier varieties were worn down to VG to Fine in some instances.

In the early 1950s I spent one afternoon at the Forty Fort (Pennsylvania) State Bank and by looking through coins they had on hand I was able to completely fill two Whitman folders. In that era I was quite aware of coins that could be found in circulation. Among half dollars Barber coins of the 1892 to 1915 design could be found occasionally. The rarest Liberty Walking halves, in terms of availability at that time, were the 1917-S with obverse mintmark and the 1938-D.

Today Liberty Walking half dollars are in the forefront of popularity and are widely collected. Most numismatists aspire to build a complete set, but some others concentrate on the later dates from 1933 onward as these are easily available in Mint State. Still others start at 1941. There are no "impossible" rarities, although many of the earlier varieties are elusive in high ranges of Mint State.

In 1986 when the Treasury Department sought a motif for its silver "eagle" bullion coins it reached back to the 1916 Liberty Walking half dollar as the best motif in its repertoire.

An American Silver Eagle bullion coin, as depicted in a U.S. Mint catalog.

Early Design Commentary

On the afternoon of May 30, 1916, Secretary of the Treasury William G. McAdoo issued a statement describing the new design:

> The obverse of the half dollar bears a full length figure of Liberty with a background of the American flag flying to the breeze. The goddess is striding toward the dawn of a new day, carrying laurel and oak branches, symbolic of civic and military glory. The reverse shows an eagle perched high up on a mountain crag, wings unfolded. Growing from a rift in the rock is a sapling of mountain pine, symbolic of America.

The *Sower* motif on a French silver 2-francs coin.

The *striding* designation was never picked up by numismatists, and *walking* became the popular adjective in books and albums. The design was based on an adaptation of Louis-Oscar Roty's 1887 painting, *La Semeuse* (*The Sower*), which had been the motif for French silver coins beginning in 1897. On the coins she appeared restyled as Marianne (the symbolic personification of Republican France), with a slimmer figure and wearing a Phrygian cap. No information has been found to identify any model who posed for Weinman when he created the 1916 half dollar.[1] The features differ somewhat from those on *The Sower*.

Mehl's Numismatic Monthly, December 1916, gave this review:

> The new fifty-cent pieces were issued the first week in January and there seems to be a great difference of opinion concerning their artistic beauty. The eagle comes in for considerable criticism. It may be ornithologically correct, but Mr. Frank M. Chapman, one of the most prominent ornithologists of this continent, criticizes it as follows: "The artist has made this bird a terrestrial fowl, striding or marching on the ground like a turkey-cock and with as much dignity as one."
>
> Another less learned critic comments: "The eagle looks as though it were wearing overalls and marching through hot tar."
>
> Still another says: "Liberty in sandals taking giant strides across its face might burn her toes, if she should step one millimeter nearer the rising sun."
>
> The new coin also has its strong admirers—many consider the new designs the most attractive that have ever figured on our coins. One thing is certain—the interest of non-collectors is aroused, and the great number of collectors will increase the more our coinage is studied.

In January 1917 *The Numismatist* noted:

> Although the new half dollar and quarter dollar have not been placed in circulation up to the time this is written, they may be issued by or shortly after the first of the year....Specimens of the new coins have been on exhibition at the American Numismatic Society in New York for several days past through the courtesy of the Treasury officials.
>
> In our opinion the new designs form the most attractive set of silver coins ever issued by this or any other government. At last we have on our coins the great American eagle in a natural lifelike form. As represented on the half dollar he is, as the small boy would say, "Some bird," and his size and proportions are in keeping with the greatness and power of the country....

Release and Distribution

In October 1916 *The Numismatist* had noted this concerning the release of the coins:

> The latest advice regarding the new silver coins is that the issue has been indefinitely postponed. This information, according to the daily press, comes from those in authority at Washington. The reason given for the postponement is said to be that much trouble has been encountered in preparing the dies, and that the same difficulty presents itself whenever designs are made by artists outside the mint not familiar with the mechanical problems to be solved. Would it not be well in the future to place the designing of our new coins in the hands of men familiar with the mechanical processes and requirements of coining, especially in view of recent developments?

The problem was not made easier by Chief Engraver Charles E. Barber, who had long resented the intrusion of outside artists into the design process. Prior to the Saint-Gaudens coinage of 1907, designing coins had been the privilege of engravers on the Mint staff. Barber was justified in his resentment, however, as most of the designs by private artists had difficulties with the relief being too high in certain areas. This would have made large-scale production difficult or impossible, and could introduce the challenge of coins not stacking easily.

The new half dollars were released into circulation after Secretary McAdoo's authorization of January 17, 1917.

A Washington news release of January 26 included this:

> Reports reached the Treasury Department today from numerous sources that sharpers have been selling at a premium the newly designed quarters and half dollars coined in 1916, representing that the new coins are rare. To correct any impression that the coins are rare, officials today authorized the statement that 2,330,000 halves and 62,000 quarters of the new design were struck off in 1916.

Liberty Walking Half Dollars in Circulation

Unlike the situation when the Mercury dime reached the channels of commerce in October 1916, the half dollar was not particularly newsworthy in early 1917. Papers and magazines were immersed in coverage of the World War, and in this year America would officially join the war.

Production continued from 1916 through 1921 at all three mints. Collector interest was minimal, and apart from mentions that partway through 1917 the D and S mintmark positions were changed from the obverse to the reverse, the varieties drew little attention. The low mintages of 1921 were not newsworthy either. The dealers who laid in stocks of current Mercury dimes and, to a lesser extent, Standing Liberty quarters, more or less ignored the half dollars as the denomination was expensive in the minds of many collectors.

After 1921, mintages were sporadic. In 1923 the San Francisco Mint produced half dollars, after which none were struck until 1927, then in 1928 more were coined, followed by a gap to 1933. In the meantime various *commemorative* half dollars were made, such as the Grant Memorial issues of 1922 and several types from 1924 to 1928. Unlike for regular issues, commemorative half dollars were widely and enthusiastically collected at the time. From 1933 to 1947 Liberty Walking half dollars were produced continuously, although not consistently at all three mints until 1941.

Beginning in the mid-1930s there developed a nationwide passion for collecting coins from circulation, spurred by the availability of albums, panels, and the *Standard Catalogue of United States Coins*, the first regularly issued book to include prices and mintage figures. In the Great Depression a half dollar represented a lot of money to many citizens. While Lincoln cents could be collected by just about anyone, half dollars were different. There was a great deal of collecting interest, although casual collectors were fewer than for the new Mercury dimes and Standing Liberty quarters, which were more affordable at face value. During the same time commemorative half dollars were in an unprecedented speculative frenzy (a market which cooled in the summer of 1936).

Starting in a large way in the early 1940s Liberty Walking half dollars became very popular, their beautiful design was appreciated more than ever, and many numismatists endeavored to build collections. It was realized that many of the varieties from 1916 to 1929 were rare in Mint State as few people had saved them. No hoards surfaced. Even a single bank-wrapped roll of any variety of these years would have been very unusual—in contrast with the dime and quarter dollar series. The survival of Mint State half dollars was strictly a matter of chance, rather than of deliberate preservation.

Worn Liberty Walking half dollars were common in circulation until after 1965, when silver coins of all denominations were melted in quantity due to the rise of the bullion price on international markets. Although most of the earlier coins had disappeared by this time, millions of coins of the 1930s and 1940s were in circulation. In the mid- and late 1970s Nelson and Bunker Hunt, Texas oil millionaires, attempted to corner the market in silver. The price rose steadily until January 21, 1980, when it peaked at $52.35 per ounce. Untold millions of circulated Liberty Walking half dollars were melted, as their bullion value (more than $18) was far greater than their numismatic worth at the time. Perhaps even the majority of such coins were lost forever. After the peak, the market crashed, and the remaining circulated coins again attracted the interest of collectors.

Aspects of Striking

This Proof 1938 half dollar provides an ideal image of a well-struck coin with Full Details. Areas that on circulation strikes are often seen weak are highlighted in red.

A typical 1927-S half dollar, a variety usually found with weakness in areas, with weak areas highlighted in red.

A 1944-D circulation-strike half dollar with about as close to Full Details as it is possible to find.

The striking sharpness or lack thereof in the Liberty Walking half dollar series has been studied by several people, notably by Jeff Ambio in *Collecting and Investing Strategies for Walking Liberty Half Dollars*, 2008, and with a nod to Dean F. Howe and his *Walking Liberty Half Dollars, An In-Depth Study*, 1989. Unlike the situation for designations such as Full Bands for Mercury dimes and Full Head for Standing Liberty quarters, the hobby has no shorthand description of the quality of strike for half dollars. If such were to be adopted, FH&H for "Full Head and Hand" would probably answer much—as this usually means the skirt lines, eagle feathers, and other details are sharp as well. In the meantime, the search for sharpness is wide open for cherrypicking!

The recessed AW monogram on the lower right of the reverse is sometimes weak or even missing, due to polishing and grinding during die preparation. Most Proofs of 1941 lack the monogram for this reason. Proofs with the monogram were made later in the year and are much scarcer. Certain 1944-D half dollars have the monogram hand-engraved and are especially interesting.

Toward a Classification of Striking Sharpness

For each of the dates and mintmarks from 1916 to 1947 a commentary concerning the sharpness of details is given as follows:

Head: The details on the head of Miss Liberty. If the head is *nearly* full this is acceptable among early (pre-1933 issues).

Left hand: The details on Miss Liberty's hand at the center. Of the features mentioned here this is one of the most critical. A poorly struck hand usually indicates a coin with generally unsatisfactory striking over all.

Skirt lines over leg: This feature is not deep in the dies, and on the best strikes the lines are light. As a general rule, if the left hand is fairly sharp the skirt lines will be well defined. If the hand is weak the lines will also be weak. As these are not a major point they are not studied coin-by-coin in the following listings. Instead, the rule given here will apply.

Eagle: The feathers on the body of the eagle. If these are somewhat weak and all obverse features are satisfactory, for pre-1933 coins this usually indicates a nice example.

Overview: Commentary on what to expect for sharpness for the issue and in some instances suggestions for cherrypicking. Except for Proofs 1936 to 1942, half dollars with needle-sharp definition of details are almost impossible to find. The answer is to find examples with a fairly well struck head and hand for starters, then evaluate the strike and visual appeal overall.

Grading Liberty Walking Half Dollars

1917. Graded MS-65.

MS-60 to 70 (Mint State)

Obverse: At MS-60, some abrasion and contact marks are evident on the higher areas, which are also the areas most likely to be weakly struck. This includes Miss Liberty's left arm, her hand, and the areas of the skirt covering her left leg. The luster may not be complete in those areas on weakly struck coins (even those certified above MS-65)—the *original planchet surface* may be revealed, as it was not smoothed out by striking. Accordingly, grading is best done by evaluating abrasion as it is observed *in the right field*, plus evaluating the mint luster. Luster may be dull or lifeless at MS-60 to 62, but should have deep frost at MS-63 or better, particularly in the lower-relief areas. At MS-65 or better, it should be full and rich. Sometimes, to compensate for flat striking, certified coins with virtually flawless luster in the fields, evocative of an MS-65 or 66 grade, are called MS-63 or a lower grade. Such coins would seem to offer a lot of value for the money, if the variety is one that is not found with Full Details (1923-S is one of many examples).

Reverse: Striking is usually better, permitting observation of luster in all areas except the eagle's body, which may be lightly struck. Luster may be dull or lifeless at MS-60 to 62, but should have deep frost at MS-63 or better, particularly in the lower-relief areas. At MS-65 or better, it should be full and rich.

1921-S. Graded AU-50.

AU-50, 53, 55, 58 (About Uncirculated)

Obverse: Light wear is seen on the higher-relief areas of Miss Liberty, the vertical area from her head down to the date. At AU-58, the luster in the field is extensive, but is interrupted by friction and light wear. At AU-50 and 53, luster is less.

Reverse: Wear is most evident on the eagle's breast immediately under the neck feathers, the left leg, and the top of the left wing. Luster is nearly complete at AU-58, but at AU-50 half or more is gone.

1919-S. Graded EF-40.

EF-40, 45 (Extremely Fine)

Obverse: Wear is more extensive, with the higher parts of Miss Liberty now without detail, and with no skirt lines visible directly over her left leg. Little or no luster is seen.

Reverse: The eagle shows more wear overall, with the highest parts of the body and left leg worn flat.

1921-S. Graded VF-20.

VF-20, 30 (Very Fine)

Obverse: Wear is more extensive, and Miss Liberty is worn mostly flat in the line from her head to her left foot. Her skirt is worn, but most lines are seen, except over the leg and to the left and right. The lower part of her cape (to the left of her waist) is worn.

Reverse: The eagle is worn smooth from the head to the left leg, and the right leg is flat at the top. Most feathers in the wings are delineated, but weak.

1918-S. Graded F-12.

F-12, 15 (Fine)

Obverse: Wear is more extensive, now with only a few light lines visible in the skirt. The rays of the sun are weak below the cape, and may be worn away at their tips.
Reverse: Wear is more extensive, with most details now gone on the eagle's right leg. Delineation of the feathers is less, and most in the upper area and right edge of the left wing are blended together.

1921-D. Graded VG-8.

VG-8, 10 (Very Good)

Obverse: Wear is slightly more extensive, but the rim still is defined all around. The tops of the date numerals are worn and blend slightly into the ground above.

Reverse: Wear is more extensive. On the left wing only a few feathers are delineated, and on the shoulder of the right wing most detail is gone. Detail in the pine branch is lost and it appears as a clump.

1917-S, Obverse Mintmark. Graded G-4.

G-4, 6 (Good)
Obverse: Miss Liberty is worn flat, with her head, neck, and arms all blended together. Folds can be seen at the bottom of the skirt, but the lines are worn away. The rim is worn done into the tops of some of the letters.
Reverse: All areas show more wear. The rim is worn down into the tops of some of the letters, particularly at the top border.

1918. Graded AG-3.

AG-3 (About Good)
Obverse: Wear is more extensive. The sun's rays are nearly all gone, the motto is very light and sometimes incomplete, and the rim is worn down into more of the letters.
Reverse: Wear is more extensive, with the eagle essentially worn flat. The rim is worn down into more of the letters.

1939. Graded PF-65.

PF-60 to 70 (Proof)
Obverse and Reverse: Proofs that are extensively cleaned and have many hairlines, or that are dull and grainy, are lower level, such as PF-60 to 62. These are not widely desired, and represent coins that have been mistreated. With medium hairlines and good reflectivity, assigned grades of PF-63 or 64 are appropriate. Tiny horizontal lines on Miss Liberty's leg, known as slide marks, from National and other album slides scuffing the relief of the cheek, are common; coins with such marks should not be graded higher than PF-64, but sometimes are. With relatively few hairlines and no noticeable slide marks, a rating of PF-65 can be given. PF-66 should have hairlines so delicate that magnification is needed to see them. Above that, a Proof should be free of any hairlines or other problems.

Being a Smart Buyer

There are enough Liberty Walking half dollars in the marketplace that with very little effort the typical or casual collector can easily acquire a full set of dates and mintmarks of the later issues from 1933 to 1947 in MS-64 or MS-65 instantly or nearly so, given the Internet. Quality, however, would be a different matter entirely. Weak striking is endemic for 1940-S. Most other issues of 1933 and later are decently struck, but cherrypicking will yield really nice coins with Full Details, including on the head, the hand, and, on the reverse, the eagle.

Half dollars of the 1916 to 1929 years are often weakly struck or have other problems. It is not possible to build a high-quality collection in a short time—which, from the aspect of the spirit of the chase, is a positive. Cherrypicking comes to the fore if you want a first-class display.

If you are a connoisseur, start by reviewing only certified coins, such as from PCGS or NGC, the two leading professional third-party grading services. Slab labels are marked with grades; there are no notations made for sharpness. A certified MS-65 1916 will usually have Full Details while a certified MS-65 1923-S will be weak in several areas. Such aspects vary from year to year and mint to mint.

However, probably 95% of the buyers in the marketplace read only the label on the holder. Sometimes plus signs, stars, or other notations are added, but these do not signify sharp striking overall. You are on your own! Again, this is desirable—the thrill of the chase. When you do find one with Full Details it will cost no more! I hasten so say that some varieties do not exist with Full Details. As an example, I have never seen a 1923-S with such. In these instances, select the sharpest you can find.

Eye appeal is another consideration. A certified MS-65 half dollar can be dark, splotchy, or downright ugly, in which case you should avoid it. I would rather have a beautiful MS-63 coin than an unattractive MS-65.

Among Mint State coins look for pieces that have rich frosty mint luster and are brilliant or with light iridescent toning. Bear in mind that so-called coin doctors feel that "better coins can be made through chemistry," as I have mentioned for Mercury dimes and Standing Liberty quarters—most "rainbow" toning seen on Liberty Walking half dollars is artificial. Also note that "gradeflation" (a relaxation of strict grading standards) has resulted in many of yesteryear's MS-63 and 64 coins being certified 65 and 66 today.

While it is nice to collect early issues in Mint State, not everyone can afford this unless they specialize only in Liberty Walking halves and do not spend money on other series. If you like to cast a wider collecting net, cherrypick nice VF, EF, or AU coins with care, selecting only coins with nice eye appeal. Then you can afford to collect Mercury dimes, Standing Liberty quarters, and other series as well.

Take your time. All the coins that meet your particular requirements are in the marketplace, certain varieties that do not exist with Full Details excepted, but to find them may take a few weeks or months. Study each coin carefully before making a purchase decision.

Liberty Walking Half Dollars

1916 Liberty Walking Half Dollar

Circulation-strike
mintage:
608,000

Notes. Liberty Walking half dollars dated 1916 were released into circulation following the Treasury Department announcement of January 17, 1917. They slipped
into the channels of commerce without much notice being given to them in the
media. Many citizens in general and numismatists in particular saved them due to
their novelty.

Key to Collecting. Characteristics of striking—*Head:* Usually quite good with 80%
to 90% or more. *Left hand:* Usually quite good with 70% or more details. *Eagle's left
leg:* Usually with most feathers.

Overview: Half dollars of this year usually have particularly distinctive flat rims which frame the design elements nicely. The typical coin has fairly good details overall. Most Mint State coins have excellent eye appeal. Most have a satiny or matte finish rather than coruscating mint luster, a distinctive characteristic also seen on branch-mint coins as well. As the first year of the design these are in especially strong demand for inclusion in type sets.

Market Values • Circulation Strikes

G-4	VG-8	F-12	VF-20	EF-40	AU-50	AU-55
$50	$55	$90	$160	$225	$265	$290

MS-60	MS-62	MS-63	MS-64	MS-65	MS-66	
$350	$415	$550	$850	$1,850	$3,100	

Certified Populations

Fair	AG-2	G-4	VG-8	F-12	VF-20	EF-40	AU-50	MS-60
0	21	72	42	40	47	29	160	3

MS-61	MS-62	MS-63	MS-64	MS-65	MS-66	MS-67	MS-68	MS-69
36	176	262	335	152	63	9	1	0

1916-D Liberty Walking Half Dollar

Circulation-strike mintage:
1,014,400

Key to Collecting. Characteristics of striking—*Head:* Usually with 60% to 70% or more. *Left hand:* Usually with 60% or more details, although some have far less. *Eagle's left leg:* Usually with most feathers.

Overview: Half dollars of this year usually have particularly distinctive flat rims which frame the design elements nicely. The typical coin has fairly good details overall. Most Mint State coins have satiny matte fields and excellent eye appeal. The typical 1916-D is not as well struck as the Philadelphia coins of this year, but cherrypicking can yield one that is.

In May 1917 Henry Chapman advertised: "1916 half dollar. S and D mints, each $1.00." Chapman in Philadelphia and John Zug in Bowie, Maryland, were two of only a few dealers who maintained inventories of current coins.

See next page for chart.

Market Values • Circulation Strikes

G-4	VG-8	F-12	VF-20	EF-40	AU-50	AU-55
$50	$60	$85	$135	$215	$240	$275

MS-60	MS-62	MS-63	MS-64	MS-65	MS-66	
$360	$435	$600	$900	$2,200	$4,100	

Certified Populations

Fair	AG-2	G-4	VG-8	F-12	VF-20	EF-40	AU-50	MS-60
3	33	87	63	33	36	41	253	5

MS-61	MS-62	MS-63	MS-64	MS-65	MS-66	MS-67	MS-68	MS-69
70	233	222	357	179	38	9	0	0

1916-S Liberty Walking Half Dollar

Circulation-strike
mintage:
508,000

Key to Collecting. Characteristics of striking—*Head:* Usually with about 60% or more. *Left hand:* Usually with 60% or more details. *Eagle's left leg:* Usually with some feathers but not many.

    Overview: Half dollars of this year of all three mints usually have particularly distinctive flat rims which frame the design elements nicely. The typical coin has fairly good details overall, but not on a par with Philadelphia coins. Cherrypicking can yield an above-average example. Most Mint State coins have satiny matte fields and excellent eye appeal. This is the scarcest and most expensive of the three 1916 varieties.

Market Values • Circulation Strikes

G-4	VG-8	F-12	VF-20	EF-40	AU-50	AU-55
$120	$140	$275	$435	$650	$800	$925

MS-60	MS-62	MS-63	MS-64	MS-65	MS-66	
$1,200	$1,500	$2,100	$2,750	$5,800	$13,000	

Certified Populations

Fair	AG-2	G-4	VG-8	F-12	VF-20	EF-40	AU-50	MS-60
8	100	153	96	35	26	14	99	2

MS-61	MS-62	MS-63	MS-64	MS-65	MS-66	MS-67	MS-68	MS-69
25	77	89	132	58	13	1	0	0

1917 Liberty Walking Half Dollar

Circulation-strike mintage:
12,292,000

Key to Collecting. Characteristics of striking—*Head:* Usually with about 70% or more. *Left hand:* Usually with 80% or more details, among the best of the era. *Eagle's left leg:* Usually with most feathers.

Overview: 1917 half dollars made early in the year have flat rims that nicely frame the motifs and, if you're given a choice, are more desirable. Later coins, constituting most of the production, have rounded rims as also used on later coins through 1947. Most early coins have satiny or matte surfaces. Due to the high mintage, examples are easily found in the marketplace.

Market Values • Circulation Strikes

G-4	VG-8	F-12	VF-20	EF-40	AU-50	AU-55
$18	$19	$19.50	$21	$40	$70	$85

MS-60	MS-62	MS-63	MS-64	MS-65	MS-66
$150	$175	$210	$325	$900	$1,950

Certified Populations

Fair	AG-2	G-4	VG-8	F-12	VF-20	EF-40	AU-50	MS-60
0	2	3	1	2	12	12	303	2

MS-61	MS-62	MS-63	MS-64	MS-65	MS-66	MS-67	MS-68	MS-69
90	332	447	673	225	39	4	0	0

1917-D Obverse Mintmark Liberty Walking Half Dollar

Circulation-strike
mintage:
765,400

Key to Collecting. Characteristics of striking—*Head:* Usually with about 70% or more. *Left hand:* Usually with 60% or more details; sharpness of this feature can vary widely. *Eagle's left leg:* Usually with perhaps half of the feathers visible but satisfactory.

Overview: Many but not all have flat rims and matte or satiny surfaces. The typical Mint State coin has excellent eye appeal. Cherrypicking for sharpness of details will be rewarding.

Market Values • Circulation Strikes

G-4	VG-8	F-12	VF-20	EF-40	AU-50	AU-55
$25	$35	$80	$150	$240	$325	$425

MS-60	MS-62	MS-63	MS-64	MS-65	MS-66
$600	$875	$1,300	$2,200	$7,500	$17,500

Certified Populations

Fair	AG-2	G-4	VG-8	F-12	VF-20	EF-40	AU-50	MS-60
1	5	33	38	25	25	31	204	2

MS-61	MS-62	MS-63	MS-64	MS-65	MS-66	MS-67	MS-68	MS-69
59	150	150	165	53	4	0	0	0

1917-D Reverse Mintmark Liberty Walking Half Dollar

Circulation-strike mintage:
1,940,000

Key to Collecting. Characteristics of striking—*Head:* Usually with about 70% or more. *Left hand:* Usually with 70% or more details. *Eagle's left leg:* Usually with most of the feathers visible.

Overview: Most coins are quite well struck, although there are exceptions. Finding an attractive example will be easy enough to do.

Market Values • Circulation Strikes

G-4	VG-8	F-12	VF-20	EF-40	AU-50	AU-55
$18	$19	$45	$145	$280	$515	$600

MS-60	MS-62	MS-63	MS-64	MS-65	MS-66	
$950	$1,500	$2,200	$3,450	$16,000	$29,000	

Certified Populations

Fair	AG-2	G-4	VG-8	F-12	VF-20	EF-40	AU-50	MS-60
0	1	8	16	8	33	47	160	0

MS-61	MS-62	MS-63	MS-64	MS-65	MS-66	MS-67	MS-68	MS-69
26	62	73	105	25	3	1	0	0

1917-S Obverse Mintmark Liberty Walking Half Dollar

Circulation-strike
mintage:
952,000

Key to Collecting. Characteristics of striking—*Head:* Usually with about 70% or more. *Left hand:* Usually with 60% or more details. *Eagle's left leg:* Usually with most of the feathers present.

Overview: This is one of the key issues in Mint State among early Liberty Walking half dollars. High-grade examples are hard to find in the marketplace for this reason (already being secured in collections), and when located are expensive. Many but not all have flat rims and matte or satiny surfaces. The typical Mint State coin has excellent eye appeal. Cherrypicking for sharpness of details will be rewarding. In the 1950s and early 1960s, when Liberty Walking half dollars were still in circulation, the hardest early issues to find were the 1917-S with mintmark on obverse and the three varieties of 1921.

Market Values • Circulation Strikes

G-4	VG-8	F-12	VF-20	EF-40	AU-50	AU-55
$27	$50	$140	$375	$750	$1,300	$1,500

MS-60	MS-62	MS-63	MS-64	MS-65	MS-66	
$2,350	$3,500	$4,750	$6,200	$18,000	$33,000	

Certified Populations

Fair	AG-2	G-4	VG-8	F-12	VF-20	EF-40	AU-50	MS-60
0	11	29	44	36	44	33	98	1

MS-61	MS-62	MS-63	MS-64	MS-65	MS-66	MS-67	MS-68	MS-69
11	46	44	97	30	3	0	0	0

1917-S Reverse Mintmark
Liberty Walking Half Dollar

Circulation-strike
mintage:
5,554,000

Key to Collecting. Characteristics of striking—*Head:* Usually with about 70% or more. *Left hand:* Usually with 50% or more details; sharpness of this feature can vary widely, and there are some that are poorly struck at the center. *Eagle's left leg:* Usually with fewer than half of the feathers visible.

Overview: Striking quality varies from quite good to miserable. As certified holders make no mention of this, cherrypicking will pay rewards at no extra cost.

On June 15, 1917, I. Leland Steinman of San Francisco sent this letter to *The Numismatist:* "A bit of numismatic news which I think would be of value to readers has recently come to my attention. Beginning this month the San Francisco Mint has changed the position of the S on the half dollar from the obverse to the reverse. As it stood formerly the S appeared under the date. Now it appears to the left of the eagle on the reverse and under the cactus branch which the talons of the bird are clutching."

With possibly effaced mintmark S on obverse: Lot 2144 in the Louis E. Eliasberg Collection, Bowers and Merena Galleries, 1997, was described as follows: "1917-S Mintmark on Reverse. MS-64/65. Possibly struck from a Mint-altered 1917-S Mintmark on Obverse die!...Quite possibly a major new discovery, a 1917-S mintmark on *obverse* die altered by removing the S, so it could be combined with an S-mintmark reverse and create coins with just one (instead of two) mintmarks. Under high-powered magnification the obverse of this piece is very unusual. There are many *raised* die lines under the line WE TRUST, which is in stark contrast to most of the rest of the surface of the die which seems to have been somewhat polished. The countless raised lines in that area of the coin indicate that the die was scraped and tooled. These lines are not parallel to each other, although they are oriented more or less in the same direction, although some are in random directions and some others take the form of cross-hatching. This suggests a hypothetical scenario which, if accurate, would position the present piece as being of absolutely extraordinary importance."

See next page for chart.

Market Values • Circulation Strikes

G-4	VG-8	F-12	VF-20	EF-40	AU-50	AU-55
$18	$19	$20	$35	$70	$170	$250

MS-60	MS-62	MS-63	MS-64	MS-65	MS-66
$425	$1,175	$2,000	$3,000	$14,000	$30,000

Certified Populations

Fair	AG-2	G-4	VG-8	F-12	VF-20	EF-40	AU-50	MS-60
0	1	12	5	9	19	25	192	2

MS-61	MS-62	MS-63	MS-64	MS-65	MS-66	MS-67	MS-68	MS-69
47	150	113	295	25	3	2	0	0

1918 Liberty Walking Half Dollar

Circulation-strike
mintage:
6,634,000

Key to Collecting. Characteristics of striking—*Head:* Usually with about 80% or more details. *Left hand:* Usually with 70% or more details, although some are flat strikes. *Eagle's left leg:* Usually with most feathers.

Overview: The sharpness of most examples is excellent. Finding one with a nice strike and good eye appeal will not be much of a challenge.

Market Values • Circulation Strikes

G-4	VG-8	F-12	VF-20	EF-40	AU-50	AU-55
$18	$19	$20	$65	$155	$265	$325

MS-60	MS-62	MS-63	MS-64	MS-65	MS-66
$625	$775	$975	$1,300	$3,400	$9,000

Certified Populations

Fair	AG-2	G-4	VG-8	F-12	VF-20	EF-40	AU-50	MS-60
0	1	0	5	3	33	42	153	0

MS-61	MS-62	MS-63	MS-64	MS-65	MS-66	MS-67	MS-68	MS-69
44	78	88	223	102	7	0	0	0

1918-D Liberty Walking Half Dollar

Circulation-strike
mintage:
3,853,040

Key to Collecting. Characteristics of striking—*Head:* Occasionally with at least 80% details, but most are far below this standard. *Left hand:* Sometimes with 70% or more details, although some are flat strikes. *Eagle's left leg:* Usually with most feathers.

Overview: Sharpness varies from quite good and with rich luster, on a par with the Philadelphia Mint coins, to unsatisfactory. Cherrypicking is the order of the day.

Walter Breen's Complete Encyclopedia of U.S. and Colonial Coins, 1988, includes this: "Without AW monogram. Presently Ex. rare, 4–6 known? Varying degrees of weak AW monograms exist throughout the series, due to die preparation, not the striking of the coins. At this time the only AW variations of general interest to collectors are the 1941 Proof without the monogram and the 1944-D with hand-engraved monogram."

Market Values • Circulation Strikes

G-4	VG-8	F-12	VF-20	EF-40	AU-50	AU-55
$18	$19	$38	$100	$250	$475	$750

MS-60	MS-62	MS-63	MS-64	MS-65	MS-66	
$1,300	$1,950	$3,150	$5,200	$21,500	$40,000	

Certified Populations

Fair	AG-2	G-4	VG-8	F-12	VF-20	EF-40	AU-50	MS-60
0	1	2	13	23	56	37	149	4

MS-61	MS-62	MS-63	MS-64	MS-65	MS-66	MS-67	MS-68	MS-69
30	76	90	263	12	2	0	0	0

1918-S Liberty Walking Half Dollar

Circulation-strike
mintage:
10,282,000

Key to Collecting. Characteristics of striking—*Head:* Usually with about 70% or more details. *Left hand:* Usually with 70% or more details, although some are flat strikes. *Eagle's left leg:* Usually with about half of the feathers.

Overview: Sharpness varies more than is the case for the coins of the other two mints. Finding one with a nice strike and good eye appeal will take time, but is doable.

Market Values • Circulation Strikes

G-4	VG-8	F-12	VF-20	EF-40	AU-50	AU-55
$18	$19	$20	$35	$80	$200	$310

MS-60	MS-62	MS-63	MS-64	MS-65	MS-66
$525	$1,225	$2,100	$3,200	$16,000	$45,000

Certified Populations

Fair	AG-2	G-4	VG-8	F-12	VF-20	EF-40	AU-50	MS-60
0	3	5	8	11	27	38	194	5

MS-61	MS-62	MS-63	MS-64	MS-65	MS-66	MS-67	MS-68	MS-69
42	120	134	257	33	4	0	0	0

1919 Liberty Walking Half Dollar

Circulation-strike
mintage:
962,000

Key to Collecting. Characteristics of striking—*Head:* Usually with about 70% or more details. *Left hand:* Usually with 70% or more details, although some are flat strikes. *Eagle's left leg:* Usually with most feathers, but others have few.

    Overview: Most Mint State 1919 half dollars are fairly sharp and have good luster, but a percentage are weak in areas. Once again, cherrypicking will pay dividends.

Market Values • Circulation Strikes

G-4	VG-8	F-12	VF-20	EF-40	AU-50	AU-55
$25	$32	$78	$265	$515	$825	$1,035

MS-60	MS-62	MS-63	MS-64	MS-65	MS-66
$1,350	$2,550	$3,500	$4,200	$6,800	$10,000

Certified Populations

Fair	AG-2	G-4	VG-8	F-12	VF-20	EF-40	AU-50	MS-60
0	3	15	37	53	70	35	75	1

MS-61	MS-62	MS-63	MS-64	MS-65	MS-66	MS-67	MS-68	MS-69
12	39	58	97	32	12	0	0	0

1919-D Liberty Walking Half Dollar

Circulation-strike mintage:
1,165,000

Key to Collecting. Characteristics of striking—*Head:* Usually with 50% or fewer details. *Left hand:* Usually with 50% or fewer details. *Eagle's left leg:* Usually weak and with few feathers.

    Overview: From the standpoint of sharpness the 1919-D is the most unsatisfactory up to that date. Finding a coin with sharper details can be done, but don't expect 80% or more details. Cherrypicking is recommended to avoid a flat strike. The plus part of the equation is that a nicer coin will cost no more, as the certification services take no note of sharpness or lack thereof.

See next page for chart.

Market Values • Circulation Strikes

G-4	VG-8	F-12	VF-20	EF-40	AU-50	AU-55
$26	$40	$115	$345	$825	$1,675	$2,750

MS-60	MS-62	MS-63	MS-64	MS-65	MS-66	
$5,900	$9,000	$17,500	$27,000	$115,000	$265,000	

Certified Populations

Fair	AG-2	G-4	VG-8	F-12	VF-20	EF-40	AU-50	MS-60
0	5	26	60	56	70	38	97	2

MS-61	MS-62	MS-63	MS-64	MS-65	MS-66	MS-67	MS-68	MS-69
32	106	57	82	4	0	0	0	0

1919-S Liberty Walking Half Dollar

Circulation-strike
mintage:
1,552,000

Key to Collecting. Characteristics of striking—*Head:* Usually with about 70% or more details. *Left hand:* Usually with 50% or more details, although some are flat strikes. *Eagle's left leg:* Usually with up to half of the feathers.

Overview: In Mint State the 1919-S is considered to be the key to the series, the most expensive. Sharpness varies all over the place. Luster is usually fairly good. Cherrypicking will pay dividends once again.

In the 1950s Arthur M. Kagin said he was offered a bag of Mint State 1919-S half dollars. I endeavored to follow up on this afterward, but nothing more was learned, and no unusual quantity appeared on the market.

Market Values • Circulation Strikes

G-4	VG-8	F-12	VF-20	EF-40	AU-50	AU-55
$20	$30	$85	$275	$815	$1,600	$2,250

MS-60	MS-62	MS-63	MS-64	MS-65	MS-66	
$3,250	$5,500	$8,750	$11,000	$18,000	$26,000	

Certified Populations

Fair	AG-2	G-4	VG-8	F-12	VF-20	EF-40	AU-50	MS-60
0	5	9	40	46	79	59	80	0

MS-61	MS-62	MS-63	MS-64	MS-65	MS-66	MS-67	MS-68	MS-69
8	23	32	66	21	9	1	0	0

1920 Liberty Walking Half Dollar

Circulation-strike
mintage:
6,372,000

Key to Collecting. Characteristics of striking—*Head:* Usually with about 50% or more details. *Left hand:* Usually with 60% or more details, although some are flat strikes. *Eagle's left leg:* Usually with about half or more of the feathers.

Overview: Striking varies from fairly good, in the minority, to average or flat. This is an era in which the quality of Liberty Walking half dollars can vary widely. Cherrypicking for eye appeal and strong strike is recommended and will yield good results. The secret is that you will have little competition in such a search as most people are satisfied with the labels on holders and go no further.

Market Values • Circulation Strikes

G-4	VG-8	F-12	VF-20	EF-40	AU-50	AU-55
$18	$19	$20	$45	$80	$160	$225

MS-60	MS-62	MS-63	MS-64	MS-65	MS-66
$325	$525	$700	$1,200	$4,400	$11,500

Certified Populations

Fair	AG-2	G-4	VG-8	F-12	VF-20	EF-40	AU-50	MS-60
0	0	4	4	5	17	18	147	5

MS-61	MS-62	MS-63	MS-64	MS-65	MS-66	MS-67	MS-68	MS-69
39	109	158	278	40	5	0	0	0

1920-D Liberty Walking Half Dollar

Circulation-strike
mintage:
1,551,000

Key to Collecting. Characteristics of striking—*Head:* Usually with about 70% or more details. *Left hand:* Usually with 70% or more details, although some are flat strikes. *Eagle's left leg:* Usually with about half or more of the feathers.

Overview: Most 1920-D half dollars are quite well struck, a great contrast to the Philadelphia coins of this year. There are some flat strikes, so examine any offerings very carefully.

Market Values • Circulation Strikes

G-4	VG-8	F-12	VF-20	EF-40	AU-50	AU-55
$18	$20	$75	$250	$450	$925	$1,100

MS-60	MS-62	MS-63	MS-64	MS-65	MS-66	
$1,550	$3,150	$3,850	$6,150	$16,500	$27,500	

Certified Populations

Fair	AG-2	G-4	VG-8	F-12	VF-20	EF-40	AU-50	MS-60
0	1	9	16	39	51	27	35	0

MS-61	MS-62	MS-63	MS-64	MS-65	MS-66	MS-67	MS-68	MS-69
7	26	29	102	16	1	0	0	0

1920-S Liberty Walking Half Dollar

Circulation-strike
mintage:
4,624,000

Key to Collecting. Characteristics of striking—*Head:* Usually with about 50% or more details. *Left hand:* Usually with 60% or more details, although some are flat strikes. *Eagle's left leg:* Usually with about half or more of the feathers.

Overview: The narrative for the 1920 Philadelphia half dollar fits well with the 1920-S as well. The usually seen coin is weakly struck in the key areas. Cherrypicking for an above-average example is recommended, but the best you can find will only have partial details in the key areas.

Market Values • Circulation Strikes

G-4	VG-8	F-12	VF-20	EF-40	AU-50	AU-55
$18	$18.50	$23	$90	$230	$475	$675

MS-60	MS-62	MS-63	MS-64	MS-65	MS-66	
$875	$2,100	$3,000	$4,150	$13,750	$26,500	

Certified Populations

Fair	AG-2	G-4	VG-8	F-12	VF-20	EF-40	AU-50	MS-60
0	2	3	7	18	57	31	107	0

MS-61	MS-62	MS-63	MS-64	MS-65	MS-66	MS-67	MS-68	MS-69
18	45	49	104	39	10	1	0	0

1921 Liberty Walking Half Dollar

Circulation-strike mintage:
246,000

Key to Collecting. Characteristics of striking—*Head:* Usually with about 60% to 70% or more details. *Left hand:* Usually with 70% or more details, although some are flat strikes. *Eagle's left leg:* Usually with most of the feathers.

Overview: Most Mint State 1921 half dollars are fairly well struck and have good luster. There are many with weakness, and these should be avoided. The low mintage figure of this and the other half dollars of 1921 have made them the focal point of interest for many years.

See next page for chart.

Market Values • Circulation Strikes

G-4	VG-8	F-12	VF-20	EF-40	AU-50	AU-55
$175	$220	$350	$775	$1,700	$2,750	$3,150

MS-60	MS-62	MS-63	MS-64	MS-65	MS-66
$5,000	$7,000	$7,750	$10,000	$20,000	$32,500

Certified Populations

Fair	AG-2	G-4	VG-8	F-12	VF-20	EF-40	AU-50	MS-60
9	92	314	249	101	72	41	43	1

MS-61	MS-62	MS-63	MS-64	MS-65	MS-66	MS-67	MS-68	MS-69
8	26	42	78	35	2	0	0	0

1921-D Liberty Walking Half Dollar

Circulation-strike
mintage:
208,000

Notes. The 1921-D has the lowest mintage figure of any Liberty Walking half dollar.

Key to Collecting. Characteristics of striking—*Head:* Usually with about 60% or more details. *Left hand:* Usually with 60% or more details, although some are flat strikes. *Eagle's left leg:* Usually with about half of the feathers.

Overview: Most Mint State 1921-D half dollars are quite well struck, but cherrypicking will result in finding examples with better head, hand, and feather definition. The low mintage figure has made the 1921-D endlessly popular and in demand.

Market Values • Circulation Strikes

G-4	VG-8	F-12	VF-20	EF-40	AU-50	AU-55
$325	$375	$525	$850	$2,300	$3,300	$3,850

MS-60	MS-62	MS-63	MS-64	MS-65	MS-66
$5,500	$8,750	$13,000	$14,500	$24,000	$39,500

Certified Populations

Fair	AG-2	G-4	VG-8	F-12	VF-20	EF-40	AU-50	MS-60
13	83	403	340	135	70	34	43	2

MS-61	MS-62	MS-63	MS-64	MS-65	MS-66	MS-67	MS-68	MS-69
16	22	38	79	18	3	0	0	0

1921-S Liberty Walking Half Dollar

Circulation-strike
mintage:
548,000

Key to Collecting. Characteristics of striking—*Head:* Usually with about 60% or more details. *Left hand:* Usually with 60% or more details, although some are flat strikes. *Eagle's left leg:* Usually weak with few feathers visible.

Overview: More so than for the other two varieties of this year the 1921-S invites cherrypicking and connoisseurship. The striking can vary widely, and with some searching examples with better head and hand features can be found. The feathers are only partial on even the best strikes seen. Traditionally the 1921-S was considered to be the rarest and most valuable variety in the series, but in later years the 1919-S has taken over that position due to published population reports.

Market Values • Circulation Strikes

G-4	VG-8	F-12	VF-20	EF-40	AU-50	AU-55
$48	$80	$250	$800	$4,500	$8,300	$10,000

MS-60	MS-62	MS-63	MS-64	MS-65	MS-66	
$14,750	$22,500	$28,500	$41,000	$100,000	$200,000	

Certified Populations

Fair	AG-2	G-4	VG-8	F-12	VF-20	EF-40	AU-50	MS-60
1	28	149	255	228	196	54	42	0

MS-61	MS-62	MS-63	MS-64	MS-65	MS-66	MS-67	MS-68	MS-69
4	4	15	56	19	1	0	0	0

1923-S Liberty Walking Half Dollar

Circulation-strike
mintage:
2,178,000

Key to Collecting. Characteristics of striking—*Head:* Usually with about 50% or more details, although many are below that level. *Left hand:* Usually with 40% or fewer details, flat on some. *Eagle's left leg:* The feathers are mostly absent, and weakness is usually seen at the eagle's shoulder as well.

Overview: Half dollars of this date and mint are usually poorly struck. Finding one that is better than average will be a challenge, but none with excellent details on both sides has ever been reported.

Market Values • Circulation Strikes

G-4	VG-8	F-12	VF-20	EF-40	AU-50	AU-55
$13	$15	$30	$110	$365	$800	$1,050
MS-60	MS-62	MS-63	MS-64	MS-65	MS-66	
$1,500	$2,600	$3,700	$4,500	$14,500	$29,000	

Certified Populations

Fair	AG-2	G-4	VG-8	F-12	VF-20	EF-40	AU-50	MS-60
0	1	3	13	23	53	30	79	2
MS-61	MS-62	MS-63	MS-64	MS-65	MS-66	MS-67	MS-68	MS-69
19	34	54	80	26	4	1	0	0

1927-S Liberty Walking Half Dollar

Circulation-strike
mintage:
2,392,000

Key to Collecting. Characteristics of striking—*Head:* Usually with about 50% or more details. *Left hand:* Usually with 40% or more details, although some are completely flat strikes. *Eagle's left leg:* Usually flat with few feathers.

Overview: Striking quality varies widely with this issue. Accordingly, cherrypicking for quality will pay dividends at no extra cost.

Market Values • Circulation Strikes

G-4	VG-8	F-12	VF-20	EF-40	AU-50	AU-55
$13	$15	$18	$50	$160	$400	$575
MS-60	**MS-62**	**MS-63**	**MS-64**	**MS-65**	**MS-66**	
$950	$1,500	$2,050	$3,400	$9,000	$23,000	

Certified Populations

Fair	AG-2	G-4	VG-8	F-12	VF-20	EF-40	AU-50	MS-60
0	0	3	2	12	34	36	83	1
MS-61	**MS-62**	**MS-63**	**MS-64**	**MS-65**	**MS-66**	**MS-67**	**MS-68**	**MS-69**
15	50	132	211	40	0	0	0	0

1928-S Liberty Walking Half Dollar

Circulation-strike mintage:
1,940,000

Key to Collecting. Characteristics of striking—*Head:* Usually with about 60% or more details. *Left hand:* Usually with 50% or more details, although some are flat strikes. *Eagle's left leg:* Usually flat with few feathers.

Overview: Striking varies from weak to fairly good. Try to find one with most of the head and hand details visible. No overall sharp strike has been seen.

See next page for chart.

Market Values • Circulation Strikes

G-4	VG-8	F-12	VF-20	EF-40	AU-50	AU-55
$13	$15	$19	$75	$180	$435	$575

MS-60	MS-62	MS-63	MS-64	MS-65	MS-66
$950	$1,575	$2,750	$4,000	$8,250	$22,500

Certified Populations

Fair	AG-2	G-4	VG-8	F-12	VF-20	EF-40	AU-50	MS-60
1	1	1	3	20	34	22	87	0

MS-61	MS-62	MS-63	MS-64	MS-65	MS-66	MS-67	MS-68	MS-69
17	42	59	166	39	4	0	0	0

1929-D Liberty Walking Half Dollar

Circulation-strike
mintage:
1,001,200

Key to Collecting. Characteristics of striking—*Head:* Usually with about 60% or more details. *Left hand:* Usually with 50% or more details, although some are flat strikes. *Eagle's left leg:* Usually with about half or more of the feathers.

Overview: Most 1929-D half dollars are fairly well struck, but some are sharper than others. Eye appeal and mint luster are usually quite good.

1929-D half dollars were available at face value plus postage from the Treasury Department at a later time, per a notice received by the American Numismatic Association on April 23, 1932.

Market Values • Circulation Strikes

G-4	VG-8	F-12	VF-20	EF-40	AU-50	AU-55
$13	$15	$18	$30	$100	$190	$260

MS-60	MS-62	MS-63	MS-64	MS-65	MS-66
$385	$575	$750	$1,175	$2,700	$4,500

Certified Populations

Fair	AG-2	G-4	VG-8	F-12	VF-20	EF-40	AU-50	MS-60
0	0	0	3	3	37	46	224	2

MS-61	MS-62	MS-63	MS-64	MS-65	MS-66	MS-67	MS-68	MS-69
29	86	121	200	86	15	0	0	0

1929-S Liberty Walking Half Dollar

Circulation-strike
mintage:
1,902,000

Key to Collecting. Characteristics of striking—*Head:* Usually with about 60% or more details. *Left hand:* Usually with 60% or more details, although some are flat strikes. *Eagle's left leg:* Usually with about half of the feathers.

Overview: The quality of strike varies widely on this issue. Some are almost flat in head and hand details. Many fairly good strikes exist, so it will not be difficult to find a far-above-average example.

1929-S half dollars were available at face value plus postage from the Treasury Department at a later time, according to a notice received by the American Numismatic Association on April 23, 1932.

Market Values • Circulation Strikes

G-4	VG-8	F-12	VF-20	EF-40	AU-50	AU-55
$13	$15	$18	$35	$115	$230	$280

MS-60	MS-62	MS-63	MS-64	MS-65	MS-66
$410	$690	$900	$1,350	$2,850	$4,800

Certified Populations

Fair	AG-2	G-4	VG-8	F-12	VF-20	EF-40	AU-50	MS-60
0	0	3	8	10	32	42	136	2

MS-61	MS-62	MS-63	MS-64	MS-65	MS-66	MS-67	MS-68	MS-69
13	56	93	214	134	32	4	0	0

1933-S Liberty Walking Half Dollar

Circulation-strike
mintage:
1,786,000

Key to Collecting. Characteristics of striking—*Head:* Usually with about 70% or more details. *Left hand:* Usually with 60% or more details. *Eagle's left leg:* Usually with about half of the feathers.

Overview: Most Mint State 1933-S half dollars are nicely struck and have excellent luster and eye appeal. This issue begins the later range of Liberty Walking half dollars for which all dates and mintmarks are readily available in the marketplace, although those of the 1940s are much more plentiful than are those of the mid-1930s.

Market Values • Circulation Strikes

G-4	VG-8	F-12	VF-20	EF-40	AU-50	AU-55
$13	$15	$18	$20	$60	$240	$440

MS-60	MS-62	MS-63	MS-64	MS-65	MS-66	
$635	$875	$1,200	$1,400	$3,200	$4,400	

Certified Populations

Fair	AG-2	G-4	VG-8	F-12	VF-20	EF-40	AU-50	MS-60
0	0	1	2	12	38	60	265	1

MS-61	MS-62	MS-63	MS-64	MS-65	MS-66	MS-67	MS-68	MS-69
32	97	92	148	113	82	5	0	0

1934 Liberty Walking Half Dollar

Circulation-strike
mintage:
6,964,000

Key to Collecting. Characteristics of striking—*Head:* Usually with about 70% or more details. *Left hand:* Usually with 70% or more details. *Eagle's left leg:* Usually with most of the feathers

   Overview: These are readily available with good strike and excellent eye appeal.

Market Values • Circulation Strikes

G-4	VG-8	F-12	VF-20	EF-40	AU-50	AU-55
$13	$15	$16	$17.50	$19	$26	$50

MS-60	MS-62	MS-63	MS-64	MS-65	MS-66	
$75	$90	$110	$130	$400	$515	

Certified Populations

Fair	AG-2	G-4	VG-8	F-12	VF-20	EF-40	AU-50	MS-60
0	0	1	1	0	2	7	213	1

MS-61	MS-62	MS-63	MS-64	MS-65	MS-66	MS-67	MS-68	MS-69
38	165	313	692	589	282	97	9	0

1934-D Liberty Walking Half Dollar

Circulation-strike
mintage:
2,361,000

See next page for chart.

Key to Collecting. Characteristics of striking—*Head:* Usually with about 60% or more details. *Left hand:* Usually with 70% or more details. *Eagle's left leg:* Usually with most of the feathers.

Overview: These are readily available with good strike and excellent eye appeal.

Market Values • Circulation Strikes

G-4	VG-8	F-12	VF-20	EF-40	AU-50	AU-55
$13	$15	$18	$20	$35	$85	$110

MS-60	MS-62	MS-63	MS-64	MS-65	MS-66
$150	$180	$235	$350	$1,400	$2,050

Certified Populations

Fair	AG-2	G-4	VG-8	F-12	VF-20	EF-40	AU-50	MS-60
0	0	0	1	2	1	14	133	0

MS-61	MS-62	MS-63	MS-64	MS-65	MS-66	MS-67	MS-68	MS-69
26	121	238	567	208	32	1	0	0

1934-S Liberty Walking Half Dollar

Circulation-strike mintage:
3,652,000

Key to Collecting. Characteristics of striking—*Head:* Usually with about 70% or more details. *Left hand:* Usually with 70% or more details. *Eagle's left leg:* Usually with about half of the feathers.

Overview: Most examples of 1934-S are fairly well struck and are lustrous. Avoid those that are weak, most noticeable on the head and hand.

Market Values • Circulation Strikes

G-4	VG-8	F-12	VF-20	EF-40	AU-50	AU-55
$13	$15	$16	$17.50	$30	$90	$200

MS-60	MS-62	MS-63	MS-64	MS-65	MS-66
$325	$525	$800	$1,150	$3,700	$4,950

Certified Populations

Fair	AG-2	G-4	VG-8	F-12	VF-20	EF-40	AU-50	MS-60
0	0	1	2	1	10	21	201	0

MS-61	MS-62	MS-63	MS-64	MS-65	MS-66	MS-67	MS-68	MS-69
26	82	109	256	119	43	6	0	0

1935 Liberty Walking Half Dollar

Circulation-strike
mintage:
9,162,000

Key to Collecting. Characteristics of striking—*Head:* Usually with about 60% or more details. *Left hand:* Usually with 60% or more details. *Eagle's left leg:* Usually with about half of the feathers.

Overview: The strike varies, but there enough coins in the marketplace that a fairly sharp example can be found. A few have almost complete head details.

Market Values • Circulation Strikes

G-4	VG-8	F-12	VF-20	EF-40	AU-50	AU-55
$13	$15	$16	$17.50	$19	$25	$35

MS-60	MS-62	MS-63	MS-64	MS-65	MS-66	
$45	$60	$80	$95	$260	$450	

Certified Populations

Fair	AG-2	G-4	VG-8	F-12	VF-20	EF-40	AU-50	MS-60
0	1	0	1	0	6	8	150	1

MS-61	MS-62	MS-63	MS-64	MS-65	MS-66	MS-67	MS-68	MS-69
24	148	298	823	692	226	32	0	0

1935-D Liberty Walking Half Dollar

Circulation-strike
mintage:
3,003,800

See next page for chart.

229

Key to Collecting. Characteristics of striking—*Head:* Usually with about 50% or more details. *Left hand:* Usually with 50% or more details. *Eagle's left leg:* Usually flat.

Overview: Weak strikes are the rule for 1934-D. There are exceptions in the marketplace, and it will take some searching to find them. The good news is that you will not have much competition, for the label on a holder satisfies most buyers.

Market Values • Circulation Strikes

G-4	VG-8	F-12	VF-20	EF-40	AU-50	AU-55
$13	$15	$16	$17.50	$30	$65	$100

MS-60	MS-62	MS-63	MS-64	MS-65	MS-66
$140	$200	$300	$475	$2,000	$4,050

Certified Populations

Fair	AG-2	G-4	VG-8	F-12	VF-20	EF-40	AU-50	MS-60
0	0	0	1	1	5	8	105	2

MS-61	MS-62	MS-63	MS-64	MS-65	MS-66	MS-67	MS-68	MS-69
16	98	137	456	153	6	0	0	0

1935-S Liberty Walking Half Dollar

Circulation-strike
mintage:
3,854,000

Key to Collecting. Characteristics of striking—*Head:* Usually with about 60% or more details. *Left hand:* Usually with 60% or more details. *Eagle's left leg:* Usually with about half of the feathers.

Overview: Striking varies but on average is quite good.

Market Values • Circulation Strikes

G-4	VG-8	F-12	VF-20	EF-40	AU-50	AU-55
$13	$15	$16	$17.50	$26	$95	$170

MS-60	MS-62	MS-63	MS-64	MS-65	MS-66
$250	$350	$465	$650	$2,800	$3,450

Certified Populations

Fair	AG-2	G-4	VG-8	F-12	VF-20	EF-40	AU-50	MS-60
0	0	0	2	1	10	14	106	2

MS-61	MS-62	MS-63	MS-64	MS-65	MS-66	MS-67	MS-68	MS-69
12	61	111	319	176	47	3	0	0

1936 Liberty Walking Half Dollar

Circulation Strike

Circulation-strike mintage:
12,614,000

Proof mintage:
3,901

Proof

Key to Collecting. Characteristics of striking—*Head:* Usually with about 60% or more details. *Left hand:* Usually with 60% or more details. *Eagle's left leg:* Most feathers are usually present.

Overview: Striking varies, but most are fairly sharp.

Proofs. Well struck. Some of the earlier strikes are less mirrorlike. This is the rarest of the Proofs. Availability is proportional to the quantity made.

Market Values • Circulation Strikes and Proof Strikes

G-4	VG-8	F-12	VF-20	EF-40	AU-50	AU-55	MS-60	MS-62
$13	$15	$16	$17.50	$18	$25	$35	$45	$55

MS-63	MS-64	MS-65	MS-66	PF-64	PF-65	PF-66	PF-67	
$75	$90	$210	$325	$2,500	$3,250	$4,500	$12,500	

Certified Populations

Fair	AG-2	G-4	VG-8	F-12	VF-20	EF-40	AU-50	MS-60	MS-61	MS-62	MS-63	MS-64	MS-65
0	0	1	6	2	1	14	165	0	22	118	286	926	1,130

MS-66	MS-67	MS-68	MS-69	PF-60	PF-61	PF-62	PF-63	PF-64	PF-65	PF-66	PF-67	PF-68	PF-69
564	112	6	0	1	5	45	117	402	357	319	82	—	—

1936-D Liberty Walking Half Dollar

Circulation-strike
mintage:
4,252,400

Key to Collecting. Characteristics of striking—*Head:* Usually with about 70% or more details. *Left hand:* Usually with 70% or more details. *Eagle's left leg:* Most feathers are usually present.

Overview: Striking varies, but the majority of examples are fairly sharp.

Market Values • Circulation Strikes

G-4	VG-8	F-12	VF-20	EF-40	AU-50	AU-55
$13	$15	$16	$17.50	$20	$50	$60

MS-60	MS-62	MS-63	MS-64	MS-65	MS-66	
$85	$100	$120	$130	$400	$775	

Certified Populations

Fair	AG-2	G-4	VG-8	F-12	VF-20	EF-40	AU-50	MS-60
0	0	0	1	1	7	13	79	0

MS-61	MS-62	MS-63	MS-64	MS-65	MS-66	MS-67	MS-68	MS-69
15	78	160	585	522	203	27	0	0

1936-S Liberty Walking Half Dollar

Circulation-strike
mintage:
3,884,000

Key to Collecting. Characteristics of striking—*Head:* Usually with about 60% or more details. *Left hand:* Usually with 60% or more details. *Eagle's left leg:* Usually with about half of the feathers.

   Overview: Striking varies, but there are enough coins available that finding one with above average sharpness will be easy enough to do.

Market Values • Circulation Strikes

G-4	VG-8	F-12	VF-20	EF-40	AU-50	AU-55
$13	$15	$16	$17.50	$22	$60	$100

MS-60	MS-62	MS-63	MS-64	MS-65	MS-66	
$130	$160	$200	$260	$750	$1,025	

Certified Populations

Fair	AG-2	G-4	VG-8	F-12	VF-20	EF-40	AU-50	MS-60
0	0	0	3	2	10	9	47	1

MS-61	MS-62	MS-63	MS-64	MS-65	MS-66	MS-67	MS-68	MS-69
5	32	97	446	457	148	17	0	0

1937 Liberty Walking Half Dollar

Circulation-strike mintage:
9,522,000

Circulation Strike

Proof mintage:
5,728

Proof

See next page for chart.

Key to Collecting. Characteristics of striking—*Head:* Usually with about 70% or more details. *Left hand:* Usually with 70% or more details. *Eagle's left leg:* Usually with most of the feathers.

   Overview: Striking is usually quite good. Mint State coins typically have rich luster and excellent eye appeal.

Proofs. Well struck. This is the second-rarest of the Proofs. Availability is proportional to the quantity made.

Market Values • Circulation Strikes and Proof Strikes

G-4	VG-8	F-12	VF-20	EF-40	AU-50	AU-55	MS-60	MS-62
$13	$15	$16	$17.50	$18	$25	$30	$40	$55
MS-63	**MS-64**	**MS-65**	**MS-66**	**PF-64**	**PF-65**	**PF-66**	**PF-67**	
$70	$85	$215	$325	$750	$850	$1,150	$1,600	

Certified Populations

Fair	AG-2	G-4	VG-8	F-12	VF-20	EF-40	AU-50	MS-60	MS-61	MS-62	MS-63	MS-64	MS-65
0	0	0	1	1	5	14	175	1	18	121	280	956	1,015
MS-66	**MS-67**	**MS-68**	**MS-69**	**PF-60**	**PF-61**	**PF-62**	**PF-63**	**PF-64**	**PF-65**	**PF-66**	**PF-67**	**PF-68**	**PF-69**
351	95	3	0	2	13	37	74	345	379	402	237	27	—

1937-D Liberty Walking Half Dollar

Circulation-strike
mintage:
1,676,000

Key to Collecting. Characteristics of striking—*Head:* Usually with about 70% or more details. *Left hand:* Usually with 70% or more details. *Eagle's left leg:* Usually with about half of the feathers.

   Overview: Striking is usually quite good, but cherrypicking will result in finding ones that are above average, including with more feathers on the eagle's leg.

Market Values • Circulation Strikes

G-4	VG-8	F-12	VF-20	EF-40	AU-50	AU-55
$13	$15	$16	$18	$32	$100	$150

MS-60	MS-62	MS-63	MS-64	MS-65	MS-66	
$215	$245	$265	$300	$600	$825	

Certified Populations

Fair	AG-2	G-4	VG-8	F-12	VF-20	EF-40	AU-50	MS-60
0	0	0	0	1	10	18	91	0

MS-61	MS-62	MS-63	MS-64	MS-65	MS-66	MS-67	MS-68	MS-69
15	58	93	345	331	156	36	1	0

1937-S Liberty Walking Half Dollar

Circulation-strike
mintage:
2,090,000

Key to Collecting. Characteristics of striking—*Head:* Usually with about 70% or more details. *Left hand:* Usually with 60% or more details, not as sharp as coins from the other mints. *Eagle's left leg:* Usually with most of the feathers.

Overview: There are many 1937-S half dollars available, and most are attractive. Cherrypicking is advised to find one with a sharper-than-average strike.

Market Values • Circulation Strikes

G-4	VG-8	F-12	VF-20	EF-40	AU-50	AU-55
$13	$15	$16	$17.50	$25	$60	$110

MS-60	MS-62	MS-63	MS-64	MS-65	MS-66	
$165	$185	$210	$255	$625	$875	

Certified Populations

Fair	AG-2	G-4	VG-8	F-12	VF-20	EF-40	AU-50	MS-60
0	0	0	2	1	2	13	54	2

MS-61	MS-62	MS-63	MS-64	MS-65	MS-66	MS-67	MS-68	MS-69
4	41	116	433	403	141	11	0	0

1938 Liberty Walking Half Dollar

Circulation Strike

Proof

Circulation-strike
mintage:
4,110,000

Proof mintage:
8,152

Key to Collecting. Characteristics of striking—*Head:* Usually with about 70% or more details. *Left hand:* Usually with 60% or more details. *Eagle's left leg:* Usually with most of the feathers.

Overview: Most are very attractive. Cherrypicking is advised to find one with a sharper-than-average strike on the obverse.

Proofs. Well struck. Availability is proportional to the quantity made.

Market Values • Circulation Strikes and Proof Strikes

G-4	VG-8	F-12	VF-20	EF-40	AU-50	AU-55	MS-60	MS-62
$13	$15	$16	$18	$20	$45	$55	$70	$115

MS-63	MS-64	MS-65	MS-66	PF-64	PF-65	PF-66	PF-67	
$160	$180	$300	$450	$550	$725	$900	$1,300	

Certified Populations

Fair	AG-2	G-4	VG-8	F-12	VF-20	EF-40	AU-50	MS-60	MS-61	MS-62	MS-63	MS-64	MS-65
0	0	2	4	6	8	14	130	0	18	85	181	661	753

MS-66	MS-67	MS-68	MS-69	PF-60	PF-61	PF-62	PF-63	PF-64	PF-65	PF-66	PF-67	PF-68	PF-69
284	37	1	0	3	3	27	84	323	449	577	298	58	—

1938-D Liberty Walking Half Dollar

Circulation-strike mintage:
491,600

Key to Collecting. Characteristics of striking—*Head:* Usually with about 70% or more details. *Left hand:* Usually with 60% or more details. *Eagle's left leg:* Usually about half of the feathers.

Overview: Striking sharpness varies. Look for an example with better-than-average details. The 1938-D is the key issue among Liberty Walking half dollars of the 1930s and 1940s. In the 1950s, when bank-wrapped rolls of issues of the 1930s were available, particularly for those 1935 and later, I only ever saw one roll of the 1938-D.

Market Values • Circulation Strikes

G-4	VG-8	F-12	VF-20	EF-40	AU-50	AU-55
$75	$100	$110	$135	$175	$250	$350

MS-60	MS-62	MS-63	MS-64	MS-65	MS-66
$500	$560	$625	$725	$1,450	$2,400

Certified Populations

Fair	AG-2	G-4	VG-8	F-12	VF-20	EF-40	AU-50	MS-60
0	1	36	172	277	611	240	190	2

MS-61	MS-62	MS-63	MS-64	MS-65	MS-66	MS-67	MS-68	MS-69
14	56	113	414	404	107	21	0	0

1939 Liberty Walking Half Dollar

Circulation Strike

Proof

Circulation-strike
mintage:
6,812,000

Proof mintage:
8,808

Key to Collecting. Characteristics of striking—*Head:* Usually with about 70% or more details. *Left hand:* Usually with 70% or more details. *Eagle's left leg:* Usually with most of the feathers.

Overview: Nearly all are well struck and attractive.

Proofs. Well struck. Availability is proportional to the quantity made.

Market Values • Circulation Strikes and Proof Strikes

G-4	VG-8	F-12	VF-20	EF-40	AU-50	AU-55	MS-60	MS-62
$13	$15	$16	$17.50	$18	$26	$30	$40	$55
MS-63	MS-64	MS-65	MS-66	PF-64	PF-65	PF-66	PF-67	
$65	$85	$155	$255	$450	$650	$750	$1,000	

Certified Populations

Fair	AG-2	G-4	VG-8	F-12	VF-20	EF-40	AU-50	MS-60	MS-61	MS-62	MS-63	MS-64	MS-65
0	0	0	1	1	4	9	185	0	27	115	237	784	1,140
MS-66	MS-67	MS-68	MS-69	PF-60	PF-61	PF-62	PF-63	PF-64	PF-65	PF-66	PF-67	PF-68	PF-69
775	306	20	0	0	7	22	64	287	436	648	377	96	1

1939-D Liberty Walking Half Dollar

Circulation-strike
mintage:
4,267,800

Key to Collecting. Characteristics of striking—*Head:* Usually with about 70% or more details. *Left hand:* Usually with 60% or more details. *Eagle's left leg:* Usually most of the feathers.

Overview: Striking sharpness varies, but as Mint State coins are common there will be no difficulty finding one that is better than average.

Market Values • Circulation Strikes

G-4	VG-8	F-12	VF-20	EF-40	AU-50	AU-55
$13	$15	$16	$17.50	$18	$25	$32

MS-60	MS-62	MS-63	MS-64	MS-65	MS-66	
$43	$65	$75	$95	$180	$325	

Certified Populations

Fair	AG-2	G-4	VG-8	F-12	VF-20	EF-40	AU-50	MS-60
0	0	0	1	3	4	13	88	0

MS-61	MS-62	MS-63	MS-64	MS-65	MS-66	MS-67	MS-68	MS-69
7	57	175	712	1,147	565	86	2	0

1939-S Liberty Walking Half Dollar

Circulation-strike
mintage:
2,552,000

See next page for chart.

Key to Collecting. Characteristics of striking—*Head:* Usually with about 70% or more details. *Left hand:* Usually with 70% or more details. *Eagle's left leg:* Usually with most of the feathers.

Overview: Finding a nice example of this common issue will be easy.

Market Values • Circulation Strikes

G-4	VG-8	F-12	VF-20	EF-40	AU-50	AU-55
$13	$15	$16	$17.50	$26	$70	$100

MS-60	MS-62	MS-63	MS-64	MS-65	MS-66
$140	$150	$180	$200	$300	$525

Certified Populations

Fair	AG-2	G-4	VG-8	F-12	VF-20	EF-40	AU-50	MS-60
0	0	0	0	3	6	20	51	0

MS-61	MS-62	MS-63	MS-64	MS-65	MS-66	MS-67	MS-68	MS-69
8	34	66	319	753	552	121	0	0

1940 Liberty Walking Half Dollar

Circulation Strike

Proof

Circulation-strike mintage:
9,156,000

Proof mintage:
11,279

Key to Collecting. Characteristics of striking—*Head:* Usually with about 70% or more details. *Left hand:* Usually with 70% or more details. *Eagle's left leg:* Usually with most of the feathers.

Overview: Finding a nice example of this common issue will be easy.

Proofs. Well struck. Availability is proportional to the quantity made.

Market Values • Circulation Strikes and Proof Strikes

G-4	VG-8	F-12	VF-20	EF-40	AU-50	AU-55	MS-60	MS-62
$13	$15	$16	$17.50	$18	$22	$27	$35	$45
MS-63	MS-64	MS-65	MS-66	PF-64	PF-65	PF-66	PF-67	
$55	$70	$145	$245	$450	$575	$700	$900	

Certified Populations

Fair	AG-2	G-4	VG-8	F-12	VF-20	EF-40	AU-50	MS-60	MS-61	MS-62	MS-63	MS-64	MS-65
0	0	0	0	2	6	10	154	0	23	167	322	984	1,315
MS-66	MS-67	MS-68	MS-69	PF-60	PF-61	PF-62	PF-63	PF-64	PF-65	PF-66	PF-67	PF-68	PF-69
758	235	15	1	0	8	30	80	345	616	782	369	59	—

1940-S Liberty Walking Half Dollar

Circulation-strike mintage:
4,550,000

Key to Collecting. Characteristics of striking—*Head:* Usually with about 60% or more details. *Left hand:* Usually with 60% or more details. *Eagle's left leg:* Usually flat with few feathers.

Overview: This is *the* challenging coin of the 1940s to find with a decent strike, as most are weak. To find one with just a good strike—not even necessarily a full strike—you will need to review dozens of coins.

See next page for chart.

Market Values • Circulation Strikes

G-4	VG-8	F-12	VF-20	EF-40	AU-50	AU-55
$13	$15	$16	$17.50	$18	$35	$40

MS-60	MS-62	MS-63	MS-64	MS-65	MS-66
$45	$60	$80	$110	$300	$875

Certified Populations

Fair	AG-2	G-4	VG-8	F-12	VF-20	EF-40	AU-50	MS-60
0	0	0	1	0	2	9	69	11

MS-61	MS-62	MS-63	MS-64	MS-65	MS-66	MS-67	MS-68	MS-69
30	128	357	1,419	782	176	10	0	0

1941 Liberty Walking Half Dollar

Circulation Strike

Proof

Circulation-strike
mintage:
24,192,000

Proof mintage:
15,412

Key to Collecting. Characteristics of striking—*Head:* Usually with about 70% or more details. *Left hand:* Usually with 70% or more details. *Eagle's left leg:* Usually with most of the feathers.

Overview: Finding a nice example of this common issue will be easy. This year begins the date range for a "short set" of Liberty Walking half dollars—brought about by the second of two Whitman folders for the series starting with this year. Furthermore, building a set of high-grade coins of the 1941 to 1947 years is easy to do. Striking sharpness is another matter, as discussed under the individual entries on the following pages.

Proofs. Well struck. Availability is proportional to the quantity made. Also see below.

Proofs without AW monogram: Proofs issued during the year from January until about October have the AW monogram missing. It was removed from the die by over-polishing. Later Proofs, perhaps 15% to 20% of the total, have the AW sharp. Although the monogram-less variety has been known for many years there has been little market notice of it, nor have the rarer with-monogram coins attracted much attention. In a letter published in *The Numismatic Scrapbook Magazine* in February 1942, Chief Engraver John R. Sinnock explained the missing monogram: "I wish to say that since these are raised in relief in the die they tend to become softened with each polishing. The average number of coins struck between each polishing is about 500 on the reverse of half dollars. This particular detail of the design (initials) becomes more faint each time the die is polished. The impressions which you describe must have been made from a die which had been polished several times. There were three reverse half dollar dies used for Proof half dollars in 1941."

Market Values • Circulation Strikes and Proof Strikes

G-4	VG-8	F-12	VF-20	EF-40	AU-50	AU-55	MS-60	MS-62
$13	$15	$17	$17.50	$18	$22	$27	$35	$45

MS-63	MS-64	MS-65	MS-66	PF-64	PF-65	PF-66	PF-67	
$55	$75	$150	$235	$450	$575	$700	$900	

Certified Populations

Fair	AG-2	G-4	VG-8	F-12	VF-20	EF-40	AU-50	MS-60	MS-61	MS-62	MS-63	MS-64	MS-65
0	0	1	2	2	9	22	539	4	103	403	872	2,502	3,302

MS-66	MS-67	MS-68	MS-69	PF-60	PF-61	PF-62	PF-63	PF-64	PF-65	PF-66	PF-67	PF-68	PF-69
2,344	643	25	0	0	3	27	96	506	757	781	358	55	1

1941-D Liberty Walking Half Dollar

Circulation-strike
mintage:
11,248,400

See next page for chart.

Key to Collecting. Characteristics of striking—*Head:* Usually with about 70% or more details. *Left hand:* Usually with 70% or more details. *Eagle's left leg:* Usually with most of the feathers.

Overview: Finding a nice example of this common issue will be easy.

Market Values • Circulation Strikes

G-4	VG-8	F-12	VF-20	EF-40	AU-50	AU-55
$13	$15	$16	$17.50	$18	$22	$28

MS-60	MS-62	MS-63	MS-64	MS-65	MS-66
$38	$50	$65	$87	$160	$245

Certified Populations

Fair	AG-2	G-4	VG-8	F-12	VF-20	EF-40	AU-50	MS-60
0	0	0	2	2	2	11	201	1

MS-61	MS-62	MS-63	MS-64	MS-65	MS-66	MS-67	MS-68	MS-69
40	149	348	1,388	2,189	1,223	189	3	0

1941-S Liberty Walking Half Dollar

Circulation-strike
mintage:
8,098,000

Key to Collecting. Characteristics of striking—*Head:* Usually with about 60% or more details. *Left hand:* Usually with 60% or more details. *Eagle's left leg:* Usually flat with few feathers.

Overview: The 1941-S is usually seen with an indifferent strike. Finding a sharp one will be a challenge, as few exist. Be patient.

Market Values • Circulation Strikes

G-4	VG-8	F-12	VF-20	EF-40	AU-50	AU-55
$13	$15	$16	$17.50	$18	$26	$50

MS-60	MS-62	MS-63	MS-64	MS-65	MS-66
$75	$95	$120	$225	$850	$1,700

Certified Populations

Fair	AG-2	G-4	VG-8	F-12	VF-20	EF-40	AU-50	MS-60
0	0	0	1	2	2	25	435	5

MS-61	MS-62	MS-63	MS-64	MS-65	MS-66	MS-67	MS-68	MS-69
82	352	900	2,700	923	224	21	0	0

1942 Liberty Walking Half Dollar

Circulation-strike mintage:
47,818,000

Circulation Strike

Proof mintage:
21,120

Proof

Key to Collecting. Characteristics of striking—*Head:* Usually with about 70% or more details. *Left hand:* Usually with 70% or more details. *Eagle's left leg:* Usually with most of the feathers.

Overview: As with all half dollars of this era, striking varies. Finding a nice one will be no difficulty as there are so many from which to choose.

Proofs. Well struck. Availability is proportional to the quantity made. This is the last Proof issue in the series.

Market Values • Circulation Strikes and Proof Strikes

G-4	VG-8	F-12	VF-20	EF-40	AU-50	AU-55	MS-60	MS-62
$13	$15	$16	$17.50	$18	$22	$30	$40	$45

MS-63	MS-64	MS-65	MS-66	PF-64	PF-65	PF-66	PF-67	
$60	$70	$150	$230	$450	$575	$700	$900	

Certified Populations

Fair	AG-2	G-4	VG-8	F-12	VF-20	EF-40	AU-50	MS-60	MS-61	MS-62	MS-63	MS-64	MS-65
0	0	0	8	2	9	34	1,038	11	151	763	1,486	4,344	5,033

MS-66	MS-67	MS-68	MS-69	PF-60	PF-61	PF-62	PF-63	PF-64	PF-65	PF-66	PF-67	PF-68	PF-69
2,681	386	4	0	1	10	58	138	655	971	1,355	909	185	4

1942-D Liberty Walking Half Dollar

Circulation-strike
mintage:
10,973,800

Key to Collecting. Characteristics of striking—*Head:* Usually with about 70% or more details. *Left hand:* Usually with 60% or more details. *Eagle's left leg:* Usually with about half of the feathers.

Overview: Cherrypicking is essential to find an above-average strike.

Market Values • Circulation Strikes

G-4	VG-8	F-12	VF-20	EF-40	AU-50	AU-55
$13	$15	$16	$17.50	$18	$20	$30

MS-60	MS-62	MS-63	MS-64	MS-65	MS-66
$40	$60	$75	$100	$215	$280

Certified Populations

Fair	AG-2	G-4	VG-8	F-12	VF-20	EF-40	AU-50	MS-60
0	0	0	2	3	2	8	149	1

MS-61	MS-62	MS-63	MS-64	MS-65	MS-66	MS-67	MS-68	MS-69
24	106	287	1,038	1,548	880	133	6	0

1942-S Liberty Walking Half Dollar

Circulation-strike
mintage:
12,708,000

Key to Collecting. Characteristics of striking—*Head:* Usually with about 60% or more details. *Left hand:* Usually with 60% or more details. *Eagle's left leg:* Usually flat.

Overview: Most 1942-S half dollars are indifferent in sharpness. Some effort will be required to find an exception.

Market Values • Circulation Strikes

G-4	VG-8	F-12	VF-20	EF-40	AU-50	AU-55
$13	$15	$16	$17.50	$18	$22	$30

MS-60	MS-62	MS-63	MS-64	MS-65	MS-66
$40	$60	$80	$120	$425	$1,200

Certified Populations

Fair	AG-2	G-4	VG-8	F-12	VF-20	EF-40	AU-50	MS-60
0	0	0	1	2	3	12	161	1

MS-61	MS-62	MS-63	MS-64	MS-65	MS-66	MS-67	MS-68	MS-69
31	137	495	2,218	1,136	210	8	0	0

1943 Liberty Walking Half Dollar

Circulation-strike mintage:
53,190,000

Key to Collecting. Characteristics of striking—*Head:* Usually with about 70% or more details. *Left hand:* Usually with 70% or more details. *Eagle's left leg:* Usually with most of the feathers.

Overview: As with all half dollars of this era, striking varies. Finding a nice 1943 will be no difficulty as there are so many from which to choose. Many have wide rims on the reverse.

Note: Some accounts of a 1943/2 overdate have been published, but their existence is controversial. David W. Lange and Bill Fivaz both consider that the coins called "1943/2" overdates were in fact simply exhibiting die doubling.[2]

See next page for chart.

Market Values • Circulation Strikes

G-4	VG-8	F-12	VF-20	EF-40	AU-50	AU-55
$13	$15	$16	$17.50	$18	$20	$30

MS-60	MS-62	MS-63	MS-64	MS-65	MS-66
$35	$40	$48	$60	$150	$230

Certified Populations

Fair	AG-2	G-4	VG-8	F-12	VF-20	EF-40	AU-50	MS-60
0	0	0	5	7	29	31	998	5

MS-61	MS-62	MS-63	MS-64	MS-65	MS-66	MS-67	MS-68	MS-69
143	683	1,514	4,326	4,740	2,912	565	16	0

1943-D Liberty Walking Half Dollar

Circulation-strike
mintage:
11,346,000

Key to Collecting. Characteristics of striking—*Head:* Usually with about 70% or more details. *Left hand:* Usually with 70% or more details. *Eagle's left leg:* Usually with most of the feathers.

Overview: The 1943-D half dollars are usually very attractive, and most are fairly well struck.

Market Values • Circulation Strikes

G-4	VG-8	F-12	VF-20	EF-40	AU-50	AU-55
$13	$15	$16	$17.50	$18	$24	$38

MS-60	MS-62	MS-63	MS-64	MS-65	MS-66
$48	$65	$73	$85	$200	$275

Certified Populations

Fair	AG-2	G-4	VG-8	F-12	VF-20	EF-40	AU-50	MS-60
0	0	0	2	0	2	10	155	1

MS-61	MS-62	MS-63	MS-64	MS-65	MS-66	MS-67	MS-68	MS-69
14	101	252	1,035	1,740	1,362	319	5	0

1943-S Liberty Walking Half Dollar

Circulation-strike
mintage:
13,450,000

Key to Collecting. Characteristics of striking—*Head:* Usually with about 60% or more details. *Left hand:* Usually with 50% or more details. *Eagle's left leg:* Usually with about half of the feathers.

   Overview: To find a nice 1943-S will be a challenge. Most of them lack significant detail in the important areas, but, happily, there are occasional exceptions.

Market Values • Circulation Strikes

G-4	VG-8	F-12	VF-20	EF-40	AU-50	AU-55
$13	$15	$16	$17.50	$18	$25	$35

MS-60	MS-62	MS-63	MS-64	MS-65	MS-66	
$42	$50	$60	$85	$300	$650	

Certified Populations

Fair	AG-2	G-4	VG-8	F-12	VF-20	EF-40	AU-50	MS-60
0	0	1	1	1	7	7	120	2

MS-61	MS-62	MS-63	MS-64	MS-65	MS-66	MS-67	MS-68	MS-69
19	127	462	2,477	1,526	314	25	0	0

1944 Liberty Walking Half Dollar

Circulation-strike
mintage:
28,206,000

See next page for chart.

249

Key to Collecting. Characteristics of striking—*Head:* Usually with about 60% or more details. *Left hand:* Usually with 60% or more details. *Eagle's left leg:* Usually with most of the feathers.

Overview: Most 1944 half dollars fall short of excellence in their strike, but there are so many around that with some searching you will easily find one that is above average.

Market Values • Circulation Strikes

G-4	VG-8	F-12	VF-20	EF-40	AU-50	AU-55
$13	$15	$16	$17.50	$18	$20	$28

MS-60	MS-62	MS-63	MS-64	MS-65	MS-66
$35	$40	$50	$70	$150	$230

Certified Populations

Fair	AG-2	G-4	VG-8	F-12	VF-20	EF-40	AU-50	MS-60
0	0	0	0	1	9	14	458	7

MS-61	MS-62	MS-63	MS-64	MS-65	MS-66	MS-67	MS-68	MS-69
84	410	1,036	3,196	3,137	956	91	2	0

1944-D Liberty Walking Half Dollar

Circulation-strike
mintage:
9,769,000

Key to Collecting. Characteristics of striking—*Head:* Usually with about 70% or more details. *Left hand:* Usually with 70% or more details. *Eagle's left leg:* Usually with most of the feathers.

Overview: As with all half dollars of this era, striking varies. Some are fairly indistinct at the head and hand. Finding a nice 1944-D will be no difficulty as there are so many from which to choose.

Hand-engraved AW monogram: On at least five different dies used to coin 1944-D half dollars the AW monogram is hand-engraved.[3] This feature was missing on the original dies. Coins with this feature identified sell for multiples of regular values. Cherrypicking (searching a dealer's inventory for a coin that has the hand-

Regular AW monogram on a
1944-D half dollar.

Hand-engraved AW monogram on
a 1944-D half dollar.

engraved monogram but isn't identified as such) may be a less expensive way to go.
Bill Fivaz stated in 2006: "Other dates and mints within the series are known and will
be added to our listings as we can examine them," but in response to a query, on
October 26, 2014, he said that no other dates or mintmarks had been found with this
feature. (FS-50-1944D-901)

Market Values • Circulation Strikes

G-4	VG-8	F-12	VF-20	EF-40	AU-50	AU-55
$13	$15	$16	$17.50	$18	$20	$30

MS-60	MS-62	MS-63	MS-64	MS-65	MS-66
$40	$50	$58	$70	$160	$230

Certified Populations

Fair	AG-2	G-4	VG-8	F-12	VF-20	EF-40	AU-50	MS-60
0	0	0	1	2	2	7	128	2

MS-61	MS-62	MS-63	MS-64	MS-65	MS-66	MS-67	MS-68	MS-69
27	105	331	1,421	2,425	1,362	242	1	0

1944-S Liberty Walking Half Dollar

Circulation-strike
mintage:
8,904,000

Key to Collecting. Characteristics of striking—*Head:* Usually with about 60% or
more details. *Left hand:* Usually with 60% or more details. *Eagle's left leg:* Usually flat
with just a few feathers.

See next page for chart.

251

Overview: Most 1945-S half dollars have weak areas. Cherrypicking for a fairly sharp one is advised.

Market Values • Circulation Strikes

G-4	VG-8	F-12	VF-20	EF-40	AU-50	AU-55
$13	$15	$16	$17.50	$18	$24	$32

MS-60	MS-62	MS-63	MS-64	MS-65	MS-66	
$40	$55	$63	$85	$350	$1,000	

Certified Populations

Fair	AG-2	G-4	VG-8	F-12	VF-20	EF-40	AU-50	MS-60
0	0	0	0	3	1	4	83	1

MS-61	MS-62	MS-63	MS-64	MS-65	MS-66	MS-67	MS-68	MS-69
20	162	744	3,464	1,284	217	6	0	0

1945 Liberty Walking Half Dollar

Circulation-strike
mintage:
31,502,000

Key to Collecting. Characteristics of striking—*Head:* Usually with about 70% or more details. *Left hand:* Usually with 70% or more details. *Eagle's left leg:* Usually with most of the feathers.

Overview: Striking varies, but as Mint State 1945 coins exist in large numbers finding a sharp one will be easy enough to do.

Market Values • Circulation Strikes

G-4	VG-8	F-12	VF-20	EF-40	AU-50	AU-55
$13	$15	$16	$17.50	$18	$20	$25

MS-60	MS-62	MS-63	MS-64	MS-65	MS-66	
$35	$40	$50	$75	$150	$230	

Certified Populations

Fair	AG-2	G-4	VG-8	F-12	VF-20	EF-40	AU-50	MS-60
0	0	0	3	7	20	20	493	4

MS-61	MS-62	MS-63	MS-64	MS-65	MS-66	MS-67	MS-68	MS-69
85	485	1,378	4,419	4,471	1,518	118	0	0

1945-D Liberty Walking Half Dollar

Circulation-strike
mintage:
9,966,800

Key to Collecting. Characteristics of striking—*Head:* Usually with about 70% or more details. *Left hand:* Usually with 70% or more details. *Eagle's left leg:* Usually flat with few feathers.

Overview: Cherrypicking to find a 1945-D with better feather definition that average will be worthwhile, but relatively few coins are better strikes.

Market Values • Circulation Strikes

G-4	VG-8	F-12	VF-20	EF-40	AU-50	AU-55
$13	$15	$16	$17.50	$18	$20	$28

MS-60	MS-62	MS-63	MS-64	MS-65	MS-66
$35	$45	$55	$70	$150	$230

Certified Populations

Fair	AG-2	G-4	VG-8	F-12	VF-20	EF-40	AU-50	MS-60
0	0	0	0	1	2	8	127	1

MS-61	MS-62	MS-63	MS-64	MS-65	MS-66	MS-67	MS-68	MS-69
17	75	377	1,985	3,737	2,159	223	2	0

1946 Liberty Walking Half Dollar

Circulation-strike
mintage:
12,118,000

Key to Collecting. Characteristics of striking—*Head:* Usually with about 70% or more details. *Left hand:* Usually with 70% or more details. *Eagle's left leg:* Usually with most of the feathers.

Overview: Most 1946 half dollars are very nice. Avoid the exceptions.

Market Values • Circulation Strikes

G-4	VG-8	F-12	VF-20	EF-40	AU-50	AU-55
$13	$15	$16	$17.50	$18	$20	$28

MS-60	MS-62	MS-63	MS-64	MS-65	MS-66
$37	$45	$50	$75	$160	$325

Certified Populations

Fair	AG-2	G-4	VG-8	F-12	VF-20	EF-40	AU-50	MS-60
0	0	0	0	4	6	13	243	3

MS-61	MS-62	MS-63	MS-64	MS-65	MS-66	MS-67	MS-68	MS-69
37	251	714	2,496	2,220	616	45	1	0

1946-D Liberty Walking Half Dollar

Circulation-strike mintage:
2,151,000

Key to Collecting. Characteristics of striking—*Head:* Usually with about 60% or more details. *Left hand:* Usually with 60% or more details. *Eagle's left leg:* Usually flat, with just a few feathers.

Overview: The typical 1946-D leaves a lot to be desired in terms of sharpness. However, despite their low mintage they are very common, and finding an above-average coin will be easy to do.

Market Values • Circulation Strikes

G-4	VG-8	F-12	VF-20	EF-40	AU-50	AU-55
$13	$15	$16	$17.50	$22	$32	$40

MS-60	MS-62	MS-63	MS-64	MS-65	MS-66
$47	$55	$60	$70	$150	$230

Certified Populations

Fair	AG-2	G-4	VG-8	F-12	VF-20	EF-40	AU-50	MS-60
0	0	0	0	1	0	2	45	0

MS-61	MS-62	MS-63	MS-64	MS-65	MS-66	MS-67	MS-68	MS-69
4	53	417	3,298	6,521	2,387	120	0	0

1946-S Liberty Walking Half Dollar

Circulation-strike
mintage:
3,724,000

Key to Collecting. Characteristics of striking—*Head:* Usually with about 60% or more details. *Left hand:* Usually with 60% or more details. *Eagle's left leg:* Usually flat, with just a few feathers.

Overview: Although the typical 1946-S will win no ribbon for sharpness, enough are enough in the marketplace that finding one with better details can be done.

Market Values • Circulation Strikes

G-4	VG-8	F-12	VF-20	EF-40	AU-50	AU-55
$13	$15	$16	$17.50	$18	$25	$35

MS-60	MS-62	MS-63	MS-64	MS-65	MS-66
$43	$50	$58	$75	$150	$250

Certified Populations

Fair	AG-2	G-4	VG-8	F-12	VF-20	EF-40	AU-50	MS-60
0	0	0	0	0	0	3	45	2

MS-61	MS-62	MS-63	MS-64	MS-65	MS-66	MS-67	MS-68	MS-69
12	47	326	2,499	4,078	1,334	71	0	0

1947 Liberty Walking Half Dollar

Circulation-strike
mintage:
4,094,000

Key to Collecting. Characteristics of striking—*Head:* Usually with about 60% or more details. *Left hand:* Usually with 60% or more details. *Eagle's left leg:* Usually flat with just a few feathers.

Overview: Striking quality is very average for this issue, making cherrypicking quite rewarding.

Market Values • Circulation Strikes

G-4	VG-8	F-12	VF-20	EF-40	AU-50	AU-55
$13	$15	$16	$17.50	$18	$25	$38

MS-60	MS-62	MS-63	MS-64	MS-65	MS-66
$48	$55	$60	$75	$160	$325

Certified Populations

Fair	AG-2	G-4	VG-8	F-12	VF-20	EF-40	AU-50	MS-60
0	0	0	0	1	2	1	148	4

MS-61	MS-62	MS-63	MS-64	MS-65	MS-66	MS-67	MS-68	MS-69
29	165	617	2,700	2,819	728	74	0	0

1947-D Liberty Walking Half Dollar

Circulation-strike mintage:
3,900,600

Key to Collecting. Characteristics of striking—*Head:* Usually with about 70% or more details. *Left hand:* Usually with 70% or more details. *Eagle's left leg:* Usually with about half of the feathers.

Overview: The typical 1947-S in the marketplace is quite attractive. Some searching will yield a better-than-average coin from the aspect of strike.

Market Values • Circulation Strikes

G-4	VG-8	F-12	VF-20	EF-40	AU-50	AU-55
$13	$15	$16	$17.50	$18	$30	$36

MS-60	MS-62	MS-63	MS-64	MS-65	MS-66
$45	$55	$60	$70	$150	$280

Certified Populations

Fair	AG-2	G-4	VG-8	F-12	VF-20	EF-40	AU-50	MS-60
0	0	0	0	3	0	8	58	0

MS-61	MS-62	MS-63	MS-64	MS-65	MS-66	MS-67	MS-68	MS-69
6	66	353	2,503	4,142	977	55	1	0

Three Valuable Books for Every Stage of Your Hobby

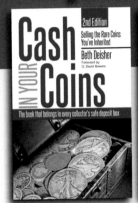 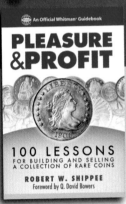 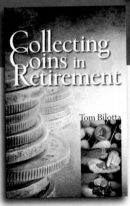

Don't leave your heirs in the dark. *Cash In Your Coins: Selling the Rare Coins You've Inherited* is for anyone who's inherited or found a collection of old coins. How rare are they? What are they worth? Should you sell? Where do you even begin? If you're a coin collector, you want your heirs to make smart, confident decisions—and avoid expensive mistakes. Keep a copy of this book with your collection for the benefit of your loved ones. Updated and expanded 2nd edition. **304 pages, 6 x 9 inches, full color • $9.95**

In *Pleasure and Profit: 100 Lessons for Building and Selling a Collection of Rare Coins*, Robert W. Shippee shares hands-on hobby advice, but his text is also about golf, whisky, friendships, and other good things in life that are attached to the experience of collecting coins. His relaxed storyteller's wit makes the lessons fun and interesting. Q. David Bowers says, "*Pleasure and Profit* is one of the most useful books in American numismatics. It will change your buying strategies." **320 pages, 6 x 9 inches, full color • $9.95**

"Coin collecting during retirement poses specialized challenges and opportunities," says numismatist Tom Bilotta. In *Collecting Coins in Retirement,* he covers these issues in depth and guides you toward building your enjoyment of the hobby. In addition to addressing active collectors, he gives valuable real-world advice to inheritors on how to manage the disposition of rare coins and other collectibles. **288 pages, 6 x 9 inches, full color • $19.95**

Order individually, or
SPECIAL OFFER for readers of this book
get all three titles, a $39.85 value, for just $30 postpaid.

Mention code MD.
Order by phone at 1-866-546-2995,
online at Whitman.com,
or email customerservice@Whitman.com

appendix

A

The Coin Designers

Adolph A. Weinman

Adolph Alexander Weinman, designer of the 1916 Mercury dime and Liberty Walking half dollar, was born in Durmersheim, Baden, Germany, on December 11, 1870. He came to America when he was 10 years old. As a teenager he was apprenticed to Frederick Kaldenberg, a sculptor in wood and ivory. In this field he studied in the evening at Cooper Union in New York City.

Adolph A. Weinman in his studio with models for the 1916 half dollar.

Weinman is best remembered today for his coin designs and medals. His interest in the field was well documented in his time. On January 17, 1910, he was named a member of the American Numismatic Society. After the two coins he designed were publicized, he was featured nationwide in that connection. He protested this emphasis and declared that he was first and foremost a sculptor for architectural projects. His work in that area was extensive and well admired, but outside of scholars of civic sculptures he is little remembered in that context today. He made small bronze reproductions of many of his sculptures and sold them widely. *Descending Night*, created for the Panama-Pacific International Exposition of 1915, was a particular favorite. The original is now in the Metropolitan Museum of Art.

In 1916 the *American Journal of Numismatics* told this:

> Adolph Alexander Weinman, designer of the new half-dollar and dime, has kindly furnished the following information as to his course of study and the work he has so far accomplished:
>
> "After a five years' apprenticeship with Kaldenberg in carving in wood and ivory, during which period I studied drawing in Cooper Union, I entered the studio of Philip Martiny, and under him and at the Art Students' League I continued my studies for several years. Later I worked as assistant under Olin Warner, Augustus Saint-Gaudens, Charles H. Niehaus and Daniel C. French. The St. Louis Exposition offered the first opportunity for individual work in a commission for a large group, *The Destiny of the Red Man*. Shortly thereafter I won in competition the commission for the monument to General Alexander Macomb, for Detroit, and following it, the Maryland *Union Soldiers and Sailors Monument* for Baltimore.
>
> "Among my most important other works are: The Lincoln statue at Hodgenville, Kentucky. The Lincoln statue in Frankfort, Kentucky. Decorative sculpture and statue of Alexander Cassatt. Pennsylvania Railroad Terminal, New York. Sculpture in the façade and surmounting tower of Municipal Building, New York. Panels in façade of the library of

A full-size version of *Descending Night* was originally commissioned for the Panama-Pacific International Exposition of 1915 in San Francisco. The winged figure is a personification of the waning hours of daylight. The version pictured is a 26-inch reduction from the Metropolitan Museum of Art in New York.

J. Pierpont Morgan, Esq. Monument to Lieut. Col. William F. Vilas, National Military Park, Vicksburg, Mississippi. Pediment sculpture in the façade of the Madison Square Presbyterian Church, New York. Pediment sculpture in the façade of Senate wing of Wisconsin State Capitol, at Madison. Sphinxes flanking the entrance to the Scottish Rite Temple, Washington, D.C. Fountains of *The Rising Sun* and *The Setting Sun* for the Panama-Pacific International Exposition, San Francisco.

"I designed the gold Medal of Honor for the American Institute of Architects, the National Institute of Arts and Letters medal of awards, the Louisiana Purchase Exposition medal, and the United States Medal for Life Saving on Railroads.

"I received the silver medal awarded at the Louisiana Purchase Exposition; the silver medal, Brussels International Exposition, 1910; the gold Medal of Honor of Honor for Sculpture presented by the Architectural League of New York, 1913...."

The *Union Soldiers and Sailors Monument*, commemorating the Union military personnel of the Civil War, is located in Baltimore, Maryland. It depicts Bellona, the goddess of war, and the personification of Victory together with a citizen-soldier as he dons a uniform. The monument was dedicated on November 6, 1909.

At a special meeting of the American Numismatic Society, sculptors Hermon A. MacNeil and Adolph A. Weinman discussed their creation of new 1916 silver coin designs. The Society had encouraged their efforts. (See Howard L. Adelson, *The American Numismatic Society, 1858–1958*, page 196.)

Galvano for the 1904 Louisiana Purchase Exposition medal. (Engraving Department, U.S. Mint, Philadelphia)

Finished products of Weinman's medallic work for the Louisiana Purchase Exposition.

In 1904 Weinman opened a studio in New York City, where he did work for the Louisiana Purchase Exposition that opened in St. Louis that year. Many of his civic and commercial sculpture commissions in and near New York City were from the prominent architectural firm of McKim, Mead, and White. He was active in the National Sculpture Society and was its president from 1927 to 1930, overlapping his tenure on the Commission of Fine Arts from 1929 to 1933. The CFA was a group that advised the government concerning coin designs, including the Washington quarter of 1932.

After Weinman's dime and quarter appeared, he was mentioned in many numismatic publications. *Mehl's Numismatic Monthly*, February 1917, included the following in an article, "The Men Who Designed Our New Coins."

> About two months ago the new dimes appeared. Those who have admired them have doubtless noticed the small "W" indicating the name of the sculptor, Adolph Alexander Weinman. Because of some United States law, only the first issue of the coins is permitted this distinguishing mark. Last month the new half dollar has appeared, designed by the same sculptor.
>
> Mr. Weinman was born in Germany, but has lived in this country for many years and has executed many groups of statuary, especially memorial pieces, that are scattered through the country. There is hardly a great park or city of the country but has some of his handiwork. He made the *Lincoln Memorial* for Hodgenville, Kentucky, and the Lincoln statue for the State Capitol of Kentucky. His sculptures ornament the facade of the new Municipal Building in New York City. His studio and home are in old Chelsea Village section of New York City. He is devoted to his children, and, in contradiction of the theory that an artist is not domestic, his home life is ideal.

Two months later, B. Max Mehl published this, derived from the *New York Sun*:

How Our Coins Are Made

> Smoothing out the wrinkles in Miss Liberty's dress and keeping the die makers from cutting off the tips of her fingers took seven months of the hardest kind of work on the part of Adolph A. Weinman, who designed the new dimes and half dollars, which, if you are fortunate, you are now jingling in your pockets. Sitting in his studio, says the *New York Sun*, the artist who began last spring the work of designing new coins for Uncle Sam, told how the work was done.
>
> "The first task is to make a detailed sketch of the design. From this sketch is made a finished model from modeling wax. Some men work with small models; some with large. The models made for the coins were 14 or 15 inches in diameter.
>
> "When this model is completed it is necessary to make a reduced model from it by means of a mechanical device by which one needle traces the large model, and another, connected with it, but moving

on a reduced area, reproduces the original. This reduced model was, in this case, five times the size of the coin. From this smaller model a bronze alloy cast is made.

"This is used by the Mint identically as the original large model was used to make a further reduction the exact size of the proposed coin. This reduction is cut on a soft steel 'hub' and the design is reproduced in relief—not as a sunken model. This steel relief is called the 'master die' although it is not a die at all, but a relief model.

"The steel of which it is made is then tempered and made very hard; is placed in a 'chuck' and a piece of soft steel is forced down upon it with terrific pressure. This produces the final die, which in turn is hardened, and from it the coins are struck. These dies will strike from 100 to 120 [thousand] coins before being defaced. It is necessary, therefore, continually to take new dies from the 'master die' to keep up the coinage. Only a single stroke of the die machine is necessary to make the impression."

Weinman died in Port Chester, New York, on August 8, 1952, at the age of 81. He was buried in Calvary Cemetery in Queens, New York. His papers are preserved in

The "Genesis / Web of Destiny" medal by Weinman, no. 39 in the Society of Medalists series, 1949.

Pegasus from the façade of the sculptor's studio, Forest Hills, New York. (Brookgreen Gardens)

Pediment of the National Archives Building, Pennsylvania Avenue, Washington, D.C.

the Smithsonian Institution. A selection of his sculptures is on display at Brookgreen Gardens in South Carolina. His son Robert was a sculptor as well and designed the 1936 Long Island commemorative half dollar and medals for the Society of Medalists, among other works.

Hermon Atkins MacNeil

Riders of the Dawn, located in Brookgreen Gardens, South Carolina, depicts two riders on charging horses over the rayed disc of the rising sun. Weinman won the National Academy's Watrous Gold Medal for *Riders of the Dawn* in 1945.

Hermon Atkins Mac-Neil, born in Everett, Massachusetts, on February 27, 1866, became an accomplished sculptor. He is best remembered today as the creator of the Standing Liberty quarter dollar. After his elementary and high-school education he pursued his career as a designer and sculptor at the Normal Art School in Boston. MacNeil taught industrial art at Cornell University from 1886 to

Hermon A. MacNeil in his studio.

1889. He then went to Europe and worked with Henri Chapu at the Académie Julian and with Alexandre Fulguière at the École des Beaux-Arts in Paris. After returning to America in 1891 he settled in Chicago to assist Philip Martiny for a year by making sketches for architectural and other art for the World's Columbian Exposition. MacNeil also opened a studio and taught at the Chicago Art Institute. Afterward he traveled to the Southwest to study Indian culture. This catalyzed an interest that inspired him to feature Native Americans in a number of works, including a medal for the Society of Medalists based on a dance he had witnessed in northern Arizona.

His wife, née Carol Brooks, was a talented artist and sculptor in her own right, having studied under her artist father and also in Paris and in America, under sculptor Lorado Taft. They married on Christmas Day 1895. Their union produced two children. Carol was well known for her work and received many commissions and awards. She died in 1944.

MacNeil's "Hopi Prayer for Rain" medal, 1931, the third in the Society of Medalists series.

MacNeil worked in Rome from 1896 to 1900 as one of the first two winners of the Rinehart Scholarship in Sculpture. He then went to New York, where he opened a studio. Beginning with the McKinley Memorial in 1907 (depicted on the reverse of the U.S. Mint's 1916 and 1917 commemorative gold dollars) he received many commissions for memorials and statuary groups. In 1916 he had studios at 160 Fifth Avenue (on the roof with natural lighting, where he designed the quarter) in New York City and at his home in College Point, Long Island. For a time was an instructor at the Pratt Institute in Brooklyn. In 1923 the American Numismatic Society awarded him the J. Sanford Saltus medal. For the society he designed the medal to commemorate the 300th anniversary of the purchase of Manhattan by the Dutch.

The McKinley Memorial is a monumental grouping of statues by MacNeil honoring the 25th U.S. president, William McKinley. On each side of the memorial are two groups of statues, each depicting an adult and a child. The memorial was unveiled in Columbus, Ohio, in 1906.

Hermon A. MacNeil circa 1907.

He was a member of the American Academy of Arts and Letters, the National Academy of Design, the National Institute of Arts and Letters, the Architectural League of New York, and the Municipal Arts Society, and he served as president of the National Sculpture Society. At the World's Columbian Exposition in Chicago in 1893 he was awarded a medal for design, at the Paris Exhibition in 1900 he was given a silver medal for his *The Sun Vow* and *Last Act of the Moqui Snake Dance* groups. At the Pan-American Exposition in Buffalo in 1901 he was awarded a gold medal, and many other honors could be mentioned.

For the Louisiana Purchase Exposition in St. Louis in 1904 MacNeil designed the Fountain of

General George Washington as commander in chief, Washington Arch, New York City.

MacNeil completed *The Sun Vow* in 1899 at the American Academy in Rome. He was inspired by a trip made to the American West in 1895, during which time he visited several Native American tribes. This sculpture depicts a rite of passage in which a boy must shoot an arrow directly into the sun in order to be accepted as a warrior.

Liberty, one of the prime attractions there. Among a long list of civic sculptures are *Coming of the White Man* for City Park, Portland, Oregon; the McKinley Memorial, Columbus, Ohio (depicted on the reverse of the 1916 and 1916 commemorative gold dollars); Justice, the Guardian of Liberty, on the United States Supreme Court building (considered by some to be his best work); General George Washington for the Washington Arch in Washington Square in New York City; and various military memorial sculptures.

Pony Express Rider, located in St. Joseph, Missouri, was one of MacNeil's final works. It was dedicated in 1940. Picturing a mail carrier mid-run, this statue commemorates the Pony Express, a mail service run from Missouri to California by horseback in 1860 and 1861. It was the most direct means of east–west communication before the telegraph was established.

Hermon MacNeil died on October 2, 1947. After his passing, the contents of his home-studio were about to be discarded when a neighbor, commercial illustrator John A. Coughlin, rescued many items including letters and scrapbooks, now mostly preserved in the Smithsonian Institution. Certain of his casts and models were scattered. His ideal design for the 1916 quarter, with dolphins and other touches (see chapter 4), turned up in a yard sale in 2001.

NATIONAL SCULPTURE SOCIETY
EXHIBITION OF 1923

Exhibitor's Name *H. A. MacNeil*
Address *College Point N.Y.*
Agent
Address
Full Title *4 studies (Reverse)*
Quarter Dollar U.S.A.

LABEL—To be attached to exhibit.
Fill in by printing, not writing. This label must correspond with Entry Slip.
The National Sculpture Society will not be responsible for the loss of, or any damage to, any of the exhibits arising from any cause whatsoever during carriage or while in its custody.

Tag on the back of a plaster for a quarter dollar design that MacNeil exhibited some years later in 1923.

appendix B

Mints for the 1916–1947 Coins

U.S. coins have been struck at eight different mints over the years (or nine, including the Manila Mint, which made United States / Philippine coins under American sovereignty). Three of these that struck the new silver designs introduced in 1916—Denver, Philadelphia, and San Francisco—are discussed separately below. The others are summarized here:

Charlotte Mint (1838–1861): In 1838 a branch mint was opened in Charlotte, North Carolina, for the purpose of producing gold coins from metals extracted from mines and streams of the area. This and the Dahlonega and New Orleans mints were authorized by the Coinage Act of 1835. $1, $2.50, and $5 pieces were produced there from 1838 until the Civil War started in 1861, after which the mint closed.

Charlotte coins are identified by the mintmark C, as, for example, 1843-C. All coins struck at Charlotte are either scarce or rare today.

Dahlonega Mint (1838–1861): The history of the Dahlonega Mint is similar to that of Charlotte. Gold produced in the Dahlonega area of northern Georgia was converted into $1, $2.50, $3, and $5 pieces from the period 1838 through 1861. The mint closed after the advent of the Civil War.

Dahlonega coins have the mintmark D, not to be confused with the same mintmark later used for Denver coins, for the Dahlonega Mint operated in a different time frame, decades before the Denver Mint opened. All Dahlonega gold coins are either scarce or rare and as a class are more elusive than their Charlotte Mint counterparts.

New Orleans Mint (1838–1909): Due to increasing commerce on the Mississippi River and in the Gulf of Mexico, a mint was opened in 1838 at the foremost trading center in the area: New Orleans, Louisiana. Coins were produced at this facility from 1838 until the Civil War started in 1861, and again from 1879 through 1909. In 1861 the mint was seized by the State of Louisiana and was later operated for a short time under the auspices of the Confederate States of America.

The mintmark O appears on coins struck there. Pieces produced at New Orleans were in silver and gold metals; no copper coins were struck. A coin struck at the New Orleans Mint is described as follows, for example: 1879-O.

Carson City Mint (1870–1893): In 1870 a mint was otpened in Carson City, Nevada, to take advantage of silver and gold mined in the Comstock Lode about 15 miles away, discovered in 1858. In the early years of mining the precious metal was shipped by rail to the San Francisco Mint. It was expected that the Carson City Mint would offer convenience and take over much of the business. This did not work out, as Abram Curry, partner in the largest mine in the area, was the first mint superintendent—to the displeasure of his competitors in the silver business. Moreover, the greatest call for coins was on the West Coast, not in the mining camps of Nevada. Most coins minted in Carson City had to be shipped to California anyway.

The result was that production of silver and gold coins in Carson City was low in comparison to that of San Francisco. The mint ceased coining partway through 1885, then opened again in 1889 and closed forever in 1893. Today the mint building serves as the Nevada State Museum.

Bearing CC mintmarks (the only mintmark with more than one letter) these coins are very popular today. While there are many rare issues, Morgan silver dollars of certain dates were stored in quantity by the Treasury Department in bags of 1,000 coins. These were produced under the Bland-Allison Act of February 28, 1878, enacted due to pressure on Congress by Western mining interests. Countless millions were minted, although there was hardly any demand for them in the channels of commerce. Many years later in the 1950s and 1960s hundreds of thousands of Mint State CC dollars were released to the delight of numismatists.

Manila Mint (1920–1941): The Philippine Islands were administered as a colony of the United States after the Spanish-American War ended in 1898, and as a U.S. commonwealth from 1936 to 1946. From 1903 to 1919 special Philippine coins bearing the words UNITED STATES OF AMERICA were struck at the Philadelphia and San Francisco mints. In the first part of 1920, one-centavo coins were struck in San Francisco; later in the year a new mint facility, the Mint of the Philippine Islands, was opened in Manila, and from that point into 1941 Philippine coins of one, five, ten, twenty, and fifty centavos were struck there. The coins produced at the Manila Mint in 1920, 1921, and 1922 bore no mintmark. No Philippine coins were struck in 1923 or 1924. The Manila Mint reopened in 1925; from then through 1941 its coinage featured an M mintmark. The Manila Mint shut down during World War II, after the Japanese occupation began in 1941. The Denver and San Francisco mints would be used for Philippine coinage in the final years of the war, 1944 and 1945, while the islands were still under Japanese occupation.

West Point Mint (1984 to date): Beginning in 1984 a special minting facility at West Point, New York (home of the Military Academy), has been used to produce certain gold commemorative coins, silver and gold bullion coins, and some other issues. The distinguishing mintmark W characterizes these pieces. In the 1960s Lincoln cents were made there, but without a mintmark, to help ease a nationwide coin shortage.

Denver Mint

The Denver Mint.

The Denver Mint had its origin on April 21, 1862, when the Treasury Department bought the minting and assaying business of Clark, Gruber & Co., in Denver. They renamed the facility the Denver Mint, a notation that afterward appeared in all *Annual Reports of the Director of the Mint*. However, that Denver Mint acted only as an assay office and depository. No coins were ever struck there.

At the turn of the 20th century construction began for a new Denver Mint at a different location in the city. It officially opened for business on New Year's Day 1906. During the next several weeks coinage was limited to quarters and half dollars. Coins produced there bear a D mintmark on the reverse, not to be confused with the D for the Dahlonega Mint used from 1838 to 1861. An addition to the Denver Mint was built in 1936 and occupied in 1937.

During the era of the Mercury dime, Standing Liberty quarter, and Liberty Walking half dollar coinages, 1916 to 1947, the Denver Mint was the second-highest-volume producer, after Philadelphia and ahead of San Francisco. Its coins were usually distributed in the Rocky Mountain states and in the Midwest. The most famous of the issues is the rare 1916-D Mercury dime. Cents, nickels, silver dollars (1921 to 1934), and gold coins (1906 to 1931) were also made at Denver during this time period.

In addition to regular U.S. coinage, the Denver Mint produced coins for various foreign countries over the years.

Philadelphia Mint

The third Philadelphia Mint.

In 1792 the U.S. government acquired a plot of land and several buildings in Philadelphia and set up the first federal facility for the production of coins. In the meantime in July of that year about 1,500 silver half dismes were struck in a private shop using equipment intended for the Mint. The foundation stones for the mint facility were laid on July 31. Equipment was moved into the facility starting in September—two of the buildings remaining from earlier uses. In autumn and early winter of that year limited numbers of pattern coins were struck there. Copper cents, the first coins made in quantity for general circulation, were issued in March 1793, followed by the first silver coins in 1794 and the first gold coins in 1795.

On July 4, 1829, the cornerstone for the second Philadelphia Mint was laid. A number of silver half dimes were struck for use at the ceremony. In 1832 the new facility opened for operations. In ensuing decades it struck coins of many denominations and also supplied dies for the various branches beginning with Charlotte, Dahlonega, and New Orleans in 1838. The mint also performed assays, storage, and other functions. The engraving department created new designs and motifs. Proof coins for presentation and for collectors were struck there from about 1820 onward, with mintages expanding greatly after 1857 when numismatics became a widely popular hobby. The Mint Cabinet, a display initiated in 1838, was a focal point for numismatists. The last full year of operation for the second Philadelphia Mint was 1900.

In 1901 the third Philadelphia Mint was opened. In this facility Mercury dimes, Standing Liberty quarters, and Liberty Walking half dollars were coined along with cents, nickels, silver dollars, and $2.50, $5, $10, and $20 coins. The last gold coins were struck in 1933. Vast quantities of earlier-minted gold coins were stored in vaults until in 1937 they were shipped to the new Treasury repository at Fort Knox, Kentucky, and melted.

In addition to standard U.S. coins, the Philadelphia Mint produced hundreds of kinds of coins for dozens of foreign countries, starting in the 1830s.

Philadelphia coins bore no mintmark until certain wartime silver five-cent pieces of 1942 to 1945 used a large P. In recent decades this distinguishing letter has appeared on the obverse of all coins struck at the Philadelphia Mint.

The fourth and current Philadelphia Mint was opened in 1967 on Independence Square, not far from the Liberty Bell and other historic attractions.

San Francisco Mint

The second (1874–1937) San Francisco Mint.

The first San Francisco Mint opened in March 1854 in a building that had been slightly expanded after the Treasury purchased it from Curtis, Perry, & Ward, private assayers and minters of gold coins. During the first year gold $1, $2.50, $5, $10, and $20 denominations were struck there. Its first silver coins were minted in 1855. Cramped and poorly ventilated, the San Francisco Mint served its purpose but from the beginning was unsatisfactory in many ways. In time silver coins from the trime to half dollar and gold coins from the dollar to the double eagle were produced.

In 1870 the cornerstone for the second San Francisco Mint was laid. Opened in 1874, it produced silver and gold coins exclusively until the first bronze cents were struck there in 1908. Nickel five-cent pieces followed in 1912. After the San Francisco earthquake and fire of April 1906 the mint was the only building left standing in its

The third San Francisco Mint, opened in 1937.

district. It became the headquarters for security and other government and banking activities while the rubble was cleared and other arrangements were made. Gold coins were last struck there in 1930. In addition to federal coins the mint also struck coins for Hawaii, Japan, the Philippines, and certain Latin American countries. It also served as a storage depot for large quantities of silver dollars and gold coins. Mercury dimes were made there from 1916 to 1937, Standing Liberty quarters from 1917 to 1930, and Liberty Walking half dollars from 1916 to 1937.

In 1937 the third and current San Francisco Mint was opened on Duboce Street. The footprint of the building is 185 by 208 feet. Built on a hill of solid rock, it offered state-of-the-art security and was constructed to withstand fires and earthquakes. Mercury dimes were struck there from 1937 to 1945 and Liberty Walking half dollars from 1937 to 1946. After coining cents and dimes in 1955 the Treasury Department discontinued mintage operations. In 1962 it was renamed the San Francisco Assay Office. In the mid-1960s there was a nationwide coin shortage, and planchets were made at San Francisco to be shipped to the Denver Mint. The Coinage Act of 1965 provided that its coining facilities be reactivated. In 1968 the Assay Office began striking coins for Proof sets—an operation earlier conducted only in Philadelphia. On March 31, 1988, the *San Francisco Mint* name was officially restored.

In recent decades the facility has made commemorative and Proof coins and other special issues as well as selected regular denominations, the latter usually in lower quantities than have been made in Denver and San Francisco.

Mint Directors and Superintendents, 1916–1947

Mint Directors

In the era of the Mercury dime, Standing Liberty quarter, and Liberty Walking half dollar, the office of the director of the Mint was located in the Treasury Building in Washington, D.C., having been relocated there from Philadelphia in 1873. The nomination was made by the president of the United States, usually nodding to political considerations, and the appointment confirmed by Congress. The director was responsible for the Denver, Philadelphia, and San Francisco mints. The superintendents of those facilities reported to him or her. The director reported to the secretary of the Treasury. He or she was often called on by various congressional committees regarding coinage and monetary matters.

There was often a small gap between the term of one director and that of his or her successor. In such times the office would be filled by an appointed acting director. The Mint's fiscal year ran from July 1 of one year into June 30 of the next. Most accounts and reports were on a fiscal-year basis, supplemented by some numbers calculated into calendar years, the latter necessary for numismatists interested in mintage figures, the number of dies used in a calendar year, and related aspects. The *Annual Report of the Director of the Mint* was compiled by staff, starting after the close of the fiscal year and published months later.

Director Robert W. Wooley facilitated the development of the 1916 coinage designs.

Mint Directors and Their Terms

March 1915 to July 1916: Robert W. Woolley, nominated by Woodrow Wilson.

September 1916 to February 1917: Friedrich J.H. von Engelken, nominated by Woodrow Wilson.

March 1917 to March 1922: Raymond T. Baker, nominated by Woodrow Wilson.

March 1922 to September 1923: Frank E. Scobey, nominated by Warren G. Harding.

November 1923 to May 1933: Robert J. Grant, nominated by Calvin Coolidge.

May 1933 to April 1953: Nellie Tayloe Ross, nominated by Franklin D. Roosevelt.

Mint Superintendents

Each of the three mints active during the 1916 to 1947 era was under the day-to-day direction of an appointed superintendent, again usually a reward for good deeds to the party in control of Congress or to the president. Superintendents reported to the director of the Mint in Washington, D.C. The superintendent had charge of operations, including the processing of metal and planchets, coining to meet the requirements requested by the Treasury Department, and all other activities and departments.

The most important superintendency was that of the Philadelphia Mint, where the Engraving Department was located and where dies for all three mints were made. Philadelphia's superintendent managed these important departments and corresponded much more frequently with the Mint director than did those of Denver and San Francisco. Each year he helped organize the U.S. Assay Commission to review the previous year's coinage of precious metals.

Mint Superintendents and Their Terms

Denver Mint

August 1913 to July 1921: Thomas Annear.

July 1921 to November 1923: Robert J. Grant.

November 1923 to June 1933: Frank E. Shepard.

June 1933 to December 1942: Mark A. Skinner.

April 1943 to April 1952: Moses E. Smith.

Philadelphia Mint

July 1914 to March 1921: Adam M. Joyce.

April 1921 to January 1934: Freas M. Styer.

January 1934 to April 1935: A. Raymond Raff.

April 1935 to July 1953: Edwin H. Dressel.

San Francisco Mint

August 1913 to June 1921: T.W. Shanahan.

July 1921 to June 1933: M.J. Kelly.

July 1933 to December 1944: P.J. Haggerty.

May 1945 to November 1947: N.H. Callaghan.

Adam M. Joyce was superintendent of the Philadelphia Mint when the new coins of 1916 debuted. His salary was $4,500, equivalent to roughly $96,000 in 2015 dollars.

Edwin H. Dressel was the Philadelphia Mint's superintendent in 1947, when the last of the suite of 1916 coins (the Liberty Walking half dollars) rolled off the presses. In this January 11, 1937, photograph, Dressel discusses with Mint Director Nellie Tayloe Ross the upcoming transfer of Philadelphia's gold reserves to Fort Knox, Kentucky.

appendix

D

Pattern Coins of 1916

History and Overview

Several varieties of patterns were made for the Mercury dime during which the relief was adjusted and other refinements were made.[1]

Today nearly all of the existing dime and half dollar patterns of the 1916 types show wear, from light to extensive. One possible explanation is that Secretary of the Treasury William Gibbs McAdoo had a box of these patterns in his home in Virginia. His residence was burgled and the coins were stolen; the thieves, not being aware of their significance, may have spent them and they entered circulation as regular pocket change.[2]

During 1916 various patterns were made for the new quarter. Most of these were done without consulting designer Hermon MacNeil—a unique situation among the various relationships with outside artists and the Engraving Department at the Mint. No official records have been found about the production quantities or details.

 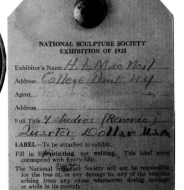

Plaster models for a pattern 1916 quarter made by Hermon A. MacNeil and exhibited at the National Sculpture Society. The exhibit tag is on the back of the model for the reverse.

In early 1916 the Engraving Department at the Mint produced a number of different patterns with variations on Adolph Weinman's half dollar design. No specific records have been found concerning these. Little was known about them in numismatic circles either. *The Numismatist* printed this in April 1937:

Plaster model by Hermon A. MacNeil of a design not known to have been made in pattern form. The date is in Roman numerals. (Roger W. Burdette, *Renaissance of American Coinage 1916–1921*).

A Pattern Half Dollar of 1916

Collectors generally are not aware of the existence of a pattern half dollar of 1916 the first year of issue of the current type. At least two specimens of the pattern are known. One of these is in the national collection at the Smithsonian Institution, in Washington, D.C., and the other is owned by a collector in Philadelphia.

It differs from the adopted type only in the placing of the inscriptions. On the obverse the words "Liberty" and "In God We Trust" are placed in the right of the field instead of the word "Liberty" around the upper circumference. On the reverse the words "Half Dollar" are between the eagle and "United States of America," and "E Pluribus Unum" follows the lower circumference instead of being to the left of the eagle's head.

Today more varieties are known, as described in the following pages. All are extreme rarities.

In the charts in this appendix, **Judd #** refers to the pattern's Judd catalog number in United States Pattern Coins, 10th edition. **Metal** indicates the metal the pattern was struck in. In all cases for 1916 patterns, the **Edge** is reeded. **Number Known** is an estimate of the number of pattern coins believed to exist. The **MS-60**, **MS-63**, and **MS-65** values are retail/auction approximations.

One obverse die has the T in LiberTy overly large, perhaps copied from the logotype of the Rudolph Wurlitzer Company, which used it prior to 1916.[3]

Patterns of 1916
J-1981: 1916 Dime

Pattern 1916 dime, Judd-1981 as cataloged in *United States Pattern Coins* by Dr. J. Hewitt Judd.

Listed as J-1794 prior to the eighth edition of the Judd reference on patterns. Made from unpolished as well as polished dies; the latter have thinner letters. Two examples are in the Smithsonian Institution.

Obverse: No AW initials. When the motto is oriented horizontally, the Liberty Head tilts slightly downward, and the L and Y (of LIBERTY) appear to be balanced. Compared to the regular issue: The neck truncation is larger, is shaped slightly differently, and extends closer to the border. The legends appear thin and delicate. The motto letters have serifs. The date is smaller and fits entirely under the truncation. More of the E (in LIBERTY) is visible, and the T is distant from the back of the cap. On pieces struck from polished dies, the dots otherwise visible between the words in the motto do not show.

Reverse: Details of the branch are different from the regular issue, and the border inscription is closer to the rim.

Judd #	Metal	Edge	Number Known	MS-60	MS-63	MS-65
1981	Silver	Reeded	4 to 6	$65,000	$110,000	—

J-1982: 1916 Dime

Pattern 1916 dime, Judd-1982.

Listed as J-1794 prior to the eighth edition of Judd's book. Notable for bold relief to the motifs and lettering. Two examples are confirmed.

Obverse: No AW initials. Similar to J-1981, but the Liberty Head is larger, with the top wing feather on the cap extending well past the R in LIBERTY. Less of the E is visible, and the legends are bolder.

Reverse: The die is similar to that of Judd-1981, but strengthened.

Judd #	Metal	Edge	Number Known	MS-60	MS-63	MS-65
1982	Silver	Reeded	4 to 6	—	—	—

J-1983: 1916 Dime

Listed as J-1794 prior to the eighth edition of Judd's book. Two examples are confirmed.

Pattern 1916 dime, Judd-1983.

Obverse: No AW initials. Similar to J-1982, but the neck truncation is notably shorter and distant from the rim, and the motto letters have no serifs.

Reverse: The die is similar to that of Judd-1981, but strengthened.

Judd #	Metal	Edge	Number Known	MS-60	MS-63	MS-65
1983	Silver	Reeded	4 to 6	$19,000	—	—

J-1984: 1916 Dime

Listed as J-1794 prior to the eighth edition of Judd's book. The motifs and letters are in higher relief than on any other pattern dime.

Pattern 1916 dime, Judd-1984.

Obverse: Similar to that of the regular issue, but in higher relief; the rim is extremely narrow; the AW initials are equidistant between the date and the Y of LIBERTY; and the neck truncation is slightly larger and closer to the rim. As with the regular issue, the motto letters have no serifs; when the motto is oriented horizontally, the Liberty Head tilts slightly upward; and the L of LIBERTY appears higher than the Y.

Reverse: Similar to that of the adopted issue, but the border letters touch the rim.

Judd #	Metal	Edge	Number Known	MS-60	MS-63	MS-65
1984	Silver	Reeded	4 to 6	—	$115,000	$173,000

J-1988: 1916 Quarter Dollar

Listed as J-1796a prior to the eighth edition of Judd's book.

Pattern 1916 quarter, a Mint modification of MacNeil's design—Judd-1988, as attributed in *United States Pattern Coins* by Dr. J. Hewitt Judd.

Obverse: Hermon MacNeil's full-length figure of Miss Liberty, her head turned to the left (viewer's right), stepping through a gateway, her left arm upraised, bearing a shield from which the covering is being drawn, and with an olive branch in her right hand (slightly different from the regular-issue style). In an arc at the top border is LIBERTY. At the top of the wall, interrupted by the gateway, is IN GOD / WE TRUST. The date 1916 is on a step under Liberty's feet. On this pattern, unlike the regular issue, there is no M on the base of the right portal. The details are in very shallow relief.

Reverse: An eagle in flight to the right. Above the eagle is UNITED STATES OF AMERICA, beneath which is E PLURIBUS UNUM in smaller letters. Curved along the bottom border is QUARTER DOLLAR. The details are in shallow relief. An olive branch is at the left border and another is at the right border. The eagle is higher in the field than it is on the regular issue.

Judd #	Metal	Edge	Number Known	MS-60	MS-63	MS-65
1988	Silver	Reeded	4 to 6	$215,000	—	—

J-1989: 1916 Quarter Dollar

Listed as J-1795 prior to the eighth edition of Judd's book. The Jimmy Hayes specimen is the only one seen in modern times.

Pattern 1916 quarter, Judd-1989.

Obverse: Style as the regular-issue die, but with important differences, including a different treatment of the olive branch, no initial M, and certain other adjustments. **Reverse:** Regular die. An eagle in flight to the right. Above the eagle is UNITED STATES OF AMERICA, beneath which is E PLURIBUS UNUM in smaller letters. Curved along the bottom border is QUARTER DOLLAR. At the left border are seven stars and on the right are six stars.

Judd #	Metal	Edge	Number Known	MS-60	MS-63	MS-65
1989	Silver	Reeded	4 to 6	—	—	$475,000

J-1991: 1916 Half Dollar

Pattern 1916 half dollar, a Mint modification of MacNeil's design—Judd-1991, as attributed in *United States Pattern Coins* by Dr. J. Hewitt Judd.

Listed as J-1798 prior to the eighth edition of Judd's book. This pattern is believed to have been struck between May 29 and June 21, 1916; it is accordingly given the first position in this list. It w as struck from polished as well as unpolished dies.

chart on next page

Obverse: Full-length figure of Miss Liberty striding toward the rising sun with rays, carrying branches of laurel and oak in her left hand, her right hand outstretched with the palm forward. Behind her, a cape in the form of a flag with 13 stars. Arranged in a semicircle around the border is LIBERTY in widely spaced letters. Low to the right in the field is IN GOD WE TRUST in small, well-made letters. The lettering is thin and in low relief. The date 1916 is centered at the bottom border.

Reverse: A perched eagle, as on the regular issue, but with many differences. The eagle has more feathers than on the adopted version, but on the pattern they are mostly indistinctly defined. UNITED STATES OF AMERICA / HALF DOLLAR is at the top border in two concentric arcs. E PLURIBUS UNUM is in tiny letters at the bottom border. There is no AW monogram.

Judd #	Metal	Edge	Number Known	MS-60	MS-63	MS-65
1991	Silver	Reeded	4 to 6	$84,000	$130,000	$240,000

J-1992: 1916 Half Dollar

Pattern 1916 half dollar, Judd-1992.

Listed as J-1797 prior to the eighth edition of Judd's book. This pattern is believed to have been struck between July 27 and August 18, 1916.

Obverse: Adolph A. Weinman's full-length figure of Miss Liberty striding toward the rising sun with 13 rays, carrying branches of laurel and oak in her left hand, her right hand outstretched with the palm forward. Behind her is a cape in the form of a flag with 13 stars. The figure is tall, with the head nearly touching the top border. In the right field is LIBERTY in large letters, below which is IN GOD WE TRUST in thick medium-size letters. The date 1916 is centered at the bottom border.

Reverse: A perched eagle, as on the regular issue, but with many differences. The eagle has more feathers than on the adopted version, but on the pattern they are mostly indistinctly defined. UNITED STATES OF AMERICA / HALF DOLLAR is at the top border in two concentric arcs. E PLURIBUS UNUM is in tiny letters at the bottom border. There is no AW monogram.

Judd #	Metal	Edge	Number Known	MS-60	MS-63	MS-65
1992	Silver	Reeded	4 to 6	$50,000	$85,000	$142,000

J-1993: 1916 Half Dollar

Pattern 1916 half dollar, Judd-1993.

This pattern is believed to have been struck after August 21 and before September 20, 1916.

Obverse: Adolph A. Weinman's full-length figure of Miss Liberty striding toward the rising sun with 13 rays, carrying branches of laurel and oak in her left hand, her right hand outstretched with the palm forward. Behind her is a cape in the form of a flag with 13 stars. The figure is tall, with the head nearly touching the top border. In the right field is LIBERTY in large letters, below which is IN GOD WE TRUST in thick medium-size letters. The date 1916 is centered at the bottom border.

Reverse: Similar to the regular die, but with some slight differences due to the size-reduction process and a lack of details in cutting the hub. With the AW monogram as approved by the secretary of the Treasury on August 10, 1916.

Judd #	Metal	Edge	Number Known	MS-60	MS-63	MS-65
1993	Silver	Reeded	4 to 6	$80,000	$150,000	$225,000

J-1994: 1916 Half Dollar

Pattern 1916 half dollar, Judd-1994.

Listed as J-1801 prior to the eighth edition of Judd's book. This pattern is believed to have been struck between September 25 and October 21, 1916. All known specimens have a die crack above the R in LIBERTY, and another downward from the Y.

Obverse: Somewhat similar to the adopted issue, but the date is small and compact and the letters in LIBERTY are heavy.
Reverse: Similar to the die of Judd-1993, but of slightly reduced scale. No AW.

Judd #	Metal	Edge	Number Known	MS-60	MS-63	MS-65
1994	Silver	Reeded	4 to 6	$80,000	$150,000	$225,000

J-1995: 1916 Half Dollar

Pattern 1916 half dollar, Judd-1995.

Listed as J-1799 prior to the eighth edition of Judd's book. This pattern is believed to have been struck between October 1 and 21, 1916.

Obverse: Somewhat similar to the adopted design, but with differences. LIBERTY is in thin letters. IN GOD WE TRUST is in small, irregular letters. The date is large, with the digits 9 and 6 open; the second 1 leans left. The sun is with ray 1 mis-shapen and connected to the sun. The foot at lower right has an especially prominent slope in the background.

Reverse: Similar to the die of Judd-1994, but with a slight reduction in the size of the design; the letters are farther from the rim. No AW.

Judd #	Metal	Edge	Number Known	MS-60	MS-63	MS-65
1995	Silver	Reeded	4 to 6	$60,000	$90,000	$150,000

J-1996: 1916 Half Dollar

Pattern 1916 half dollar, Judd-1996.

Listed as J-1800 prior to the eighth edition of Judd's book. This pattern is believed to have been struck between October 21 and November 11, 1916.

Obverse: Similar to the preceding, but with the date in larger numerals; the E in LIBERTY is differently positioned in relation to the top of Liberty's head; and there is a beaded border (instead of plain).
Reverse: Similar to the adopted design in general concept, but with smaller letters around the periphery and with a beaded border. Considerable hand engraving on the hub/die.

Judd #	Metal	Edge	Number Known	MS-60	MS-63	MS-65
1996	Silver	Reeded	4 to 6	$68,000	$112,000	$185,000

appendix E

Misstruck and Error Coins of 1916–1947

The U.S. Mint is an awe-inspiring factory—an impressive model of precise and accurate high-speed production. In recent decades the Mint has turned out *billions* of coins every year. Some are made specifically for collectors, in an array of alloys and attractive finishes and formats. More significantly, the Mint produces ton after ton of coins to facilitate everyday commerce.

Even in the production era of the Mercury dime, Standing Liberty quarter, and Liberty Walking half dollar, 70 to 100 years ago, the nation's mints were cranking out coins by the millions annually. With production reaching such numbers, it is understandable that a few irregular pieces (of all denominations) would escape inspection and inadvertently be released, usually in original (mint-sewn) bags or rolls of new coins. To err is human, it is said, and to forgive divine; for coin collectors, for the Mint to err is divine—no forgiveness needed! Today, mint errors of the early to mid-1900s, elusive as a class, are eagerly sought, not only for the light they shed on minting techniques but also as fascinating variations from normal date-and-mintmark collecting.

Mercury dime, Standing Liberty quarter, and Liberty Walking half dollar errors are decidedly uncommon. For the larger coins, Nicholas P. Brown, David J. Camire, and Fred Weinberg, writing in *100 Greatest U.S. Error Coins*, note that because of their size, such error coins "were easily spotted by the mint personnel who inspected coins after striking." For example, describing a Peace dollar struck on a quarter dollar planchet (the coin ranked number 5 in their book), they write, "The fact that there are no other Morgan or Peace dollar off-metal or wrong-planchet errors in existence is a testimony to the effectiveness of the Mint's inspection process for silver dollar coins."

Most larger error coins of that era have been found by dealers and collectors opening original bags, as opposed to having entered circulation and being noticed in the course of day-to-day business transactions.

When it comes to the scarcity of mechanical errors (the number known) across all series, Liberty Walking half dollars are second only to Standing Liberty quarter dollars. For the half dollars, even double strikes, broadstrikes, brockages, and partial-collar misstrikes are very scarce.

A Peace dollar (1922–1935) struck on a Standing Liberty quarter dollar planchet. (Shown enlarged; and also in context with a standard Peace dollar and a standard quarter, all at actual size.) Ranked no. 5 among the *100 Greatest U.S. Error Coins.* This error coin was sold for $8,250 in the November 1985 Bowers and Merena sale of the Abe Kosoff Collection. In 1985 that was a lot of money for a mint error. Today the coin is worth more than $100,000.

A 1944 Liberty Walking half dollar struck on a quarter dollar planchet. This oddity occurred when a quarter planchet (intended for the Washington quarter then in production) was somehow fed into the striking chamber and collar setup used to produce Liberty Walking half dollars. About a dozen such errors are known, and they can be worth $25,000 or more, with overall eye appeal and the presence or absence of a visible date being factors in value.

289

A Liberty Walking half dollar struck on a 1943 steel Lincoln cent planchet, ranked no. 8 among the *100 Greatest Error Coins*. Only two examples are known of this amazing error. Another example found today would fetch an auction price upward of $100,000, perhaps more. (Error shown enlarged, and also alongside a regular half dollar and steel cent at actual size.)

These two wrong-planchet errors were both struck on Mercury dime planchets. The Standing Liberty quarter is worth $35,000 to $50,000, and the Liberty Walking half dollar $25,000 to $40,000. The Standing Liberty quarter series has the fewest errors of any coin type of the 20th century. Liberty Walking half dollars struck on planchets smaller than a quarter are exceedingly rare.

This is actually a double error. First, a Liberty Walking half dollar was struck on a silver quarter planchet. Then, instead of being ejected into a tote bin like normal, it was struck a second time with a newly fed planchet lying on top of its obverse. An "S" mintmark is visible, so we know the error occurred at the San Francisco Mint. Dating the error is trickier, however; the year is not visible, so this misstrike could have occurred in 1917, in 1946, or any year in between when San Francisco was producing half dollars. Its value is from $75,000 to $95,000.

Major mechanical errors like this dramatic multiple-strike are very rare among Liberty Walking half dollars. Perhaps five or six double-struck errors are known of this type. A multiple-struck coin occurs when a finished coin is not ejected properly from the press, but remains in place, perhaps slightly off orientation, and is struck again with the same dies. This 1945-S error coin, struck 60% off center at 9 o'clock, is worth from $25,000 to $35,000.

This 1943-S Walking Liberty half dollar was struck on a planchet for a Peruvian half-sol coin. The San Francisco Mint (and other U.S. mint facilities) produced coins for various foreign countries during World War II, and a coinage blank intended for Peru ended up in the hopper for U.S. half dollars, either accidentally or as a worker's lark. The resulting error is about 3 mm smaller than a normal half dollar, and—with an alloy of .700 copper and .300 zinc—has a brassy yellow color. Its value is about $20,000.

Three more wartime errors: a Mercury dime struck on a planchet for a 10-cent coin of the Netherlands East Indies; another struck on a Peruvian 5-centavo planchet; and a third struck on a Netherlands 10-cent planchet. Because the dime was (and remains) the smallest-diameter U.S. coin, any wrong-planchet or off-metal strike had to be on a planchet intended for another country's coinage. It would be mechanically impossible for a larger planchet to be set into the press for striking dimes.

An off-center coin is one that was struck out of collar and incorrectly centered, with the result that part of the design is missing. This off-center Liberty Walking half dollar has wear from circulation or from being carried around as a pocket piece. This is a visually dramatic example of this kind of error; about a half dozen are known in the Liberty Walking series, and most are less than 25% off center. This one is 40% off center at 12 o'clock, with the date (1944) clearly visible. It is worth about $8,000 to $10,000. Collectors should be aware of the difference between a true off-center error and an uncentered broadstrike (which is typically worth far less). On a broadstruck coin, none of the design is missing, although the coin is slightly off center and spread out larger (the result of having been struck without being contained in the retaining collar die). Broadstrikes lack the normal reeded edge of a finished coin.

appendix F

The American Silver Eagle Redesign

The American Silver Eagle is a .999 fine bullion coin that the U.S. Mint introduced in 1986. Its obverse design is modeled after Adolph Weinman's Liberty Walking motif, and the reverse features a heraldic eagle by John M. Mercanti. The coins are 40.6 mm in diameter—about one-third larger than the half dollar's 30.6 mm. Since they debuted, eager collectors and investors worldwide have bought more than 350 million of these popular silver pieces.

In *American Silver Eagles: A Guide to the U.S. Bullion Coin Program*, retired U.S. Mint chief engraver Mercanti discusses the process by which Weinman's original half dollar design was updated into the obverse of the one-ounce silver bullion piece.

"For the first few years of American Silver Eagle production," he writes, "Weinman's obverse Walking Liberty was used without any modifications, and there were what are referred to in the industry as 'fill problems' related to modeling and basin issues. Also, the cry from headquarters was, 'We need to see more detail.'"

In response, Mercanti and his team created enlarged 12-inch epoxy models of Weinman's original 6-inch plasters. They modified details in Weinman's coinage model by giving more definition to all the stars in the flag, the oak leaves, the lines in Miss Liberty's skirt, and her sandals, "so that everything was as clear as we could make it at that scale." After refining the design details, they reduced the models to 6 inches again. From there, new dies were cut with the increased detail.

The results are easy to see when a Liberty Walking half dollar and an American Silver Eagle are examined side by side.

Enlargements of the two coins. Note the differences in definition in
Miss Liberty's skirt, the flag, the oak-leaf cluster, and other details.

appendix

G

Centennial Coins of 2016

In early August 2014, at the American Numismatic Association World's Fair of Money, the U.S. Mint hinted that 2016 might bring a special celebration of the 100th anniversary of the debut of the coins of 1916. On August 28 the Mint conducted a survey among several hundred of its customers to gauge their opinions of a gold version of the Mercury dime and Liberty Walking half dollar.

The following month, in September 2014, the Mint revealed that it was considering .9999 fine (24k) gold versions of the dime and half dollar. The Standing Liberty quarter at first was not included in these discussions, but on September 23 the Mint announced that it was also considering a 2016 version of the quarter. *Coin World* senior staff writer Paul Gilkes reported on September 23, 2014, that "A decision has not been determined whether to employ artist/sculptor Herman A. MacNeil's original Bared Breast obverse from 1916, or the modified Mailed Breast subtype introduced in 1917, should plans proceed to produce a centennial quarter dollar."

At that point the alloy of any such quarter was also uncertain.

After more focus-group study, the Mint's plans firmed up and in *Coin World*'s January 28, 2015, online edition, Washington correspondent Bill McAllister was able to report the breaking news: "Mint reveals details of 2016 gold coins to mark 1916 silver issues." McAllister was reporting on the January 28 meeting of the Citizens Coinage Advisory Committee, which meets to discuss and advise the secretary of the Treasury on coin and medal designs. "Members of the panel reacted with great joy to the proposal," he noted, with historian Herman Viola calling it "a brilliant proposal" and numismatic curator Robert Hoge pronouncing it "a wonderful idea." The committee encouraged the Mint to issue the new coins in either silver or platinum as well as gold. In response, they were advised by a Mint attorney that the secretary of the Treasury only has authority to issue gold coins, and that silver versions would require congressional action.

The Mint's initial plans called for the coins to be issued in fractions of an ounce of gold, with the date 2016, and a statement of their fineness (as seen on gold bullion coins). Members of the CCAC objected to the proposed intrusion of a phrase (such as .9999 GOLD) into the coins' classic designs, suggesting instead a more minimalist approach—a small privy mark, or edge lettering—to protect the designs from becoming cluttered.

The Mint confirmed that the coins would be issued in their 1916 denominations, in their original sizes. They would also have their original designs (except for the new date and any additional indication of fineness). In the case of the quarter, that would be the Variety 1 design with Miss Liberty's breast exposed, and no stars below the eagle. Proof and Uncirculated versions were both under consideration in these early discussions.

Artist's conception of the 2016 gold coins.

50th Anniversary Kennedy half dollar, gold.

The 2016 centennial gold coins have a recent precedent in the U.S. Mint's 2014 tribute to the Kennedy half dollar. A .9999 fine gold version (containing three-quarters of an ounce of gold) was struck at the Philadelphia Mint to mark the 50th anniversary of the coin. It used the original 1964 coinage portrait of President John F. Kennedy (which had been modified slightly over the years), and the regular reverse design, but featured a dual 1964–2014 date on the obverse.

The gold Kennedy half dollar was very popular, sparking great enthusiasm within the hobby community and even making national headlines in the mainstream media. Collectors and speculators formed long lines at coin shows to make their purchases.

Techniques of Smart Buying

The main chapters of this book contain much information on how to be a smart collector—what to look for in terms of grade, sharpness, eye appeal, and more. In this appendix I discuss the art and techniques of *buying*—how to spend your money most effectively when you bid in an auction, or write a check, or otherwise actually acquire the Mercury dimes, Standing Liberty quarters, and Liberty Walking half dollars you desire. (This advice is useful for not only the three coins showcased in this book, but for most other series as well.)

Conventional wisdom is that sellers want the highest price while buyers want to pay as little as possible. This may be true for some buyers and sellers in other venues—new and used cars, real estate, and the like. However, it seems to me that in numismatics the situation is different, because the human element intervenes. Coin collecting is a hobby, or a combination of a hobby and an investment, and in most instances both the buyer and the seller want the other party to have a pleasant experience and would like to develop a continuing relationship. If both buyer and seller enjoy the transaction, the two will meet again in the future. If the buyer feels that he or she has been pressed to the very limit of price, or if the seller is exhausted after a round of dickering, neither will look forward to a future encounter—and there might not be one.

The Three Elements of *Quality*

In numismatics, with the exception of great rarities, there are enough things available for outright purchase or at auction that you will never lack for opportunities to acquire the objects of your desire. This is true for nearly every variety of Mercury dimes, Standing Liberty quarters, and Liberty Walking half dollars. Rarely is it necessary to act in haste. For these particular three series, being a smart buyer means evaluating three main aspects.

Numerical grade: Based on your budget and desires, develop a guideline as to the typical grade you seek. It may be EF-45 more or less, MS-63, or some other level. When exploring auction catalogs, Internet listings, or other offerings, you can save time by looking for coins only in or close to that grade. There is no advice more important than this: the numerical grade on a holder is only a part of a coin's desirability, and not necessarily the most relevant.

Sharpness of strike: Except for the designations of Full Bands on Mercury dimes and Full Head on Standing Liberty quarters, holders say nothing about whether a coin is sharply or weakly struck. As mentioned earlier in the text, Full Head for a quarter usually means that the head of Liberty is fairly sharp, but not necessarily really full. Most such quarters of the Type II design, 1917–1930, that are certified as FH have some of the shield rivets weak or missing. It pays to look at the *entire* coin, not just the head.

As part of this process you need to know the territory. For example, a 1917 Type I Philadelphia Mint quarter nearly always comes with a Full Head plus full shield rivets and sharp everything else. As to a 1926-D, although you can pay a lot of money for a FH coin, I have yet to see one that is sharp in all other areas as well.

Eye appeal: Grading numbers do not help with eye appeal very much. Some + or other designations are intended to mean that within a given grade a + coin is "high end." Still, the coin may have low eye appeal, may be artificially toned, or could have other problems.

To become an expert—a connoisseur—in the above three areas, you will need to study. Images on the Internet and in auction catalogs will help you. In time you will gain knowledge that will enable you to make better purchases—of coins that are sharper and more beautiful—than the typical buyer who simply looks at the numbers on holders.

I would rather have a sharply struck MS-63 coin with superb eye appeal than a weakly struck MS-65 that is stained, dark, or otherwise unattractive. The secret is that such an MS-63 coin might cost only a fraction of what the MS-65 would!

It is relevant to say that certain of the connoisseurs who built the finest-quality collections in American numismatics considered the grade to be just the starting point—and beyond that sharpness and eye appeal were equally if not more important. D. Brent Pogue, Emery May Holden Norweb, Claude Davis, and John J. Pittman are just four of such connoisseurs I have known over a long period of time.

The above precepts apply equally well to other series from half cents to double eagles, from colonials to territorial gold.

The above said, I go on to give a basic primer concerning aspects of buying:

Do Your Homework

Before entering into any purchase, do your homework regarding the items you seek. Learn as much as you can about the coins you want to add to your collection.

Most of your competitors in the marketplace will not do much checking, but will simply read labels on holders or descriptions in auction catalogs. As they will have no strategy, they may bid 90% of market price for the unappealing 1916 Standing Liberty quarter and believe they have captured a bargain. They may bid a 50% premium for the gorgeous 1916-D Mercury dime in an Internet sale, and consider ridiculous the price of what seems to be a worn 1942, 42 Over 41, overdate.

There are three parts to gaining knowledge:

By looking: The Internet offers an easy way to do this from the comfort and convenience of your favorite chair. Examine as many coins as you can, online and at coin shows and shops.

By reading: For relatively modest expense you can build a very nice library on American coins. Several hundred dollars spent on Whitman Publishing titles will get you started. The expense is tiny in comparison to the prices of the coins you will be buying, and the knowledge you will gain is priceless.

By spending time: To become an expert buyer, a connoisseur, time is needed. Keep at the two aspects above for several months, and you will emerge as a smarter buyer than 90% of your competitors in the marketplace!

Strategies for Buying Outright

Generally, most dealers who own coins that are for sale will post an asking price on each. It has been my experience that no two dealers do this in the same way. Some simply look at the *Coin Dealer Newsletter, Coin Values,* the *Guide Book of United States Coins,* "Coin Market" (*Numismatic News*), a Web site, or some other handy guide, or use several of these, and go from there. The prices in the *Coin Dealer Newsletter* are sometimes wholesale, and a percentage can be added. Prices in most other listings are intended to be retail. In all instances, such listings are for *typical coins of average quality.* The worth of a given specimen at hand may be higher or lower, depending on factors I've already discussed—including sharpness of strike and eye appeal.

In most retail offerings, coins are priced generically. Accordingly, if a dealer has five examples of a 1940-S Liberty Walking half dollar, all graded MS-64 (Numismatic Guaranty Corporation, or NGC), his asking price is apt to be the same for each. Likewise if he has three 1926-D Standing Liberty quarters in MS-63 (ANACS), seven 1945 Mercury dimes in MS-65 (Professional Coin Grading Service, or PCGS), or whatever, the price will be the same. At the present time very few dealers with identical coins separate them by sharpness and/or eye appeal. For the varieties just mentioned there can be *vast* difference in sharpness of strike. You, as a careful buyer, have the secret advantage of being able to cherrypick for a coin of exceptional quality (assuming that such exists in a given group).

For circulation strikes of classic U.S. coins there are often differences in quality for a particular date/mintmark. Again, it is necessary to know the territory. You know from reading this book that a 1939-S Liberty Walking half dollar that is sharp is no big deal. However, if you can find a 1923-S half dollar that is far above average in sharpness, although not needle-sharp, that is an accomplishment.

It would also seem logical that a dealer might ask more for coins with the best strike and eye appeal, and less for those that are not as nice. However, dealers do not often do this because it complicates their listings or because they are not familiar with such characteristics. More than just a few "leading dealers" in rare coins have little knowledge beyond what they see on a holder and read in price lists.

Negotiating Price

The real value of the coin is most important. It's better to pay full asking price for a coin worth $1,000 than to get a 20% discount on a coin that's worth $1,000, but is priced at $1,500. Be *value* conscious, not *price* conscious.

Some dealers (particularly those setting up at shows) will set prices higher than the figures they really want, so they can give a discount—and thus the *appearance* of a good buy. In rare coins, however, the asking prices may be set high, but not super-high. Shoppers at coin shows tend to dicker more than do mail-order clients. On the other hand, dealers who publish price lists are less apt to set elevated prices for ordinary coins, for if their listed prices are too high, they won't get many orders.

Make no mistake, however. There are many occasions for which fine dealers will allow courtesy discounts for nice coins. A retail customer who offers to spend a lot of money at one time, with little discussion, complication, or hassle with the dealer, may receive a discount when asked.

Sometimes a dealer will give a special price for a quick sale, if several items are bought at once, if a customer is a friend or long-term buyer, if a coin has remained in stock too long, or if the dealer made a mistake when purchasing it. Not all dealers have ready markets for all coins.

There are no rules as to how sellers set their asking prices. Ten different dealers might price the same grade and variety of coin at 10 different prices. However, as I mentioned, it is the real value of the coin that counts. Value is not only based on the grade, but on the sharpness and eye appeal. This cannot be overemphasized.

In a phrase: If a variety that is normally found weakly struck and with poor eye appeal is discovered with sharp strike and superb eye appeal, it is probably best to pay the price asked. If it is sub-par, do not buy. If it is normally found sharp and beautiful, negotiate the best price you can—without impairing any friendship.

Promoting Long-Term Relationships

Business Etiquette. When buying something I need for my collection I pay the asking price if I consider it to be reasonable. If I do not, and a counteroffer wouldn't offend the seller, I make such an offer—but not merely to save a few dollars or to try to demonstrate that I'm a sharp buyer. Building a fine, long-term relationship with a dealer is better than being tolerated as a semi-nuisance haggler. Dealers often talk about this type of annoying buyer when they get together.

It is important to live up to your obligations. If you say that you need two weeks' time to sell some stock or raise some money in order to buy a 1927-S Liberty Walking half dollar, and will send your check for $9,000 at that time, do so on a timely basis. When you do write the check, be sure you have money in the bank to cover it.

Social Etiquette. When handling a dealer's coins, do it very carefully. Coins as well as holders should be lifted and held only by their edges. Be sure your hands are clean. If you've just had a hamburger, go wash your hands, then return to the dealer's table. If you're carrying a beverage around with you, be sure it isn't in a position to fall or spill.

Dress neatly and always in *clean* clothes. Generally, a dealer or anyone else will pay more attention to a nicely dressed man or woman than to someone wearing a food-stained T-shirt. A few years ago the Professional Numismatists Guild set up a rule that members had to dress well at coin shows. Good plan.

If a dealer is talking with someone else, wait your turn. If the conversation seems to be interminable, in a nice way get his or her brief attention and ask when a good time would be to return to the table.

If you are well financed and can buy everything you see, keep the details of your wealth to yourself or (if credit is important) limit them to conversations with the dealer. Some of the wealthiest people I know are also the most modest.

Not everyone cares about etiquette. However, a bit of care, kindness, and thoughtfulness from parties on each side of a transaction will reap great dividends in enjoyment and, probably, better bottom-line values for you as a buyer.

Buying Coins at a Shop or Office

There are many coin shops throughout the United States. Some of these are stores, with display counters, racks of books and supplies for sale, and a proprietor—sometimes backed by a staff—ready to greet walk-in visitors. Often such businesses are located on the ground floor or somewhere else easy to access. In contrast, many other dealers operate from office buildings and conduct their business quietly, perhaps keeping the coins in a nearby bank vault rather than on display. Such dealers may do business by appointment, rather than on a walk-in basis.

Once you've located a coin shop, it's a good practice to call in advance unless you know for sure that it will be open when you arrive. The owners or expert numismatists at even the most active walk-in businesses are often away at coin shows. You might also want to ask what times tend to be less busy than others. It may be easier for a shop owner to chat on Tuesday morning than on Saturday afternoon.

Upon your arrival or in your telephone inquiry, it's perfectly okay to say something such as, "I'm a newcomer to the hobby, and I'd just like to come and look around, and perhaps buy a book or two." There is no reason at all to act like you might be a "big spender." In my view, you want to go where you will be welcomed—big spender, moderate spender, or just interested in a few books or supplies.

It's good form to make at least a modest purchase as a courtesy when you visit—perhaps an inexpensive book, a magnifying glass, or something else of the sort.

Most proprietors and staff of coin shops are more than eager to see interested collectors—beginners as well as advanced specialists. While it's a popular notion that big spenders receive the best attention, in practice most shop owners are happy to talk to anyone. They also know that someone buying a common-date half dollar today may be looking for a high-grade Proof a year from now!

Much more could be said about buying. And, of course, a whole chapter or more could be written about *selling*. Along these lines you might enjoy my *Expert's Guide to Collecting and Investing in Rare Coins*, a book that has been very useful to many people.

Notes

Chapter 1

1. Alexander Hamilton was at that time secretary of the Treasury.

2. This and the following comments make it clear that the newspaper writer must have visited the Mint to examine unadopted patterns by Barber as well as the finished design by Morgan.

3. As quoted in the *American Journal of Numismatics*, April 1878.

4. R.W. Julian, letter, April 24, 1996.

5. Roger W. Burdette, *Renaissance of American Coinage 1916–1921*, pp. 14–31, gives correspondence and extensive details and is recommended as a source for additional information.

Chapter 2

1. Sources include *Mehl's Numismatic Monthly*, September and October 1919.

2. In 1936 Moritz Wormser himself would join the ranks of dealers and open the New Netherlands Coin Company in New York City.

3. In 1976 the Mint requested that the Smithsonian return the coins so they could be exhibited at the Philadelphia Mint. This caused great distress to the curators, Vladimir and Eliza Clain-Stefanelli. Harvey Stack solved the problem by persuading the heirs to the Louis E. Eliasberg estate, Louis Jr. and Richard A., to loan that collection to the Mint, which they did.

4. Partner Julius Guttag remained active in numismatics and conducted a small business, occasionally advertising, including as Guttag Brothers. In 1938 he was important in the production of the New Rochelle commemorative half dollar. The author interviewed him in the 1950s.

5. Tragically, most Schulman family members were killed in the Holocaust.

6. Letter in the *Numismatic Scrapbook Magazine*, June 1943.

7. Stuart Mosher in *The Numismatist*, January 1945.

Chapter 3

1. Provided to the author by Roger W. Burdette; from research in the National Archives.

2. This is confirmed by unpublished documents in the Library of Congress.

3. The monument was authorized by the General Assembly of Maryland on April 5, 1906, and was dedicated on November 6, 1909, in Druid Hill Park. Albert Randolf Ross assisted Weinman in the work. The sculpture is about 10 feet high, and the granite base about 12 feet. In 1959 it was moved to Wyman Park to make way for the Jones Falls Expressway.

4. Letter from Roger W. Burdette, November 29, 2003; Burdette, *Renaissance of American Coinage, 1916–1921*, 2005.

5. David M. Sundman furnished certain information regarding release and distribution.

6. Lange, The Complete Guide to Mercury Dimes, 2005.

7. Per an interview with Wayne Miller, rare-coin dealer there, who occasionally bought examples from the general public.

8. CONECA Web site, 2013.

Chapter 4

1. Booker T. Washington is said to have suggested the theme of the film. It was a counter to D.W. Griffith's racist *The Birth of a Nation*, 1915, and endeavored to show the equality of various races.

2. Sent to the author on March 20, 2007, as a contribution to educate coin buyers beyond "conventional wisdom" and grading-service labels.

3. Merkin, an accomplished clarinetist, entered professional numismatics in 1958.

Chapter 5

1. Roger W. Burdette, letter, November 29, 2003.

2. Correspondence with Lange and Fivaz, various, 2003 onward.

3. This feature was brought to the attention of many readers in an article by William T. Gibbs in *Coin World*, March 1, 2004, which mentioned that five dies had been identified. "This variety has been known for about a month."

Appendix D

1. Roger W. Burdette, *Renaissance of American Coinage 1916–1921*, gives details of the Mercury dime patterns, steps in their production, and much information that has never appeared in print before. Most of this is beyond the scope of the present book. For patterns also see J. Hewitt Judd, *United States Pattern Coins*, 10th edition.

2. Suggestion of Rogers M. Fred Jr., of Leesburg, Virginia, 1974. McAdoo's daughter Frances stated that when thieves burgled her father's house in the 1920s they took coins including 1916-dated patterns.

3. In 1966 the author showed Farny Wurlitzer, chairman emeritus of the firm, a photograph of a pattern half dollar with LiberTy and asked him if this large T had an outside origin. He said something to the effect of "our advertising department dreamed it up."

Bibliography

Ambio, Jeff. *Collecting and Investing Strategies for Walking Liberty Half Dollars*. Irvine, CA: Zyrus Press Inc., 2008.

Breen, Walter H. *Walter Breen's Complete Encyclopedia of U.S. and Colonial Coins*. Garden City, NY: F.C.I. Press Inc., 1988.

Bressett, Kenneth E., ed. *A Guide Book of United States Coins*. Various modern editions. Atlanta, GA. Earlier editions edited by Richard S. Yeoman.

Brookgreen Gardens, SC. Brochures about Adolph W. Weinman and Hermon A. MacNeil.

Burdette, Roger W. *Renaissance of American Coinage 1909–1915*. Great Falls, VA: Seneca Mills Press. 2005.

Renaissance of American Coinage 1916–1921. Great Falls, VA: Seneca Mills Press, 2006.

Coin World Almanac. Sidney, OH: Coin World, 2010.

Coin World. Sidney, OH: Amos Press, 1960 to date.

Fivaz, Bill, and J.T. Stanton. *The Cherrypickers' Guide to Rare Die Varieties*. Various editions and volumes. Atlanta, GA: Whitman Publishing.

Howe, Dean F. *Walking Liberty Half Dollars, an In-Depth Study*. Sandy, UT: Dean F. Howe Rare Coins, 1989.

Judd, J. Hewitt. *United States Pattern, Experimental and Trial Pieces*. Racine, WI, 1959. Various modern editions published as *United States Pattern Coins*. Atlanta, GA: Whitman Publishing.

Knauss, Robert H. *Standing Liberty Quarter Varieties & Errors*, second edition. Published by the author, 2014.

Lange, David W. *The Complete Guide to Mercury Dimes*. Virginia Beach, VA: DLRC Press, 1993 and 2005.

Numismatic Guaranty Corporation of America Census Report. Sarasota, FL: Numismatic Guaranty Corporation of America, various issues.

Numismatic Scrapbook Magazine. Chicago, IL, and Sidney, OH: 1935–1976.

Numismatic News. Iola, WI: Krause Publications, 1952 to date.

Numismatist, The. The American Numismatic Association. Colorado Springs, CO (and other addresses), various issues 1914 to date.

PCGS Population Report. Newport Beach, CA: Professional Coin Grading Service, various issues.

Pessolano-Filos, Francis. *Venus Numismatic Dictionary.* New York, NY: Eros Publishing Company, 1983.

Pollock, Andrew W. III. *United States Patterns and Related Issues.* Wolfeboro, NH: Bowers and Merena Galleries, 1994.

Raymond, Wayte. *Standard Catalogue of United States Coins and Paper Money* (titles vary). New York, NY: Scott Stamp & Coin Co. (and others), 1934 to 1957 editions.

Records of the Bureau of the Mint, National Archives.

Schwarz, Ted. *A History of United States Coinage.* San Diego, CA, and New York, NY: A.S. Barnes and Co., circa 1980.

Swiatek, Anthony. *The Walking Liberty Half Dollar.* New York, NY: Sanford J. Durst Publications, 1983.

Taxay, Don. *U.S. Mint and Coinage.* New York, NY: Arco Publishing, 1966.

Treasury Department, United States Mint, et al. *Annual Report of the Director of the Mint.* 1912 onward.

Vermeule, Cornelius. *Numismatic Art in America: Aesthetics of the United States Coinage.* Atlanta, GA: Whitman Publishing, 2007.

Wexler, John A. and Kevin Flynn. *Treasure Hunting Mercury Dimes.* Savannah, GA: Stanton Printing & Publishing, 1999

Credits and Acknowledgments

Karen Bridges of Stack's Bowers Galleries provided certain illustrations. **Roger W. Burdette** corresponded concerning various subjects. His 2006 book, *Renaissance of American Coinage 1916–1921*, is the master work on the title subject and was consulted frequently. Bill Fivaz furnished information about certain die characteristics and other topics. **Kevin Flynn** shared information. In 1974 **Rogers M. Fred Jr.** provided information about Treasury Secretary William McAdoo. **Bill Gibbs** of *Coin World* provided files of articles. **Heritage Auctions** was the source of illustrations for study. **R.W. Julian** shared information and insight. **David W. Lange** contributed information and insight on various matters. **Ron Pope** provided a study of the characteristics of striking Standing Liberty quarters. The photograph of Elsie Stevens in chapter 3 is courtesy of **Random House**. **David M. Sundman** shared information. **Donald Sundman** of Mystic Stamp Co. provided the first-day-of-issue envelope image in chapter 2. The **U.S. Mint** at Philadelphia was the source for an illustration.

About the Author

Q. David Bowers is chairman emeritus of Stack's Bowers Galleries and is numismatic director of Whitman Publishing, LLC. He served as president of the American Numismatic Association (1983–1985) and president of the Professional Numismatists Guild (1977–1979).

Bowers is the author of more than 50 books and several thousand articles, including columns in *Coin World* and *The Numismatist*. His books have earned more "Book of the Year Award" honors bestowed by the Numismatic Literary Guild than have those of any other author. He has been important in the sale of many of the most valuable coin collections ever sold at auction.

Bowers is a trustee of the New Hampshire Historical Society and a fellow of the American Antiquarian Society, the American Numismatic Society, and the Massachusetts Historical Society. In Wolfeboro, New Hampshire, he serves on the board of selectmen and is the town historian. He has been a consultant for the Smithsonian Institution, the Treasury Department, and the U.S. Mint, and is research editor of the *Guide Book of United States Coins* (the hobby's best-selling "Red Book").

Index